Historical Judgments Reconsidered

Historical Judgments Reconsidered

SELECTED

HOWARD UNIVERSITY LECTURES

IN HONOR OF

RAYFORD W. LOGAN

Edited by

Genna Rae McNeil and Michael R. Winston

HOWARD UNIVERSITY PRESS
WASHINGTON, D.C.
1988

Second Series of Historical Publications (Number 17)
Department of History, Howard University

Printed in the United States of America

This book is printed on acid-free paper.

LIBRARY OF CONGRESS CATALOGING-IN-PUBLICATION DATA

Historical judgments reconsidered.

(Second series of historical publications; no. 17)
Includes index.
1. Afro-Americans—History.   2. Slavery—United
States—History.   3. United States—Race relations.
4. Afro-Americans—Biography—History and criticism.
5. Logan, Rayford Whittingham, 1897–   .
I. Logan, Rayford Whittingham, 1897–   .
II. Winston, Michael R. III. McNeil, Genna Rae.
IV. Series.
E185.H54 1988   973'.0496073   88–32856
ISBN 0–88258–173–2

iv

To the memory of Rayford W. Logan (1897–1982)

whose scholarship is a cherished part of the intellectual tradition
of the Department of History of Howard University

and

To Lorraine A. Williams

under whose chairmanship the Department of History
inaugurated the Rayford W. Logan Lecture Series.

ACKNOWLEDGMENTS

Grateful acknowledgments are made to the following:

Lorraine A. Williams and the Howard University Department of History for permission to reprint "George Washington Williams and Africa" by John Hope Franklin; and "Black History's Diversified Clientele" by Benjamin Quarles from *Africa and the Afro-American Experience*. Copyright © 1971 and 1977 by the Howard University Department of History.

John W. Blassingame and Oxford University Press for permission to reprint "Sambos and Rebels: the Character of the Southern Slave" from *The Slave Community* by John W. Blassingame. Copyright © 1979 by Oxford University Press, Inc.

A. Leon Higginbotham, Jr., and Oxford University Press for permission to reprint the "Introduction" from *In the Matter of Color: Race and the American Legal Process* by A. Leon Higginbotham, Jr. Copyright © 1978 by Oxford University Press, Inc.

David Levering Lewis and the Journal of American History for permission to reprint "Parallels and Divergences: Assimilationist Strategies of Afro-American and Jewish Elites from 1910 to the Early 1930s," by David Levering Lewis from the *Journal of American History* 71(December, 1984). Copyright © 1984 by the Journal of American History.

Vincent G. Harding and the Journal of American History for permission to reprint "Beyond Amnesia: Martin Luther King, Jr., and the Future of America," by Vincent G. Harding from the *Journal of American History* 74(September, 1987). Copyright © 1987 by the Journal of American History.

C. Vann Woodward for permission to reprint "History from Slave Sources: a Review Article" by C. Vann Woodward from the *American Historical Review* 79(April, 1974). Copyright © 1974 by C. Vann Woodward.

Dodd, Mead & Co. for permission to reprint "We Wear the Mask" by Paul Laurence Dunbar from the *Paul Laurence Dunbar Reader: Selections of the Best Paul Laurence Dunbar Poetry and Prose*, edited by Jay Martin and Gossie Hudson. Copyright © 1974 by Dodd, Mead & Co.

Carl Wendell Hines, Jr., for permission to reprint "Now That He Is Safely Dead" from *Drum Major for a Dream: Poetic Tributes to Martin Luther King, Jr.*, edited by Ira G. Zepp, Jr., and Melvyn D. Palmer. Copyright © 1977 by Carl Wendell Hines, Jr.

Contents

Foreword

Howard University has a rich legacy of scholarship in the field of history. The university is especially proud of the record the Department of History has made in the development of African and Afro-American history. To those who appreciate the value of historical knowledge, the contributions of Carter G. Woodson (founder of the Association for the Study of Negro Life and History, and publisher of the *Journal of Negro History*), and William Leo Hansberry (historian of African civilizations and initiator of one of the first systematic courses in African history within the universities of Europe and the United States) are well known.

When I became president of Howard University in 1969, I was particularly interested in strengthening the social sciences and humanities at the graduate level. I was pleased by the Department of History's curricular reorganization and diversification in the first years of my presidency and the leadership of Professors Elsie M. Lewis, Harold O. Lewis, and Lorraine A. Williams. Under Professor Williams, the Doctor of Philosophy in history program, which had been established in 1962, emphasized broader presentation of timeless and contemporary issues while providing specialized training in the methodology of historical research and interpretation. The priority that I requested be placed on developing graduate training programs and advanced research was addressed by the Department of History effectively and creatively.

I am gratified that the Department of History inaugurated in 1970 a lecture series in honor of Rayford Whittingham Logan, then professor emeritus. The inaugural lecture was appropriately given by a former member of Howard University's History Department, the distinguished John Hope Franklin (then chairman of the Department of History at the University of Chicago).

Subsequent lectures have been given by other historians of great distinction such as Professor Benjamin Quarles and C. Vann Woodward as well as younger scholars, including Joseph E. Harris, John Wesley Blassingame, and Mary Frances Berry, who received their early graduate training at Howard University. I am proud to present selected Rayford W. Logan lectures in this seventy-fifth anniversary commemorative volume in the Department of History's Second Historical Series. It is fitting that a wider audience come to know the significance of this research and writing done both to honor one of our greatest historians and to increase knowledge of the history of people of African descent throughout the world.

JAMES E. CHEEK
President
Howard University
Washington, D.C.

Rayford W. Logan

(1897–1982)

Rayford Whittingham Logan, distinguished historian and educator, was born in Washington, D.C., on January 7, 1897, the second son of Martha Ann Whittingham and Arthur Charles Logan. He was educated in the city's Thaddeus Stevens School and the M Street High School (later Dunbar). He graduated from Williams College, Phi Beta Kappa, in 1917 and enlisted in the First Separate Battalion of the District of Columbia National Guard. He was promoted to first lieutenant of infantry, January, 1918, served at the front in the Argonne Forest and Camp Ancona, near Bordeaux, until his discharge in 1919. Because of his bitter experiences in a racially segregated army, he requested discharge in France, which was granted in August, 1919. He remained in France for five years, and became a leader of the Pan-African movement, assisting Dr. W. E. B. Du Bois in the organization of the Pan-African Congresses, 1921–24.

Upon his return to the United States, Rayford Logan taught briefly at Dunbar High School in Washington before joining the faculty of Virginia Union University, Richmond. From 1925 to 1930 he served there as a professor of modern languages, history, and other social sciences. With the assistance of a fellowship from the General Education Board, he attended the Graduate School of Arts and Sciences at Harvard, 1930–32, receiving the Ph.D. in history in 1936. From 1932 to 1933 Dr. Logan served as assistant to Dr. Carter G. Woodson at the Association for the Study of Negro Life and History. In 1933 he joined the faculty of Atlanta University as professor and head of the Department of History. He returned to Washington in 1938 as professor of history at Howard University, serving as head from 1942 to 1964. Appointed professor emeritus of history in 1965, he served as historian of the

Rayford W. Logan

university until 1969. While he was head of the department, the graduate program in history was strengthened significantly, culminating in the inauguration of a Ph.D. program in history in 1962.

Active in international affairs, Dr. Logan's investigation of conditions in Haiti contributed to the withdrawal of the United States military occupation in 1934. Seven years later Haiti conferred upon him the National Order of Honor and Merit with the rank of *Commandeur*. From 1941 to 1942 he worked with Nelson Rockefeller, Coordinator of Inter-American Affairs, undertaking studies in Cuba, Haiti, and the Dominican Republic. From 1940 to 1945 he was also chairman of the Committee on the Participation of Negroes in National Defense. In 1945 he was an accredited correspondent to the San Francisco Conference which organized the United Nations. He served as a member of the United States National Commission for UNESCO, 1947–50, and was a Fulbright Research Fellow in Paris, 1950–51.

A renowned teacher and lecturer, Professor Logan was also a prolific author, establishing himself as an authority in several fields, including European diplomatic history, United States history, Latin American history, and Negro history. Among his best known works are *The Diplomatic Relations of the United States with Haiti, 1776–1891* (1941); *The Negro and the Post-War World* (1945); *The African Mandates in World Politics* (1948); *The Negro in American Life and Thought* (1954); *The Negro in the United States* (1957); *Haiti and the Dominican Republic* (1968); and *Howard University: The First Hundred Years* (1969). He was also editor of *What the Negro Wants* (1944); *Memoirs of a Monticello Slave* (1951); *The Life and Times of Frederick Douglass* (1967); and *W. E. B. Du Bois: A Profile* (1971). At the time of his death he had just completed for publication, with Michael R. Winston, the *Dictionary of American Negro Biography*.

In 1965 Williams College conferred upon him an honorary Doctor of Humane Letters degree, and Howard University conferred the degree Doctor of Laws in 1972. He was appointed distinguished professor of history at Howard in 1971. In July, 1980, he was awarded the Spingarn Medal by the NAACP in recognition of his scholarship and contribution to the achievement of civil rights for all Americans.

Introduction

The emergence of the Howard University Department of History as an important center of teaching and research paralleled the gradual professionalization of history as an academic discipline in the United States. During Howard University's first forty years, 1867-1907, students learned history only as an adjunct to their studies in Latin and Greek. Modern history was initially added to the curriculum in the 1880s as a companion study for English literature. In 1892, Charles Chauveau Cook (1870-1910) professor of English literature, history, rhetoric, logic, and elocution, introduced the first courses at Howard devoted exclusively to history, "The History of Continental Europe, from the Eighth to the Middle of the Eighteenth Century" and a survey of English history. Interest in history grew steadily through Professor Cook's stimulating teaching, and in 1906 the university appointed its first professor of history, the Reverend William V. Tunnell, who taught English and United States history for twenty-two years. Professor Tunnell conducted the university's first historical seminar in 1911, a study of the Reconstruction period, which would be a continuing interest of later faculty and students.

Soon after the establishment of a professorship in history, the university considerably expanded and modernized its curriculum in the College of Arts and Sciences. As a result of this expansion, the European system of academic chairs was abandoned and the American pattern of academic departments was adopted. Thus the Department of History was established in 1913, making Howard the third university in the District of Columbia to establish such a department. A turning point in the department's history was the appointment in 1919 of Dr. Carter G. Woodson, the

Inaugural lecture of the Rayford W. Logan Lectures, May 7, 1970
Left to right: John W. Blassingame, John Hope Franklin,
Lorraine A. Williams, Rayford W. Logan, and Michael R. Winston

editor of *The Journal of Negro History,* as professor of history. In 1919 the department was comprised of four historians, Walter Mitchell Dyson, Charles Harris Wesley, William V. Tunnell, and Carter G. Woodson. Under Professor Woodson's leadership there was developed a new undergraduate and graduate curriculum of twenty-four courses in the academic year 1919–20, which had a number of notable features. In addition to the usual offerings in ancient, medieval, and modern history, there were courses on the Far East and the Negro in American history, the first such courses offered by a university in the District of Columbia. The 1919 curriculum represented simultaneously the special interest in Negro history and a broad cosmopolitan view that would become a strong tradition of the department throughout its later development.

An important addition to the department in its first decade was

William Leo Hansberry (1894-1965). He introduced at Howard the first courses on ancient and medieval African civilizations to be taught in an American university, at a time when it was widely believed that before the arrival of Europeans, Africa was a continent "without a history." In recognition of his contribution to the study of African history, the government of Nigeria established the Hansberry College of African Studies at Nsukka on September 22, 1963. In the following year, Emperor Haile Selassie of Ethiopia personally presented William Leo Hansberry with the first African Research Award for his pioneering work at Howard.

Charles Harris Wesley (1891-1987) was head of the Department of History from 1921 to 1942. During these years there was a steady growth and consolidation of the department's programs of teaching and research. From 1921 to 1930 the department issued the *Howard University Studies in History,* edited by Walter M. Dyson. A comprehensive curriculum in United States, European, Latin American, African, and Asian history was taught increasingly by specialists. Among the important additions to the faculty during this period were Harold O. Lewis in 1930, Williston H. Lofton in 1936, and Rayford W. Logan in 1938. The published research of the faculty and the record established by its graduates brought increasing professional recognition to the department. From 1920 to 1942, graduate students wrote ninety-four master's theses. Most of them were in Afro-American history and constituted a significant contribution to a field neglected until relatively recent years by the historical profession in the United States.

Rayford W. Logan (1897-1982) was head of the Department of History from 1942 to 1964. During these years there was an expansion of course offerings in diplomatic, African, and Asian history with greater specialization of courses in the United States field. This was made possible by significant additions to the faculty, including Merze Tate in 1942, John Hope Franklin in 1947, Elsie M. Lewis in 1956, Chancellor Williams in 1961, and Esther Morrison in 1963. In recognition of the department's productivity in research, and its successful master's degree program, the Howard University Board of Trustees authorized the establishment of a Ph.D. program in 1962. This was a major landmark in the department's evolution from its modest beginnings in 1913.

From 1964 to 1970, during the chairmanships of Elsie M. Lewis (1964-69) and Harold O. Lewis (1969-70), the department embarked on an effort to reorganize its teaching program to accommodate the increased needs of the graduate program and the rapidly growing demand by undergraduates for more courses in black history.

The first fifty-seven years of the Department of History's development provided a firm foundation for the innovative programs inaugurated during the chairmanship of Lorraine A. Williams (1970-74). Under her leadership the department emphasized growth in the graduate program, faculty recruitment, research and publication, and new methods of teaching.

One of the most significant of the projects of this period was the inauguration of an annual lecture series in honor of Rayford W. Logan. Proposed by two of Professor Logan's former students, Lorraine A. Williams and John W. Blassingame, the lectures were intended to provide an opportunity for the presentation of research and new points of view in the historical fields most closely associated with Howard's Department of History. In addition to honoring a senior colleague who had achieved distinction as one of the nation's leading scholars, the Logan lectures were planned also as a vehicle for objective assessments of research issues in a still emerging area of historical inquiry. The 1960s and 1970s were years in which there was not only an explosion of popular interest in black history, but also a rapidly expanding literature characterized by greater specialization and methodological innovation.

The Logan lectures were inaugurated in 1970 by John Hope Franklin, a member of Howard's faculty from 1947 to 1956 who was then the John Matthews Manly Distinguished Service Professor and chairman of the Department of History at the University of Chicago. The roster of lecturers since 1970 makes it evident that one of the objectives of the series has been met, namely, providing an appropriate forum for outstanding scholars. A second objective has, naturally, been more elusive. This is the more difficult matter of the cumulative intellectual impact of lectures that span a period of nearly two decades. It is hoped that this volume will bring to a larger audience the analyses and perspectives developed by the lecturers.

Some of the lectures selected for this volume are presented substantially as they were delivered at Howard, others were later revised as essays, and a few were expanded into full-length books. This has resulted in considerable but understandable variations in density of documentation. Nonetheless, it is the hope of the editors that the collection of these lectures will represent a contribution to the fields of research interest that they address. We believe that the Logan lectures have advanced scholarship in an evolving field. As the Department of History at Howard marks its seventy-fifth year in 1988, it is appropriate to reconsider conventional historical judgments as a tribute to a unique intellectual tradition.

I

*Perspectives on the
History of Africa*

George Washington Williams and Africa

John Hope Franklin

Speaking before a Congress on Africa in Atlanta in 1895, the Honorable John C. Smyth, a former minister to Liberia, said that "Negroes are averse to the discussion of Africa, when their relationship with that ancient and mysterious land is made the subject of discourse or reflection." More than a generation later, in 1937, the distinguished historian Dr. Carter G. Woodson said that "Negroes themselves accept as a compliment the theory of a complete cultural break with Africa, for above all things they do not care to be known as resembling in any way those 'terrible Africans'." Even Dr. W. E. B. Du Bois, in his autobiography, *Dusk of Dawn,* wrote of blacks "who had inherited the fierce repugnance toward anything African, which was the natural result of the older colonization scheme. . . . They felt themselves Americans, not Africans. They resented and feared any coupling with Africa."

These sentiments, uttered at various times during the last three quarters of a century by careful and thoroughly responsible observers, are in marked contrast to some views that Negro Americans have expressed in recent years. At the independence ceremonies in Nigeria in 1960, there were numerous Negro Americans in attendance; and they expressed almost boundless enthusiasm and delight with everything they saw. They made it quite clear that they wished to be identified with that race of

3

people who, in achieving independence, were moving to an important position on the world stage. Several years later, Negro Americans were expressing similar sentiments at the independence ceremonies of Zanzibar and of Kenya. If one such visitor found himself somewhat at a loss for words to respond to a warm greeting of one Nigerian who said, "Welcome home, brother," he appeared to have a warm feeling inside upon realizing that he could identify with his proud black brother in the once legendary "Dark Continent."

Does the rather overt if brusque manifestation of interest in Africa on the part of Negro Americans in recent years represent a significant modification of the sentiment described by Smyth, Woodson, and Du Bois in earlier years? Are the current pilgrimages to Africa on the part of Negro Americans—affluent members of the middle class as well as students working in the Peace Corps and "Operation Crossroads"—the result of a rather crude acceptance of Africans, now that they are heads of states, diplomats, delegates to the United Nations, and possible dispensers of favors and benedictions on their still rather hapless darker brothers of the New World? In one sense, the answer is yes; for the modern African states have captured the imagination of black Americans and even thrilled them in simply realizing that black peoples have risen to vaunted and enviable stations in life. Surely, in 1970, Negro Americans who could never have conceived that black peoples would ever be rulers of nations and who could not previously identify with Africans as recently as a dozen years ago are delighted to be able to say, today, "my friend, Chief so and so, is the minister of finance of the African state of X" or that "I have just returned from the African Republic of Y, where I had luncheon with the speaker of the house."

But in another sense, the answer is no. For there has always been a deep interest in the past, on the part of some Negro Americans, in Africa, in its past and present, as well as its future. Smyth, Woodson, and Du Bois were actually reproaching their fellows who seemed not to be as committed to a deep interest in Africa as they were. Even before he was minister to Liberia, Smyth manifested a deep interest in Africa. Dr. Woodson had long been a student of African history and had written about it. One of his most cherished ambitions was to compile an Encyclopedia Africana; and at the time of his death in 1950 he was working feverishly to realize this dream. Dr. Du Bois had studied African history and culture even before he published his first book on the African slave trade in 1896; and he was, in a very real way, the father of the Pan-African movement. Incidentally, it is relevant to this occasion to observe that Dr. Rayford W. Logan, who was later to write so extensively about Africa, was the principal assistant of Dr. Du Bois in planning the early Pan-African Congresses immediately following World War I.

Just as the Negro liberation movement in recent years has attracted vast numbers of people who, somehow, have lost sight of the fact that the movement is more than a century old and that it has been brought to its present stage by the untold sacrifices and efforts of thousands of pioneers, so does the current interest in Africa represent the continuation of a tradition that was begun centuries ago by highly imaginative, skillful, and resourceful Negro Americans. This interest in Africa is not new. Rather, the interest has become enlarged and now includes hundreds of thousands who a few years ago could not have dreamed that they could have any serious interest in the affairs of the so-called Dark Continent.

To recognize this recent upsurge of interest is not to reproach those who have discovered it. Negro Americans, with all their problems of survival, of gaining a measure of respectability, and of winning a semblance of their rights, had little energy and resources left to channel into the affairs of Africa. There was, moreover, the almost natural inclination—as Woodson and Du Bois implied—of avoiding identification with causes and peoples who apparently could do little if anything for them to relieve their plight. It would, nevertheless, be both unfair and inaccurate to suggest that the interest of Negro Americans in Africa is of recent origin or that it has been, from the beginning, banal and self-seeking.

There was scarcely a time when some Negroes in the New World did not entertain hopes that they would, some day, migrate to the land of their forebears. At times these hopes were inspired merely by the search for identity, for roots, for security. At other times they were viewed as the numerous manifestations of barbarity on the American scene. Paul Cuffe, the affluent Negro Quaker of Massachusetts, who early in the nineteenth century began to dream of ending his days as a migrant to Africa, held these dreams because of the nightmare of his experiences with the hypocritical claims of freedom and independence on the part of the American patriots during the American Revolution. John Russwurm, one of the first Negro college graduates and an early advocate of solving the problem of race in the United States, soon became convinced that Negroes had no future in the United States and became an ardent advocate of migration to Africa. "We consider it a waste of words to talk of ever enjoying citizenship in this country," he concluded. Thereupon, he emigrated to Liberia in 1829 to become the first superintendent of public schools in that country. In numerous other ways—as editor of the *Liberia Herald,* governor of the Maryland colony, and as a leader in the unification of Liberia—he sought to bring strength and stability to his adopted home.

Martin Delany, who had opposed colonization and had written against it, reached the conclusion in 1852 that migration to Africa was the only solution. "I am not in favor of caste," he said, "nor a separation of the brotherhood of mankind, and would as willingly live among white men as black, if I had an equal possession and enjoyment of privileges. . . . But I must admit, that I have no hopes in this country—no confidence in the American people, with a few excellent exceptions." He called on Negro Americans to join him in establishing a nation on the eastern coast of Africa. "The land is ours—there it lies with inexhaustible resources; let us go and possess it." The convention which Delany called to consider the problem met in Cleveland in 1854. Although the delegates were not specific in their desire to settle in Africa, they were enthusiastic about their African heritage, and they declared that they would not submit any longer to the domination of the white race which, after all, "constituted but one-third of the population of the globe."

It was, then, the bitter experience of Negro Americans in the United States that kept alive their interest in migrating to Africa; and that experience would continue through the nineteenth and into the twentieth century. In 1883, when the United States Supreme Court declared the Civil Rights Act of 1875 unconstitutional, Henry McNeal Turner, former chaplain of the Union Army, former member of the Georgia legislature, bishop of the AME Church, made up his mind. "There is no manhood future in the United States for the Negro," he said. "He may eke out an existence for generations to come, but he can never be a man, full, symmetrical, and undwarfed." Thousands of others reached the same conclusion. In 1877, several hundred Negro families in South Carolina joined up to go to Liberia. Later experiences moved others to resolve to go to Africa. After World War I, Marcus Garvey would point to the degradation of black Americans and call on them to join him in the most ambitious back-to-Africa scheme the world had ever seen. Within a few years millions of Negroes were talking about Garvey's Universal Negro Improvement Association, and hundreds of thousands were taking his back-to-Africa proposals seriously. Their attachment to the Garvey movement and other zionist movements reflected their despair and frustration more than it represented an active interest in migrating. In the final analysis, the interest of most of them did not seem to extend beyond the water's edge. But this was an interest that brought more Negro Americans into a closer consideration of things African than had ever before been the case.

For many years, however, there had been a small group of Negro Americans who did go beyond the water's edge, not necessarily for the purpose of migrating but to do what they could to advance and improve conditions among their African brothers. There were the religious leaders who hoped to share with Africans their own view of the better life through religion. They had little or no assistance from their white co-religionists, who seemed unable to bring themselves to join in an interracial movement to bring the light of Christianity to the Africans. Nor did the white rulers of Africa relish the idea of Negro Americans undertaking to Christianize Africans, lest they upset the white man's ideas of "how a black man was supposed to look, act, and sound." But David George went to Sierra Leone in 1792 to organize the Baptist church. Daniel Coker took Methodism there in 1821. Lott Cary, the prudent Baptist minister who saved his money and purchased his own freedom, became a leading exponent of Christian missions in following decades.

Even if Negro American missionaries did not enjoy a great success in converting their black African brothers, their presence in Africa had a profound and lasting effect on Negroes in the United States. It kept alive their interest in Africa. As missionaries returned and told of their experiences, as they sought continued support for their overseas enterprises, as they underscored the continuing cultural, racial, and even political bonds between Negro Americans and Africans, they convinced many Negro Americans that Africa was, indeed, worthy of their interest and consideration.

Perhaps the best example of the early and continuing interest, not altogether selfish, is manifested in the career of George Washington Williams, the first major Negro American historian. Williams, who was born in Pennsylvania in 1848, had little education during his early years. His parents seemed constantly on the move, from one Pennsylvania town to another, and finally to Massachusetts, where he studied for several years in the public school and academy in New Bedford. When he was fifteen, in 1863, he ran away from home, assumed the name of an uncle, and enlisted in the United States Colored Troops. The examining surgeon, aware of the fact that Williams' zeal to fight far exceeded his age, rejected him; but after much pleading by Williams, the surgeon relented. During the war Williams was severely wounded and received an honorable discharge from the service. As soon as he recovered, he reenlisted and saw action in several battles during the closing months of the war.

Shortly after the war Williams was ordered to be mustered out, but adventure and wanderlust had completely captivated him, and he enlisted in the Mexican army where he advanced from orderly sergeant to assistant-inspector general, with the rank of lieutenant colonel in the First Battery from the state of Tampico. In 1867, after the execution of Maximilian, Williams returned to the United

States and entered the cavalry service of the regular army, serving in the Comanche campaign in 1867. The following year he left the army, and after a brief sojourn in St. Louis and Quincy, Illinois, he returned East, where he resumed his studies. First, he enrolled in Howard University, but within a year he was in the Newton Theological Seminary in Cambridge, where he graduated in 1874. At the commencement exercises he delivered the class oration, "Early Christianity in Africa," in which he demonstrated an intimate knowledge of the historical development of Africa in the early centuries of the Christian era. This interest in Africa would remain throughout his life.

In the years that followed, Williams's interests shifted from religion to business, law, and politics. For a while he was store-keeper in the internal revenue department in Cincinnati. He attended lectures at the Cincinnati Law School and studied in the office of Alphonso Taft, father of the future president. In 1881 he was admitted to the Ohio bar and was later admitted to practice before the Supreme Judicial Court in Boston. Meanwhile, he had entered Republican politics and in 1879 was elected to the Ohio legislature, where he served as chairman of the Committee on the Library and on several other legislative committees. These were his busiest years. He was minister, lawyer, contributor to a newspaper, legislator, and student of history. There, he began to write his two-volume *History of the Negro Race in America,* which was published in 1883. The appearance of this work was an event of unusual significance in publishing and literary circles. Because of the nature of the work, the critics were compelled to take it seriously; and if they did not always praise it, they were forced to concede that it was a unique and important work. Five years later he. brought out his *History of the Negro Troops in the War of the Rebellion,* for which the *Literary World* offered the author "congratulations for the intelligence, discretion, and excellent workmanship with which he prepared the book."

The limited literary and financial success of his historical works by no means satisfied Williams, who was a man of burning ambition, boundless energy, and a determination to make his mark on the world. Even as he wrote his history, he continued his interest in politics; and there can be no doubt that he was ambitious for some high office, elective or appointive. He was active in Republican politics during the 1880s and was well acquainted with President Chester Arthur and with Representative James G. Blaine. In the closing days of the Arthur administration, the president nominated Williams to be minister to Haiti. The Senate confirmed him on March 3, 1885; and Williams was sworn in the following day, a few hours before Grover Cleveland was inaugurated as president. This "midnight appointment" was widely regarded as a Republican trick designed to embarrass the incoming Democratic administration; and there is reason to believe that it did embarrass the Democrats. After some equivocation, they declined to permit him to execute the required bond and to take office.

This was, for Williams, a most bitter experience. At precisely the moment that he was about to realize one of his most cherished ambitions, he discovered that he had been the victim of whimsical, partisan politics. It was enough to discourage most men. But Williams was not easily discouraged; and surely, he would not permit one setback to dispirit him. He merely used this experience as the occasion to return to one of his earliest interests, Africa. Indeed, his interest in Africa had never flagged. He had studied African history while doing research on the history of the Negro people in America. In 1884, the year following the appearance of his history, he wrote a series of articles on African geography in which he disputed the Portuguese claim to the Congo. In the same year he appeared before the Senate Committee on Foreign Relations, urging the passage of a resolution recognizing the International Association for the Congo as a friendly government. Within a few days the Senate passed such a resolution, and Williams assumed that his plea had the effect of influencing some of the senators. Greatly encouraged that United States recognition would have a salutary effect on the future of the Congo, Williams decided to take a more active part in the development of Central Africa.

In the summer of 1884 he went to Europe armed with a warm letter of introduction from the secretary of state, Frederick T.

Frelinghuysen. In August he made the first of several calls on Leopold, King of the Belgians. He consulted at length with the king about the labor system in the Congo and placed before him some suggestions for the use of black Africans and even black Americans in the development of the area. His suggestions seemed to meet with the king's approval. Doubtless, it would be good for the Belgians to have the support of a Negro American in their plans for the exploitation of the Congo, so long as he did not inspect too closely just what was going on in the Congo.

Williams was particularly concerned with the persistence of slavery and the slave trade in Africa. He hoped that if Belgium would take the lead in giving Africans in the Congo an opportunity to work as free men in the development of the region, it would be an admirable example for others to follow. He prepared an elaborate historical paper on the Congo in which he praised the establishment of the Free State in 1885 and urged the United States to join in assuming certain obligations regarding its sovereignty and neutrality. In 1889 he conferred both with President Harrison and John Sherman, chairman of the Senate Committee on Foreign Relations. Neither wanted to become involved in any scheme to guarantee the neutrality of the Congo Free State. They were, however, cordial to the idea of having an American delegate at the Anti-Slavery Conference of the European Powers, called by King Leopold.

Williams wrote and spoke against slavery in Africa and urged Americans to follow the example set by the Quakers a century earlier: "They would not buy or use rice, sugar, coffee, cotton, or any other article they knew to be the product of slave labor. We can draw inspiration and instruction from the sublime action of the American colonies which passed the Non-Importation Act. We can refuse to send rum to the Arab with which to buy slaves and drug his hapless victims. We can talk against it, and pray God for light upon this dark subject which it is our duty to aid in settling."

In the autumn of 1889 Williams spent two months in Belgium attending the Anti-Slavery Conference and conferring with the Belgians about labor problems in the Congo. In December he called at the White House and reported on the proceedings of the conference to President Harrison. He promised to prepare a memorandum containing reasons why the United States should ratify the General Act of the Conference of Berlin of 1885 recognizing the Congo Free State. Before he could complete the report, he had sailed again for Europe, en route to the Congo.

It is not clear precisely when Williams decided to visit the Congo. Surely, he had not indicated to the Belgians, during his recent visit, his intentions to go there. Perhaps he had been encouraged by certain Americans to make the visit. The president was cordial to him and apparently wanted as much information about the Congo as Williams could provide. S. S. McClure, the leading magazine editor of the time, was also interested; and he commissioned Williams to do a series of articles on Africa for his magazine. Williams also had a commission and, presumably, a healthy expense account from the railroad magnate, Collis P. Huntington, to survey the Congo and advise him on the feasibility of building a railroad across the Free State.

Williams proceeded to Brussels, where he made known his intention of visiting the Congo. Everything possible was done to dissuade him. "Officials who formerly greeted me cordially, now avoided me, and wrapped themselves in an impenetrable reserve," he reported. "An officer of the King's Household was dispatched to me for the purpose of persuading me not to visit the Congo. He dwelt upon the deadly character of the climate during the rainy seasons, the period and hardships of travelling by caravans, and the heavy expenses of the voyage. . . . I simply replied that I was going. After this the King sent for me, and received me cordially. I did not care to lead up to the conversation on the Congo, and consequently I strove to turn the conversation to other topics. But soon I saw that there was but one thing about which His Majesty cared to converse, and I made up my mind to allow him to do all the talking."

The king explained the difficulty of travelling and living in the region and urged him to postpone his trip for at least five years, and in return the king would see that Williams would receive, in Brussels, all the information he desired about the Congo. The more the effort was made to dissuade him, the more determined Williams was to go; and the king told him that if he persisted he would not be allowed to go on a state steamer.

That presented no problem to Williams. He crossed the channel to England, purchased all necessary supplies in London, and sailed from Liverpool at the end of January, 1890. The trip to Africa was the realization of a lifelong ambition for Williams, and he intended to make the most of it. The voyage from Liverpool to Boma, in the Congo Free State, occupied fifty-three days, during which time Williams was able to stop at most of the important ports on the west coast of Africa. He visited Sierra Leone; Sinoe, Liberia; Bereby, on the Ivory Coast; the Gold Coast (Ghana); the Slave Coast (Benin and Nigeria) including Calabar, and Bonny at the mouth of the River Niger in present-day Nigeria; the Cameroons; the Portuguese Island of St. Tomé; and Gabon in French Equatorial Africa. Williams was distressed to observe the selfish and oppressive rule of the Liberians. He was shocked to notice the hostility to the British on the part of the Portuguese, and he was thrilled to have an interview with an African king on the Slave Coast. He visited churches, trading posts, and villages in the hinterland; and he talked with many European businessmen trading in Africa.

Finally, he reached the Congo and spent four months travelling there. He went from the mouth of the Congo River at Banana to its headwaters at Stanley Falls; from Brazzaville on Stanley Pool to the Atlantic Ocean at Loango. In all he travelled some 3,266 miles in the Congo. It was a grueling experience, but the only complaint that Williams had was that he, together with his staff of eighty-five Congolese aides, sometimes suffered from fatigue, hunger, and heat. On one occasion it appeared that the courage of his men would "abate" and Williams considered executing two of them, but "with firmness and heroic suffering without a murmur I triumphed." "Sometimes," he said, "I was crossing plains which stretched days before me, as level as our own prairies; again I struggled for four days through the dense, dark and damp forest of Muyambu, where it rains every month in the year. Sometimes I came upon villages of friendly natives who offered me a house and food if I would honor them by remaining overnight with them; and again hostile natives warned me to move on, denying me food and entertainment. But I never consented to go. I knew too well the virtue of my modern firearms; and I usually gave them to understand that I wanted food for my people and would pay for it, and if it were not forthcoming within one hour I would come and take it. Hungry men are usually heroes for the hour, and I always got food when there was any to be had."

It was also a disenchanting experience, resulting in a public denunciation by Williams of both King Leopold and His Majesty's principal emissary in the Congo, Henry M. Stanley. In July, 1890, from Stanley Falls in the Congo, Williams wrote an "Open Letter to the King of the Belgians." At last he knew why Leopold did not want him to visit the Congo. In the first place, Leopold's title to the area was tainted by frauds of the grossest character. "Your Majesty's government is deficient in the moral, military and financial strength to govern a territory of 1,500,000 square miles," he continued; "guilty of violating its contracts made with its soldiers, mechanics, and workmen; the courts of your majesty's government are abortive, unjust, partial, and delinquent; your majesty's government is excessively cruel to its prisoners." The bill of particulars contained twelve charges of the most serious nature; and Williams concluded by telling the king, "All the crimes perpetrated in the Congo have been done in your name, and you must answer at the bar of public sentiment for the misgovernment of the peoples whose lives and fortunes were entrusted to you by the Conference of Berlin of 1884–85."

Williams wrote a lengthy report to Collis P. Huntington and his colleagues, entitled "Report on the Congo Railway." In it he reviewed the procedure by which the Free State had, in 1887, chartered the Compagnie du Congo pour le Commerce et l'Industrie to survey and build a railroad. The terms were liberal, and the company received almost a half million acres of choice land. The company had spent more time exploiting the resources of the land than in surveying and building the railroad. At the end of almost four years, "not one mile of road-bed has been laid, and only twenty miles of survey has been completed."

Williams declared that the proposed railroad was the result of the "wild, irresponsible advice" of Henry M. Stanley to King Leopold. It could not be built for the amount specified (sixteen million francs) or in the time specified (three years). It would require at least forty million francs and, under the most favorable conditions, at least eight years. Of Stanley, Williams said, "When he describes things and persons he displays the ability of an able correspondent. But the moment he attempts to deal with figures and trade, he becomes the veriest romancer. . . . Modern history records nothing equal to the speculation of Mr. Stanley. . . . And while I have an interest in the civilization of Africa equal to any person's, I cannot be silent, or suffer to pass unchallenged statements calculated to mislead and deceive the friends of humanity and civilization." He encouraged Huntington by saying, "The Congo railway ought to be built, and from the bottom of my heart I hope it will be." He clearly implied that what was needed was the genius and wealth of Collis P. Huntington and the well-remunerated advice of George Washington Williams!

The third report by Williams was written at Loanda, Angola, and was addressed to President Harrison. In it he reviewed his long interest in Africa and the president's interest in his investigations. He declared that Leopold's claim to the Congo was based on spurious treaties, supposedly made by Stanley with more than four hundred kings and chiefs. "And yet many of these people declare that they never made a treaty with Stanley, or any other white man; that their lands have been taken from them by force; and that they suffer the greatest wrongs at the hands of the Belgians." He said that he hoped that American interest in the welfare of the state and its people would continue and that this interest would be guided by noble and unselfish motives. The people of the United States, because of their earlier interest in the Congo have a "just right to know the truth . . . respecting the Independent State of Congo, an absolute monarchy, an oppressive and cruel government, an exclusive Belgian colony, now tottering to its fall. I indulge the hope that when a new government shall rise upon the ruins of the old, it will be simple, not complicated; local not European; international, not national; just, not cruel;

and casting its shield alike over black and white, trader and missionary, endure for centuries."

After Williams completed his mission in the Congo, he proceeded to Angola, Southwest Africa, where he spent several weeks resting and writing. During his sojourn in the city of Loanda, he had an opportunity to observe at close hand Portuguese rule in Southwest Africa. The black slave, he reported, had a miserable existence, but Williams was pleased to see that the considerable number that were becoming free immediately enjoyed what he described as complete equality. "There is more genuine, heartfelt democracy here," he wrote a friend, "than in your boasted America. Every black man in Loanda has a vote at the municipal elections, there are mixed schools, there are no separate churches—a great thing for the Catholic religion—there are no separate grave yards." Williams was not deluded into thinking that European rule in Africa was a good thing, however. After making his observations regarding the progress of black men in Angola, he said, "Notwithstanding all these things my cry is *Africa for the Africans!*" This conclusion was doubtless reached, in part, because of the convict system and the various labor schemes which he regarded as repressive in the extreme.

This trip, the last of his life, turned into a grand tour for Williams. Upon leaving Angola, he took a ship around the Cape of Good Hope to Algoa Bay, then up the East Coast to Zanzibar, where he lived and worked for about six weeks. While there he was entertained by the British consul general, the merchants, and other leading citizens, and was made an honorary member of the English Club. He also had a private audience with the Sultan. From Zanzibar, he proceeded northward, visiting Mombasa and Lamu in British East Africa, before going to Cairo, where he remained for several weeks in the spring of 1891. He concluded his trip by visiting Tripoli, Tunis, and Tangier.

In the late spring of 1891 Williams was back in London, doing research at the Public Records Office and preparing a lengthy manuscript on the Congo. When he left Africa his strength was greatly diminished by the strenuous activities in which he had been engaged; and old maladies, complicated by his war-time wounds, began to recur. En route to England he became friendly with a young English woman, traveling from India with her mother. By the time they reached England they had become engaged, although Williams had a wife back in Washington, D.C. When his health continued to deteriorate, the young lady and her mother accompanied Williams to Blackpool where, it was hoped, the sea air would give him strength. This move was too late; on August 2, 1891, at forty-three years of age, Williams expired.

The death of Williams made little stir in the United States. The excitement in England was over the large inventory of African curios that he brought back with him and that were now to be sold at auction. "A unique and valuable collection," the advertisement read, "comprising copper knives, quaint daggers and swords, carved spears, ornamented paddles, shields, bows and arrows, ivory tusks and trumpets, brass rings for neck, ankles and wrists, fishing spears, and other interesting objects, obtained from the natives during an extended tour of exploration by Col. George Washington Williams, an American citizen, recently deceased at Blackpool." These items, a sort of "last hurrah" for Williams, told their own story of the great variety of African cultures that Williams had come to appreciate and to respect. Soon, however, the American public would learn of his defiance and bitter condemnation of the King of the Belgians for betraying black Africans, of his advocacy of American support that might guide the Congolese to a new destiny of independence and self-respect, and of this final, heroic effort of George Washington Williams to learn more about the land of his fathers. He had not accomplished nearly as much as his boundless energy and indomitable will drove him to attempt; and in his enthusiasm he had cherished the futile hope that his own country could develop a "noble and unselfish" interest in Africa. But he had become one more witness to the continuing and increasing interest of black Americans in black Africans.

NOTE

For discussion of Professor Franklin's further research on Williams and full development of the ideas presented in this lecture, see John Hope Franklin, *George Washington Williams: A Biography* (Chicago, 1985).

The East African Slave Trade and Repatriation in Kenya

Joseph E. Harris

THE SLAVE TRADE AND ABOLITION

The slave trade from East Africa resulted from an Asian demand for labor: on the date plantations in Basra, Bandar Abbas, Minab, and along the Batinah coast of the Persian Gulf; in the pearl diving industry of Bahrein and Lingeh on the Persian Gulf; as slave soldiers in parts of Arabia, Persia, and India; as dock workers and dhow crewmen in the Indian Ocean; and as concubines, eunuchs, and domestics throughout the Muslim communities of much of Asia.[1]

The major slave dealers were the Omani Arabs. Oman held the strategic position in the naval and commercial strategy of the Middle East. Its capital, Muscat, commanded the approach to the Persian Gulf through which large numbers of African slaves were transported. And from 1784, when Omani Arabs captured Kilwa and subsequently Zanzibar, rulers of Oman claimed sovereignty over several towns on the East African mainland and intervened on many occasions to assert their control. Shortly after the turn of the nineteenth century, several Omanis moved to Zanzibar to exploit the agricultural and commercial potential of East Africa. Cloves and coconuts became major plantation industries utilizing large supplies of slave labor. Other factors contributing to the tremendous increase in the East African slave trade were the enforcement of the abolitionist treaties pertaining to the West African Coast; the gradual limitation of Arab slave depots in North Africa; the development of plantation economies by the French in the Mascarene Islands of Mauritius and Réunion.

This indeed became a big business in the nineteenth century. Although some of these slaves were transported to the Americas, the main focus was Asia. Arab merchants from Arabia and Persia sailed during the northeastern monsoon, did business along the coast of East Africa where they purchased slaves, and began their return to Asian markets with the southeastern monsoon. The season of greatest activity was during the Haj, when slave brokers from various parts of the world gathered at Mecca to conduct business with pilgrims who frequently returned home with one or two domestic slaves. The harvesting and marketing of dates in the Persian Gulf was also a busy period for slave dealers who purchased slaves with dates.

The legal abolition of the slave trade was first applied to West Africa; it later spread to the rest of the continent, mainly East Africa where the traffic had developed over nearly two thousand years. The reaction of Asian sovereigns to abolition was of course predictable. Committed both to economic gain and to Islam, which recognized slavery as a natural element in society, Muslim sovereigns viewed efforts to curtail the slave trade as threats to their religion, economy, and national sovereignty. Still, the British undertook to eliminate the trade by negotiating agreements with several sheiks on the Persian Gulf, the Shah of Persia, the King of Mukalla, and with several Somali rulers. In India, the Abolition Act of 1811 and the Indian Government Act of 1843, supplemented by British pressure on the independent Indian states, contributed to the suppression of the traffic in those areas.

The more familiar abolition agreements were the Moresby Treaty of 1822, in which the Sultan of Oman agreed to prohibit the sale of slaves to Christians; the 1845 agreement in which the Sultan acquiesced in the curtailment of the export of slaves from his African possessions (the trade could continue between the East African mainland and Zanzibar, but not to his Asian dominion);

and finally, the Treaty of 1873 which bound the Sultan to suppress the trade by sea entirely and obliged him to close the slave markets in his East African dominion. All of these agreements required the British navy for enforcement.

In addition to suppression of the trade by these measures, the British also pressed for the liberation of slaves on the Asian continent itself. From the mid-1830s, Africans liberated from dhows which violated the several agreements above, and those freed on the African mainland were channelled to three depots for settlement: Aden in Arabia, Bombay and Nasik in India, and the Seychelles in the Indian Ocean. The British resident was charged with the responsibility of finding them lodging and employment.

While a large number of those liberated Africans were assigned to individual families in Arabia and India, most of the young ex-slaves were enrolled in mission stations. The principal mission stations in India, the primary area of my concern in this essay, were the Roman Catholic orphanage at Bandora, the American mission at Poona, and the Church Missionary Society African Asylum at Nasik. In each case, the Indian government contributed a monthly allowance for the children's upkeep.

Nasik, the most relevant Asian station for this paper, is located about a hundred miles from Bombay. The Reverend William S. Price of the CMS founded the African Asylum there in 1854. It was a school and orphanage for liberated African children; there they received instruction in Bible studies and the English language. In addition, the girls were taught sewing and cooking with the hope that they would find employment as domestics. The boys were trained as carpenters, masons, and tailors.

Even before the Treaty of 1873 was negotiated, several efforts were made to have ex-slaves resettled on the East African coast; but the death of David Livingstone and the signing of that treaty both accelerated the move and resulted in specific plans for that resettlement. The best known and most successful resettlement occurred at Freretown* as an extension of the community at Nasik.

* Freretown should not be confused with Freetown, Sierra Leone.

REPATRIATION IN FRERETOWN

The genesis of the manumitted African community at Freretown occurred in 1864 when Reverend Price, then superintendent of the African Asylum at Nasik, sent two of his students, William H. Jones and Ishmael Semler, to join Johann Rebmann in missionary work at Rabai, approximately fifteen miles north of Mombasa. Jones and Semler, both Yaos, had converted to Christianity at Nasik where they were trained as a blacksmith and carpenter, respectively. They had both married Galla Ethiopian women at Nasik, so the two couples arrived in Rabai for missionary work; a Nasik colleague, George David, arrived a short while later.[2]

Jones and Semler served as missionaries at Rabai and also itinerated as ministers along the coast of East Africa. Jones in particular was a missionary in Kisulitini in 1865, at the Universities Mission in Zanzibar in 1867, as well as at Rabai. In 1871 he was sent back to Bombay to recruit additional liberated Africans to undertake missionary work in the Mombasa area. Two years later, Sir Bartle Frere, who was in East Africa to negotiate the Treaty of 1873, visited Rebmann in Rabai and noted that the Africans from Bombay were performing the tasks very well. He therefore urged that Mombasa become a place for the resettlement of manumitted Africans.

Within a short time the CMS, Universities Mission, and the Anti-Slavery Society held meetings in London on the problems of the East African slave trade. These groups also met with the British Parliament. These activities culminated in the CMS sending Reverend Price to form at Mombasa an industrial settlement for liberated Africans, to develop a Christian community at Rabai, and to establish a mission station at Kilimanjaro. Thus, in November, 1874, Price and his wife arrived in Mombasa to undertake their new tasks. Not only did they recognize several of their former students from Nasik, but three of them—Jones, Semler, and David—became the principal and most effective assistants at the station. Later that year Matthew Wellington joined the group. These four men and their families became the real

African pioneers in the establishment of Freretown and Rabai as communities for Africans liberated from the slave trade and slavery. In particular, William Jones played a major role in recruitment in India, which he visited for that purpose in 1871, 1878–81, and 1893.[3]

Before Jones first visited Mombasa in 1864, he had been married to an Anglo-Indian woman by whom he had a son, John. Jones married the Galla woman after the death of his first wife, just prior to their departure for Mombasa. He and his second wife had five children—Mary, Willie, James, Margaret, and Beatrice. All except Beatrice were educated in India and were therefore fluent in English and familiar with British culture. The two sons, Willie and James, played very important roles in Kenyan history: Willie as a pioneer in education on the coast, and James as one of the very few skilled printers in the country during the first quarter of this century.

As noted earlier, Matthew Wellington was also a pioneer Freretown settler. He was born to Yao parents in the late 1840s and was named Chengwimbe. As a child, he often heard the familiar cries of Africans trying to escape the slave catchers. He was himself captured and became a domestic slave of a Yao. In the early 1860s he was taken to Kilwa where he was sold to an Arab for a "roll of cloth," and loaded in an Arab dhow. He recalled that some two or three hundred Africans were packed in the dhow where braided palm leaves on poles separated those slaves on the top from below; several were thrown overboard when their sickness persisted. The dhow sailed first to Zanzibar, Mogadishu, and toward Arabia when it was captured by the British cruiser *Thetis*. The Africans were rescued, and within a few days they arrived in Aden; shortly thereafter two hundred of them were taken to Bombay, India. All of them entered Nasik where Chengwimbe spent nearly eight years. He was taught English, Bible studies, and carpentry. Two years after his enrollment at Nasik he was baptized and given the name Matthew; he chose the surname, Wellington.[4]

In 1874 Wellington was among five Africans at Nasik to be selected to return to East Africa to join in the search for David

Livingstone. He recalled that his first visit to Zanzibar had been as a slave; in 1872 he was there to assist in the search for a man seeking to abolish slavery. Wellington took great pride in the parallel. The five returned Livingstone's body to Bagamoyo, Tanganyika; one of the group, Jacob Wainwright, accompanied the body to England.[5]

Sometime in 1874, while Reverend Price was supervising the clearing of the site for Freretown, Wellington arrived; that reunion with his former supervisor resulted in a resumption of work begun at Nasik. In 1875 the remaining Africans at Nasik were transferred to Freretown; when they arrived on the *Thetis,* which had rescued Wellington ten years earlier, he not only welcomed his compatriots but thanked the captain for his role in liberating Africans from slavery. Wellington established his home in Freretown, had a family, continued his missionary work, and taught carpentry. In addition, he worked for the government in the Department of Public Works.[6]

Other prominent first settlers in the Bombay group included: Ishmael Semler, George David, Ishmael Mochira, Clement and Mary Farrar, Cephas and Jane Farrar, and several others. All of them had large families, and many of their descendants live in Freretown today.

Freretown also attracted settlers from surrounding areas in East Africa. The most prominent in this group are the Mbotelas, whose history reaches back to the area around Lake Malawi, then known as Lake Nyasa. Mbotela was a Yao farmer and was captured in his village by an Arab slave raiding party which marched him with other captives to the coast. Mbotela was sold and loaded on a dhow bound for Arabia when a British cruiser intercepted it and freed the Africans. Since this occurred after the British had decided to settle liberated Africans on the coast, Mbotela and others with him were eventually taken to Freretown. There they met several of their friends and relatives who had also been freed by British cruisers. This reunion was a time of great rejoicing and provided an atmosphere in which many conversions to Christianity occurred. The liberated Africans thus came to regard the British as "saviors," and Freretown as the "town of peace in the city of war."[7]

Freretown had already been established when Mbotela joined it; however, he did see some immigrants arrive from India. He recalled how they came as passengers with baggage on ships rather than as rescued Africans on cruisers. These "newcomers had been educated . . . and would be able to help understand the people of Freretown."[8] Mbotela became acquainted with the Bombay group, from whom he learned much, not only in terms of religion but also about their past experiences and the European way of life. This was especially important because, unlike the Bombay group, Mbotela's links with traditional Africa had not been severed. Consequently, he, who had been an oral historian in his village, was able to incorporate the experiences of the Bombay group with that of other groups in Freretown and pass on to posterity through his son the most complete and valuable history of the origin and development of the community. His son, James Juma Mbotela, is regarded as the "official" historian of Freretown.[9]

The following East Africans migrated to Freretown voluntarily, either for economic security during a famine or to obtain an education: Harry Stephens, a Taveta; Harry Mitchell, a Yao; Harry Banks, a Giriama; James Beauttah, a Kikuyu; Samuel Levi, a Kamba; and many others whose family histories testify to the great influence they had on Freretown in particular and Kenya generally.

Some of Freretown's immigrants came from Sierra Leone and the West Indies. Sometime during the latter part of the nineteenth century the Reverend Frederic Africana Heroe arrived from Freretown (Sierra Leone) and joined the Methodist mission at Ribe, near Rabai. He later sent for his nephew, John Clement Young, who was then in the British navy and had fought in the Boer War. When Young arrived in Freretown, Frederic was dead; however, Young remained and had a family, including Elkana Young, who later married a daughter of Cephas and Jane Farrar. They are today well known on the Mombasa coast.[10]

The following men came from the West Indies: Joseph Douglass migrated from Barbados and married one of Wellington's daughters, Florence. He worked as a mechanic on the railroad shortly after World War I. A second Barbadian was a Mr. Burke, who practiced law in Mombasa and later in Nairobi; while on the coast he gave legal advice to several Freretownians and in general made many friends there. A third Barbadian was a Doctor Bonn, who practiced medicine in Mombasa. His close personal ties with Freretownians are well remembered, especially his role in training some Freretownians as medical assistants. Some of the older residents of Freretown remember a Mr. Dopwell, a herbalist whose remedies proved very effective. He was from St. Vincent.[11]

The heterogeneity of Freretown became a source of both strength and weakness. For years there was no common language or culture among settlers from such diverse areas as India, the Kenya coast and interior (Miji Kenda, Kamba, Kikuyu), and trickles from as far away as Sierra Leone and the West Indies. While many of the early settlers knew Swahili, there were those who did not know or were not fluent in it; and a much smaller number knew English. Moreover, although there were cultural similarities, there also existed dissimilarities; and the leaders of the community were evoluées who supported missionary efforts to forge a Western-style Christian society. To accomplish this, the missionaries required all inhabitants to convert to the faith and thus accept the values of Western culture. This policy obviously gave the group from Bombay a special advantage. They had received a Western education, useful vocational skills, and other advantageous experiences in India. The Bombay group, therefore, developed a cohesiveness among themselves and cultivated close contacts with some of the Arabs, Asians, and Europeans. In short, this group of Freretownians emerged at the outset as the elite of Freretown's African society.

Within a few years, however, the bulk of the community's inhabitants came from the Miji Kenda and other mainland groups, all of whose links with neighboring indigenous peoples provided them with a kind of cultural reinforcement which helped to facilitate missionary and commercial relations with surrounding areas. At the same time, this latter group of immigrants was able to enjoy both Christian and traditional ways of life. Thus, while on the one hand they assumed the role of mission agents, they also faced the dilemma of reconciling Christian and traditional beliefs and practices. The result was that conflicts over marriage relations and obligations, inheritance procedures, etc., emerged. In a very real sense, therefore, this latter group of immigrants assured that Swahili and not English would become the principal language of the community, and that links with mainland indigenous groups would remain strong factors; this fact led to a greater unity and cooperation among large numbers of the inhabitants and a wider gulf between Africans and Europeans. It is thus no exaggeration to conclude that the settlers from the mainland by their numbers and presence determined the development of a greater African character for Freretown.

Although these diverse groups existed within the community, an element of strength lay in the fact that the Bombay group continued to attract both envy and respect within and outside Freretown. They were the ministers, teachers, artisans, and community leaders, positions the other Africans aspired to achieve and could only obtain in those early years with the assistance of the Bombay group. Likewise, this latter group, always small in number, had to cultivate close relations with the local immigrants for language and a general knowledge of the country. Those imperatives, along with the increasing awareness that the Europeans did not accept them as equals, even in the church, made the Bombay group realize that their upward mobility was also limited and that they should identify with the indigenous groups.

From about the late 1890s the Bombay group became widely dispersed along the coast and upcountry as teachers, ministers, clerks, and artisans. This not only meant that they gradually expanded their knowledge of the land and people, they also more fully identified with the local inhabitants through learning the local languages and customs. By the end of the first decade of the twentieth century, therefore, the "Bombay Africans" had become largely fused in the wider community of Africans and increasingly employed their knowledge and skills in the interest of African development and freedom.

Another aspect of this question of cross-cultural relations concerns cultural survivals, of which there is very little trace in Freretown. There are some culinary influences: pilau and jipadis are popular dishes at celebrations—birthdays, marriages, and holidays. Freretownians trace those foods to the influence of the Bombay group. On the other hand, there is virtually no trace of the Hindustani and Gujarati languages among Freretownians or Rabaians. Up to the turn of the twentieth century, several of the repatriated Africans served as interpreters and translators of those languages for the colonial administration and European business-men. However, beginning in the 1890s, Indian immigrants as-sumed those positions. Consequently, linguistic skills in Indian languages have virtually disappeared among the repatriates.

A critical factor in Freretown's growth concerns its relations with Arab neighbors. While the Sultan of Zanzibar signed major abolitionist treaties with the British in 1822, 1845, and 1873, Arabs in general continued to resist the suppression of the slave trade and slavery on both religious and economic grounds. When the Sultan signed the Treaty of 1873, however, the abolitionist movement was clearly ascendant; the legal death knell was sounded when subsequent proclamations prohibited the existence of slave markets in his dominions, although Arab resistance continued.

A very natural question at this juncture is: What were Arab reactions to the establishment of Freretown in their midst? No doubt the Arabs failed to foresee the full implications of having a community of ex-slaves founded near Mombasa. This probably was due to the careful negotiations of Bartle Frere and the Sultan, and the CMS purchase of land from the Arabs for the settlement. According to one Kenyan historian, Ahmed I. Salim, the Arab reaction "was one of general welcome," at the outset.[12] Freretown stimulated an additional demand for labor in construction and services which Mombasa supplied; the increasing number of Europeans and liberated Africans created a large consumer market for Arab businessmen; and the availability of medical facilities was appreciated by the Arab community. From these perspectives, therefore, the Freretown experiment was viewed as a mutually beneficial endeavor.

Within a year, however, relations between the Arabs and the community showed signs of tension. While some Arabs appre-ciated the economic potential of the expanding community of ex-slaves, others resented the Europeans' presence, which was regarded as the reason for the antislavery proclamations. Freretown complained that Arabs kidnapped children for an illicit slave trade; and Arabs charged that the mission harbored runaway slaves.[13] These charges and countercharges reflected economic and political jurisdictional problems that were destined to become major sources of friction between the two communities.

One of the many examples of that friction and a case which tested the commitment of the European missionaries related to the establishment of the Imperial British East Africa Company (IBEAC) in Mombasa. British Consul-General Euan-Smith at Zanzibar reported having been warned that the company would not succeed unless relations between the missionaries and Arabs improved, especially on the runaway slave issue. Euan-Smith therefore consulted with several Arab leaders and missionaries, including Reverend Price, who assured him that the cases of runaway slaves being harbored were few and that whenever a case was brought to him it received his personal attention. Believing that the Arab complaints had greater foundation than that, Euan-Smith with the Sultan's consent organized a commission of inquiry which included George S. Mackenzie, manager of the IBEAC. Much to the surprise and dismay of Price, who assisted the commission, the investigation revealed that nearly fifteen hundred male and female slaves were refuged at mission stations, about a thousand of whom were at Rabai.[14]

Mackenzie considered the mission's involvement as "a grievous moral wrong" because he regarded "slavery under existing circumstances here [as] an absolute necessity," the sudden abolition of which would ruin the country. Mackenzie thus proposed that Arab owners grant freedom to those slaves at the mission in exchange for the equivalent of twenty-five dollars per head. Price considered this "a capital stroke of policy on the part of the company." He believed it would greatly improve relations with the Arabs and at the same time have "a free community" at Rabai to draw upon for workers. The ransom was also calculated to "have a good influence on English public opinion." The ransom was thus arranged; Price and Mackenzie went to Rabai and issued an official certificate of freedom to each of the slaves on New

Year's Day, 1889; and William H. Jones preached a moving sermon in which he stressed the redeeming nature of Christian teachings. Freedom had come at last to nearly a thousand black souls at Rabai with the stroke of the pen, and a payment of £3500.

Throughout this incident William H. Jones played a key role. As a pioneer settler, an educated and articulate African who enjoyed the respect of the inhabitants both at Freretown and Rabai, Jones assumed greater autonomy than his European colleagues or IBEAC wanted. He took Christianity seriously and believed that slavery was an unjust condition which should be abolished; he also believed that Christians should be actively involved toward that end. So when he was advised by his European missionary superiors to release the fugitives at Rabai, he declared: "I will not, and I cannot hand these poor souls to their cruel and merciless master, . . . Somebody else will have to do that wicked work. How could I bear to see these poor baptized Christians, communicants, pass by me bound, beaten, abused, dragged through the village where they have lived and sung praises to the God of Heaven? If Mr. Mackenzie has come for this, then, alas, for the healing of the 'open sore' of Africa."[15]

Having personally experienced the slave trade, slavery, and freedom, Jones had committed himself to the liberation of Africans in servitude, and Christianity was his means of achieving that aim. So committed was he to the righteousness of the aim and the means he chose, that even after the British established colonial rule over the area in 1895, he continued to assume authority based on his own assessments. Some observers say that Jones was "power hungry," and he may have been; but it is clear that he was adamantly committed to the freedom of his fellow Africans in slavery; and in the history of the abolition of slavery in Kenya, Jones made a great contribution.

The freeing of the slaves at Rabai in 1889 takes its place among the several stages towards the eventual abolition of slavery in East Africa. The Zanzibar Anti-Slavery Decree of 1890 followed and provided freedom for all slaves whose owners died childless; it also provided the right for slaves to purchase their freedom. From 1896 the British consular office adopted a relaxed position on the question of harboring slaves. Then in 1897 Bishop Alfred Tucker instructed the resident missionary at Rabai not to surrender any fugitive slaves. All of these developments paved the way for the abolition of the status of slavery in the East African protectorate in 1907.

This heterogeneous settlement at Freretown gradually developed its own institutions, which provided for a measure of autonomy and self-sufficiency; at the same time those institutions afforded opportunities for a broad range of experiences not then generally available to Africans. In the economic sphere the community founded small enterprises to service local needs and to yield revenue. The basic business was the local market which facilitated the sale of local produce and goods obtained from neighboring areas; the market also sold used clothing as well as materials made by local weavers and tailors. A construction plant manufactured bricks, tiles, mats, and lumber to supply people in Freretown and Rabai. A community boat, the SS *Henry Wright,* sailed monthly between Freretown and Zanzibar. For years that was the only regular means of transport the community had for mail, supplies, and trips between the coast and the island. British cruisers regularly stopped at Zanzibar and unloaded cargo and mail for the mainland.[16]

Other economic institutions included a bank and printing press. The European missionaries encouraged the inhabitants of Freretown to deposit funds which were then invested in Indian government notes from which interest accrued to the bank depositors. The bank also served European businessmen and explorers who hired the services of African interpreters, guides, and porters. The printing press was started in 1887, and Bible tracts and educational materials were published for several missions in East Africa. There also was a community hospital to serve the needs of Freretown and nearby stations. Thus, the bank, printing press, and hospital generated income for the community and provided training for Africans as well.[17]

At the outset, Freretown was governed by a European missionary in charge, Reverend Price, who made decisions based on consultations with his European staff—chaplain, medical doctor, and a few teachers. Price also had personal ties with the Bombay group he had trained at Nasik. He therefore sought their advice on day-to-day matters, especially discipline.

As the community expanded, a more sophisticated system was established. An executive council was formed and charged with governing the community, which was divided into several districts of ten to fifteen houses and placed under African elders. All of the elders spoke English and were responsible for spiritual consultations, explanation of community policies, and general police supervision; the elders thus served as an advisory committee to the executive council and therefore became a significant component of the political frame of Freretown. Semler and David were the first elders at Freretown; Jones was the first at Rabai.[18]

Governance was based on bylaws formulated in 1888 and based on the Bible. Residence, social activities, and work were regulated by the bylaws; punishment for offenders was also stipulated by the bylaws. Enforcement of those regulations was charged to askaris (policemen) who also stood guard for the settlement. Often the askaris included Nubians and Indians on loan from the IBEAC. Freretown also maintained its own jail.[19]

Freretown and Rabai remained essentially autonomous until about the turn of the century, but they could and did occasionally appeal to the British consul at Zanzibar and to the IBEAC for support. Theoretically, the consul as representative of the British government had ultimate authority over the missions, but in reality he could not effectively administer an area 150 miles away, especially when he often was without available transportation. In addition, British authority at best was precarious up to 1890; the Sultan of Zanzibar had nominal control over the mainland but, in fact, local rulers exercised their own authority. In this context the British had neither the political nor military authority to control the missions directly. The primary role of the consul and the IBEAC was to provide askaris to the mission when requested; the consul periodically visited the community and made recommendations on a variety of issues.

Social developments were limited in Freretown during the early years. The whole atmosphere of the community was infused with the "Christian spirit"; in addition to Sunday, religious services were held several evenings each week. The playing of drums and the singing of traditional songs were prohibited. On the other hand, the mission encouraged the organization of local singing groups and a band to present Christian music. Instruments were supplied and regular rehearsals were held. The choir and band became very popular and played at receptions, holiday feasts, and on other occasions. Freretown thus became well known (and still is) for its musical performances.[20]

Marriage ceremonies became important occasions for the community. According to Mbotela, some of the men, realizing that they would have married at a young age in their traditional villages, approached Semler about the possibility of matrimony. When Semler raised the issue with the European missionaries, they told him to explain the "Biblical marriage" to the community. Semler thus conducted a few sessions on monogamous marriage; this led to the development of marriage as an institution patterned after that of Europeans. While there was little if any resistance to this at the outset, in time the practice encountered strains as immigrants from surrounding villages entered Freretown. Those newcomers had no previous contact with Christian teachings and practices, they did not have the same kind of reverence for Europeans as the Bombay group did, and many of them came to the community for reasons other than religious. They therefore felt less committed to Christian regulations.[21]

What became particularly appealing to Africans was the possibility of achieving an education in Freretown. Education accompanied the missionaries from the very beginning, and in 1884 the CMS sent Bishop James Hannington to East Africa. A Reverend Fitch, who was part of Hannington's entourage, became responsible for organizing a divinity class. He first started such a class among the Chagga around Mount Kilimanjaro, but he later moved to Freretown where, in 1903, the cornerstone for a permanent structure was laid; this was the beginning of the Freretown Divinity School. Since a primary school had already been established as part of the church, its most promising and mature students were chosen to continue studies at the Divinity School. Other students for the school were selected from among "promising" men, with or without primary education, at the several CMS schools throughout East Africa.

The primary objective of the Divinity School was to produce teacher-evangelists, the most capable of whom became ordained ministers. In 1885 Hannington ordained the first Africans in East Africa, William H. Jones and Ishmael Semler; David George would have been the third had he not died in 1884. Not surprisingly, these were Bombay trained and therefore had an edge over the other Africans. The first of the slaves liberated in East Africa to be admitted to the ministry was James Deimler, who was ordained by Bishop Tucker in 1896. Fussell Lugo Gorega Digo was ordained by Bishop Robert Peel in 1903.[22]

The Freretown Divinity School not only became the principal center for training African missionaries and ministers in East Africa, it also emerged as a center for the study of Swahili. In February, 1928, for example, sixteen students arrived from the Elgon Diocese of the Upper Nile to study Swahili, and another group arrived from Makerere University in Uganda. This was just one additional function the CMS mission discovered it could perform in the colonial context.

Since the transfer of the colonial capital from Mombasa to Nairobi in 1907, the locus of European activities had shifted upcountry among the Kikuyu. The CMS thus reassessed its position not only as a mission but also as the principal source of educated Africans who then went into the colonial government or business. That the mission could play a greater role in this regard if it moved its facilities closer to the colonial administration was evident. The climate, financial difficulties, and the offer of a large tract of land in a 999-year lease by a retired English businessman, Ernst Carr, provided all the incentive necessary to relocate in Limuru in 1930. Canon Harry Leakey played an important part in the move and provided fundees (craftsmen) to help with the construction of the school, which became St. Paul's United Theological Seminary and remains a prominent source of education in Kenya today.[23]

From 1930, therefore, African ministers assumed direct control over the Freretown church and primary schools; no European resident missionary had been appointed to Rabai since 1922. CMS interest in these two stations had clearly declined as upcountry possibilities appeared more attractive. However, CMS pursuance of upcountry interests provided the opportunity for Freretown and Rabai Africans to gain the experience and knowledge necessary to operate their own affairs; a further step in this direction occurred when the CMS sold the major part of its Freretown property in 1931 and transferred the remainder to the government in 1938. This led to the establishment in Freretown of a Local Native Council in 1940, the first step toward direct African political involvement in the colonial administration on the Kenya coast.

Freretown poses some contrasts to the cases of Sierra Leone and Liberia. First, unlike the two West African examples of repatriation, Freretown was founded by Africans who were born in East Africa, and who had been away only for up to twenty years. They retained much of their traditional culture, especially the Swahili language. Many of them had not been away long enough to sever ties with families and friends, some of whom they rejoined in Freretown and Rabai. In addition, the East African repatriates had been trained in a mission station in India which did not foster significant contacts with the larger Indian community. Thus, although they learned Hindustani and Gujarati at the mission school, they were not much influenced by Indian culture as such.

However, like their West African counterparts, the Bombay group was exposed to Western cultural values, if only for up to twenty years. They were Christians, spoke English, adopted English dress, acquired skills as blacksmiths, carpenters, masons, tailors, etc. All of those factors made them attractive potential for European missionaries seeking to spread the faith; for merchants expanding their businesses; for explorers venturing into the African interior; and for officials seeking to entrench colonial rule. Thus, some of the repatriates became missionaries and teachers along the coast of East Africa; IBEAC and other companies employed some of the repatriates as clerks and interpreters; explorers employed some to accompany caravans as guides and interpreters.

With the establishment of colonial authority, people of Freretown were recruited as clerks, interpreters, and advisers in the courts, post office, and other agencies. In fact, James Jones, nephew of William Henry Jones, became one of the few highly qualified printers in Kenya up to the 1930s; he had learned that trade in Freretown.

The mission station came to be regarded by Africans as a source of education, a place for economic survival, and as a haven for runaway slaves. Whatever the reasons, the new arrivals shared in the experiences of the community; they influenced and were influenced by it. One should note, however, that the study of Freretown points to a rather steady trend to identify with indigenous peoples, a process still in progress. This came about because the repatriates had not been completely alienated from the area and people, a point made earlier. Indeed, from a cultural standpoint the East African repatriates had more nearly been returned to their original homes than the West African repatriates had been. In addition, better preparations had been made for the return.

The fusion of the repatriates and indigenous peoples in Freretown happened partly because the local missionaries, especially the Africans, welcomed the runaway slave. Therefore, Freretown became a haven for Africans seeking escape from political and economic oppression. Very early the settlement became a mixture of several diverse ethnic groups; and although the first settlers viewed themselves and were viewed by others as a kind of elite, the fact is that all groups increasingly fused into a larger community. While it is true that the first repatriates served as a bridge between the African and European communities, those first settlers never constituted a large group and were thus dependent on both communities. The Europeans provided the opportunities for their economic and political well being, but the Africans provided a deeper cultural relationship. This became even more obvious as the repatriates were subjected to various forms of racial segregation. In the final analysis, therefore, mindful of their lack of social and economic upward mobility, the Bombay group began to organize the wider African community to demand better treatment. In time this activity galvanized into political organizations.

Indeed, during the 1890s the Freretownians organized the African Workers Council to promote the welfare of Africans working in the Mombasa CMS stations; but during the 1940s they formed a political group that had real influence on the colonial administration. Since 1900 Freretownians had begun to migrate to other areas on the coast, upcountry, and to Zanzibar. This resulted from economic opportunities in emerging cities and towns elsewhere, as well as opposition to attitudes and practices of the white missionaries. This migration led to an expansion of Freretown's influence beyond the coast and to its integration into some of the upcountry groups like the Kamba.

In sum, as the first center for sustained Western education in East Africa, Freretown had a decisive impact not only on the coast but throughout much of Kenya and in parts of Tanganyika and Zanzibar (present-day Tanzania), and Uganda. As the first African teachers, clerks, interpreters, various kinds of craftsmen, and journalists, Freretownians emerged as a professional elite whose values, goals, and achieved status made them key agents of social change. They helped to bridge the gulf between Africans and Europeans; and while they sometimes were used by Europeans to spread Western culture and influence, they also contributed immensely to the cultivation of intergroup communication and understanding which in turn led to greater inter-ethnic cooperation and unity in Kenya.

NOTES

1. This section is based on Joseph E. Harris, *The African Presence in Asia: Consequences of the East African Slave Trade* (Evanston, Illinois, 1971), chaps. 1, 4.
2. Bishop Leonard Beecher Files, Nairobi, Kenya.
3. *Ibid.*
4. W. J. Rampley, *Matthew Wellington: Sole Surviving Link with Dr. Livingstone* (London, n.d.).
5. *Ibid.*
6. *Ibid.*

7. James Juma Mbotela, *The Freeing of the Slaves in East Africa* (London, 1956), 40–55.

8. *Ibid.*, 54–63.

9. Oral testimonies, Freretown, 1972–73.

10. *Ibid.*

11. *Ibid.*

12. A. I. Salim, *Swahili-Speaking Peoples of Kenya's Coast* (Nairobi, Kenya, 1973), 48.

13. FO, 541–28, PRO, Slave Trade, "Memorial of the Arabs and the Twelve Tribes of Mombasa to Sultan Barghash," September 1, 1880, and "Liwali Ali bin Nasur to Sultan Barghash," September 8, 1880 (London).

14. *Ibid.*, Enclosure 9 in No. 303 (Memorandum by the Reverend W. Price on Runaway Slaves at Rabai), London.

15. Eugene Stock, *History of the Church Missionary Society* (London, 1899), III, 430.

16. Church Missionary Society, 1/632, Minutes Book, September, 1883.

17. *Ibid.*

18. *Ibid.*

19. Church Missionary Society, 1/632, Log Book, May, 1889 and June 25–July 1, 1904.

20. Mbotela, 72–73.

21. Stock, 87, 88.

22. "Precolonial Missionary Work, 1844–1890," unpublished notes in Church in East Africa File, St. Paul's United Theological Seminary, Limuru, Kenya; Lawrence C. T. Dena, "A Comparative Study of the Impact of the Differing Traditions of Christianity on Some of the Coastal Tribes of Kenya," unpublished paper in the Coast Folder, St. Paul's Theological Seminary.

23. Log Book, February 8 and 9, 1928 and July 11, 1930, St. Paul's Theological Seminary.

II

Reinterpretations of Slavery and Reconstruction

History from Slave Sources

C. Vann Woodward

The interviews with ex-slaves published in 1972 have been available to scholars in one form or another for some thirty years.* Sixteen of the volumes contain the interviews prepared by the Federal Writers Project (FWP) in 1936–38. The typescript was assembled, bound, and deposited for the use of readers in the rare book room of the Library of Congress in 1941 and later microfilmed for distribution. The two volumes that originated at Fisk University in 1929–30 have been available in mimeograph form since 1945. In the latter year, B. A. Botkin published a small book of excerpts from the FWP interviews consisting mainly of anecdotes and folklore, but containing quite enough material of historical value to alert the scholarly community to the character of the sources he sampled.[1]

In spite of this, historians have almost completely neglected these materials. Examining all works dealing primarily with slavery and the antebellum Negro that were reviewed in the *Journal of Negro History* during the years 1945–64, one investigator discovered that the FWP narratives had "gone virtually unexploited by serious scholars." About one-third of them cited Botkin's selection, but only one referred to the original collection and then

* George P. Rawick, general editor, *The American Slave: A Composite Autobiography* (Westport, Conn., 1972), 19 vols.

41

only in a bibliography.[2] The neglect is all the more striking because it continued almost uninterrupted through the next decade and thus through the peak of activity in black history, as well as the wave of productivity in the history of slavery. In this same period, one of the most frequent complaints was about the lack of existing evidence from the illiterate, inarticulate, voiceless mass of slaves. How was it that the historian could not escape his dependence on the testimony of the master class and the abolitionists about the experience of slavery—how it was to be a slave? The published narratives of former slaves were available, to be sure, but were they representative of the illiterate millions?

Why these questions did not stimulate extensive exploitation of the slave testimony under review is rather a puzzle. The existence of the material was widely known, and its comparative inaccessibility is not very helpful as an explanation of its neglect. It was more accessible than many manuscript and archive materials that were extensively used at the time. The questions Ulrich B. Phillips had raised about the authenticity and bias of old slave narratives published before and after the Civil War had inhibited their use for a generation.[3] But by the 1950s a neoabolitionist mood prevailed among historians of slavery, and the views of the slaves were considered at least as important to an understanding of slavery as the views of the slaveowners. Yet while the published slave narratives were increasingly used, the unpublished testimony of slaves was scarcely touched. What appears to have been the main explanation for the neglect was a prevailing suspicion of the authenticity and quality of the material itself. Grounds for some of these suspicions certainly existed. It will be one of the purposes of this essay to explore and assess the basis for these suspicions. Before doing that, however, it would be well to indicate something of the scope and character of the enterprise.

The sixteen volumes of the FWP narratives, containing about 10,000 pages and roughly 3.5 million words, are based on interviews with more than twenty-two hundred people in seventeen states. Some three hundred interviewers took part in the government-financed project. Preparation of the two remaining volumes, *Unwritten History of Slavery* and *God Struck me Dead*, was privately financed and directed at Fisk University. They are the work of a small staff and represent the records of interviews with some one hundred people in two states, Tennessee and Kentucky. The writers and editors of both projects strove with widely varying success to record the narratives in the words and dialect of the persons interviewed. George P. Rawick, nominal editor of the present publication, says that he has "left the interviews exactly as they were recorded," merely reproducing the original typescripts by photocopy. His own editorial contribution, therefore, is a brief but helpful introduction. His own monograph, *From Sundown to Sunup: The Making of the Black Community* is published as the first volume of the series.

Virtually all the significant types of slave occupations, skilled and unskilled, are represented among the people interviewed. So are all sizes of plantations and farms and all sizes of slave holdings, from one to a thousand slaves. With the exception of Louisiana, all the states and territories where slavery was still legal toward the end of the regime are represented by samples of some extent, in addition to small samples from Indiana, Kansas, and Ohio. To go beyond these few descriptive facts, however, is to begin a list of shortcomings and faults. Yet these must also be fully conceded and appreciated before any just appraisal of the merits and values of the collection can be attempted.

The claim of "a high degree of representativeness and inclusiveness"[4] that has been made in behalf of the FWP narratives is clouded by evidence of skewed sampling of several kinds. For example, the states included are very disproportionately represented. Arkansas, which never had more than 3.5 percent of the slave population, furnished about 33 percent of the ex-slaves interviewed, while Mississippi, which in 1860 contained more than 10 percent of the slaves, is represented by little more than 1 percent of those interviewed. The border states are skimpily sampled: Louisiana did not participate, and Virginia diverted all but a small portion of its collection to another publication.[5] While the number interviewed has been estimated to be approximately 2 percent of the total ex-slave population surviving at the time the interviews were taken, it cannot be assumed that this was a random sample. There is too much evidence of chance or self-selection to assure randomness. Among categories of the population represented by larger than their proportional numbers are urban residents, males, and former house servants, with a consequent under-representation of rural population, females, and former field-hands.

The very age of the former slaves at the time they were interviewed raises several serious questions—about two-thirds were eighty or more, and 15 percent were over ninety-three, with numerous centenarians (especially in Texas for unknown reasons) among the group. Not only is the question of failing memory raised but also the question of whether longevity may not be partly attributed to exceptionally good, rather than typical, treatment as slaves. Age raises other questions of typicality. The age of interviewees at the time of emancipation ranged from one to fifty. About 16 percent were under six years of age at that time, and their testimony about slavery has to be considered largely hearsay. The slave experience of the majority was, in fact, mainly that of childhood, a period before the full rigors and worst aspects of the slave discipline were typically felt and a period more likely than others to be favorably colored in the memory of the aged.[6]

Other distortions doubtlessly arise from skewed sampling and faulty memories but, in all probability, the most serious sources of distortion in the FWP narratives came not from the interviewees but from the interviewers—their biases, procedures, and methods—and the interracial circumstances of the interviews. The overwhelming majority of the interviewers were Southern whites. In several states they were almost exclusively so. While the direction and guiding spirit of the project in its formative stages was a white Southerner, John A. Lomax, the folklorist, his duties were editorial rather than administrative. Responsibility for drawing the color line in employment of interviewers lies elsewhere, but the line was drawn rather firmly. The typical circumstances, therefore, were those of a Southern white interviewing old-style blacks on their doorsteps in the Deep South in the late 1930s. Jim Crow etiquette and white supremacy attitudes prevailed virtually unchallenged in those years: segregation was at its fully developed height, lynchings were still numerous in spite of a decline, and peonage sustained by force and terror was still a way of life known to millions of blacks.[7]

In that climate of race relations, the white interrogators customarily adopted a patronizing or at best paternalistic tone and at worst an offensive condescension. They flouted very nearly every rule in the handbooks of interview procedure.[8] There were exceptions, to be sure, especially among the white interviewers in Arkansas and Georgia. But as a rule, the questions were leading and sometimes insulting, the answers routine or compliant, and the insensitivity of the interrogator and the evasiveness of the interrogated were flagrantly displayed. An occasional writer brought insight, tact, and inspired sensitivity to the task. The quality of the interview reports varied greatly, but too often they were mechanical or routine, "quaint" or "genial." The interrogator regularly got what he asked for: "Yes, sir, Boss Man, de niggers wuz treated good in slabery times en wuz trained up right, ter wuk, en obey, en ter hab good manners." Were they punished severely? "I'spects dat dey needed all de punishment what dey got."[9] The candor of Martin Jackson of Texas (age ninety) was rare: "Lots of old slaves closes the door before they tell the truth about their days of slavery. When the door is open, they tell how kind their masters was and how rosy it all was."[10]

In a few states, particularly Florida, Negro interviewers were numerous, and the two volumes of Fisk narratives were entirely their work. The distinctiveness of interviews where the interviewer and the interviewed were of the same race is readily apparent. The whole atmosphere changes. The thick dialect diminishes and so do deference and evasiveness and tributes to planter benevolence. Candor and resentment surface more frequently. There is also a fuller sense of engagement and responsiveness in the joint enterprise of seeking truth about the past. The interview could become a challenge, as it did with Margaret Nickerson (age eighty-nine or ninety) of Florida:

> Now jes listen. I wanna tell you all I kin, but I wants to tell it right; wait now, I don' wanna make no mistakes and I don' wanna lie on nobody—I ain' mad now and I know how taint no use to lie, I takin' my time. I done prayed an' got all de malice out o' my heart and I ain' gonna tell no lie fer um and I ain' gonna tell no lie on um.

She followed a chilling narrative with the statement, "Dis is what

I know, not what somebody else say. I see dis myself."[11] It would be hard to find a better witness.

Even the black interviewers had their problems. "It was with difficulty," reported one of them in Florida, "that they were prevailed upon to relate some of the gruesome details recorded here."[12] On the other hand, black interviewers also reported a good deal of apparently unaffected nostalgia for "de good ole days." After all, these were old and helpless people, often living alone in the worst years of the Great Depression, sometimes admitting they were hungry and not knowing where the next meal was coming from. And they were recalling a remote childhood when few were put to field labor before the age of ten or twelve. It is not surprising that for many the memory of slavery that often returned was that of eating and eating regularly. Slavery times and depression times were frequently compared, sometimes at the expense of the latter. Or as an ex-slave of North Carolina put it, "It's all hard, slavery and freedom, both bad when you can't eat."[13] One can never be entirely sure, but some of the testimony of internalized values of master and mistress appear to ring true enough. Abram Harris (age ninety-three) of Arkansas, for example, "kin yit see Marse Hampton" in his dreams "en er heep er times in de day when I's by myself er hoein de cotton he talks ter me plain, so's I kin understand, en he ax me iffin I's yet en still er good nigger, en tell me ter not be disencouraged."[14] There *were* such people. Father figures as well as hate images were part of their heritage from slavery.

Given the mixture of sources and interpreters, interviewers and interviewees, the times and their "etiquette," the slave narratives can be mined for evidence to prove almost anything about slavery. Hester Hunter (age eighty-five) of Marion, South Carolina, actually pronounced it "a Paradise, be dat what I call it."[15] A paradise and a hell on earth, food in plenty and daily starvation, no punishment at all and brutal beatings for no reason at all, tender care and gruesome tortures, loving family ties and forced breedings, gentle masters and sadistic monsters.

That being the case, is the traditional suspicion of this material justified? Shall historians discard the slave interviews as worthless?

Not unless they are prepared to be consistent and discard most of the other sources they habitually use. Not while they still use newspapers as sources, or, for that matter, diaries and letters and politicians' speeches and the *Congressional Record* and all those neatly printed official documents and the solemnly sworn testimony of high officials. Full of paradox and evasions, contrasts and contradictions, lies and exaggerations, pure truth and complete fabrication as they are, such sources still remain the daily bread on which historians feed. The slave narratives have their peculiarities, as all types of historical sources do, but they are not all that different from the norm. The norm for historical sources is a mess, a confusing mess, and the task of the historian is to make sense of it.

Sharing the normal shortcomings of historical sources, the slave interviews nevertheless have an unusual character. Confusing and contradictory as they are, they represent the voices of the normally voiceless, the inarticulate masses whose silence historians are forever lamenting. What would the colonial historians give for a comparable 2 percent sampling of the views of the white indentured servants of the seventeenth and eighteenth centuries, or Southern historians for similar records of the poor whites of the nineteenth century, or Indian historians for such interviews with blanket-Indian tribesmen? Would there ever have been a comparable neglect of such sources by a whole generation of historians in those fields?

As full of pitfalls as the narratives are, they contain evidence and answers of some sort for almost any kind of question that can be asked about life under slavery—any kind, that is, save those requiring quantification. Our dauntless quantifiers will probably not be stopped by this warning. But to quantify data of this sort would be attempting to quantify the memories of childhood and the lamentations of old age. Most historians still hold, however, that not all admissable evidence has to be numerical and that there are still important historical questions that are not susceptible to quantification.

To suggest a few questions on which the narratives do shed light, there are those relating to childhood, a subject to which historians have been giving increasing attention of late. These include not only nursing and infant care, but prenatal care of the mother and responsibility for discipline and training. Who taught the child to be a "good" slave? On whom did the child look as an authority figure? Master or father, father or mother, mammy or mistress? How did the father relate to the family? Wife to husband? Within the slave community, what was the relative authority or status of the black overlooker compared with the white overseer? The slave preacher compared with the white minister? Voodoo and herb doctor with white pill doctor? The house slave as against the field slave? The mulatto compared with the black? How did the social structure of the slave community look from the inside? How much solidarity and how much cleavage? Were class lines emerging? Did status and privilege relate to degree of color and racial intermixture? Was the emergence of a West Indian or Jamaica-type brown class already foreshadowed in South Carolina? How did such lines of division relate to rebelliousness or accommodation in slave discipline?

The slave interview evidence requires re-examination of many old questions and assumptions. Abolitionists agreed with pro-slavery men about the work ethic of slaves—that they were lazy, indolent, incompetent, careless, and inefficient, and worked only under the whip. This abolitionist-slaveholder stereotype is challenged by slave testimony on the variety of crafts mastered by slave artisans, the skills developed in their practice, and the pride workers took in their work and productivity. The stereotype of laziness is challenged by the sheer amount of work they did and how much of it was devoted in off-hours to self-aggrandizement and self-purchase. The old model of planter-absolutism on and off the plantation is cracked by evidence of slave bargaining power. Especially in industrial slavery and slave hiring, the lines between master-slave relations and employer-employee relations in free labor become increasingly blurred and indistinct as it becomes apparent that owners as well as employers are coping with common labor problems, sometimes in quite similar ways.

Old institutions and old assumptions about them require re-examination in light of the narratives. One instance is the old view of slave religion as an imitative parody of white evangelical Protestantism. Instead it emerges with a distinctive eschatology and theology as well as the more obviously distinctive styles of worship, preaching, hymns, and participation. A more totally religious culture is hard to imagine. Only one black atheist turned up among the twenty-three hundred interviewees, and he was the son of a white atheist father.[16] "What else good for colored folks?" demanded Anne Bell of Winnsboro, South Carolina. "I ask you if dere ain't a heaven, what's colored folks got to look forward to? They can't get anywhere down here."[17] It was a curiously joyful religion. "There is joy on the inside and it wells up so strong that we can't keep still. It is fire in the bones. Any time fire touches a man, he will jump."[18]

The stock image of immobilized slaves chained to cabin, quarters, field, and plantation gives way to contrasting figures of mobility and restlessness. America was on the move and so were they, sometimes in chains and sometimes without them. Millie Evans tells of walking from North Carolina to Arkansas at a pace of fifteen or twenty miles a day and burying her master and three slaves on the way.[19] Rachel Fairley recounts a six-week walk from Charlottesville, Virginia, to Sardis, Mississippi.[20] "Uncle" Dave, born in Virginia, fled to Key West, Florida, was shanghaied on a naval vessel, sailed around the world, was shipwrecked twice, and returned to Florida.[21] Elias Mumford, after emancipation, took his family to Africa, prospered for eight years with his own construction business, and returned to America with capital for a new start.[22] Back and forth they wandered (more of them than whites) as helpless fugitives during the Civil War, sometimes making it on their own to federal lines and freedom, sometimes with their masters, who were seeking to keep them out of the reach of the Union armies—from Alabama to Texas, from South Carolina to Oklahoma and back again. Some went as far as Antigua or St. Thomas, some to Canada and the Northern states, but few to stay, most to return to what they had learned to call "home," the South.

Any historian who attempts to make sense of emancipation and Reconstruction will have to bring his bucket to this well. It is one of the deepest reservoirs of ex-slave testimony on two of the most profound historical experiences of the race. Here are spelled out many of the meanings of freedom and how it was perceived. "I took my freedom by degrees," said Robert Glenn of Raleigh, and had trouble "taking myself into my own hands and getting out of feeling I was still under obligations to ask my master and mistress when I desired to leave the premises." He recalled vividly the first time he refused to obey an order of his former master, the first time he failed to touch his forelock on meeting him.[23] Freedom came not only by degrees but also as cataclysm, like a storm in a time of troubles. Freedom came many ways and by no means all at one time. Sometimes it was years coming after the war, and to some it never seemed to have come at all. Testimony on that experience is often as revealing as testimony on slavery.

Reconstruction had as many meanings as perceivers. But the common and earthy meaning was aptly summed up by Ambus Gray of Biscoe, Arkansas:

> The Reconstruction time was like this. You go up to a man and tell him you and your family wants to hire for next year on his place. He say I'm broke, the war broke me. Move down there in the best empty house you find. You can get your provisions furnished at a certain little store in the closest town about. You say yesser. When the crop made bout all you got was a little money to take to give the man what run you and you have to stay on or starve or go get somebody else to let you share crop wid them.[24]

And for the mass of ex-slaves, that spelled out the whole meaning of "Reconstruction."

The history of race relations should be enriched by slave testimony, especially the paradox of formal distance and physical intimacy between the races that slavery maximized. The evidence on intimacy is ample. "I nursed on one breast while that white child . . . pulled away at the other," recalled a former slave in Oklahoma.[25] "Grandma raised me on a bottle so mother could nurse Walter," the master's son. "Mother had good teeth and she chewed for us both," said another from Arkansas.[26] "Why wouldn't I love her," asked a third slave, referring to her owner, "when I sucked titty from her breast when my mammy was working in the field."[27] Love was not an invariable consequence of breast feeding. "I'm going to kill you," one slave told her master's son. "These black titties sucked you and then you come here to beat me." At the end of the encounter "he wasn't able to walk."[28]

The extended family of the planter patriarch included slaves of blood kin, and the interracial matings from which they sprang included not only casual couplings and rapes, but durable and affectionate unions. The degree of willingness partook of all the ambiguities traditionally associated with matings, and the initiative was the monopoly of neither of the races nor either of the sexes. Tempie James, white daughter of a large planter in North Carolina, was locked in her room and the head coachman sold in another state when her parents discovered she was in love with him. Tempie escaped, purchased the coachman, liberated him, married him, bore him fifteen children, and lived to bless many great grandchildren.[29] Harriet Ann Daves of the same state said her white father and owner "never denied me to anybody," and "would give me anything I asked for. He loved my mother and said if he could not marry [her] . . . he did not want to marry."[30] Another slave daughter spurned the affection of her father-master even though he supported her after her marriage, remembered her in his will, and enjoined his white son to visit her regularly after his death, which he did even after his half-sister moved to remote Oklahoma.[31]

Slave commentary on white society provides rich insights on antebellum social history. Black observers were capable of shrewd perceptions of lower class deference or subservience that punctured the myth of *Herrenvolk* democracy—the equality of all whites. One of them was amused by the conduct of a poor white overseer when visiting the quality at the big house and "use to laugh at de way he put grease on his hair, and de way he scraped one foot back'erds on de ground or de floor when they shake hands wid him. He never say much . . . [then, but] he speak a whole lot though when he git down to de quarters where de slaves live. He wasn't like the same man then."[32] Ex-slaves tended to identify

patrollers as well as overseers as poor whites and to remember
relations with them as perpetual class warfare. Their attitude was
similar to that of their descendants toward white police. "The
patrollers were for niggers just like the police and sheriffs were
for white folks. They were just poor white folks," said an Arkansas
survivor of slavery.[33] "We didn't think much of poor white men,"
said Sam Stuart of North Carolina. "He was down on us. He
was driven to it by the rich slave owner."[34]

These volumes invite attention to a relatively unexplored field
of race relations—those between Negroes and Indians. Black-red
relations had most of the complications of black-white relations,
plus peculiarities of their own. Indian masters enjoyed the reputation of being somewhat more indulgent than white masters
toward the slaves. But there were cruel and brutal Indian slave
owners as well. Recalling the beating of her uncle by one of them,
Sarah Wilson of Oklahoma declared that "if I could hate that old
Indian any more I guess I would, but I hated him all I could
already I reckon."[35] The extent of black-red interbreeding and
intermarriage needs serious research. The number of ex-slaves
who claimed Indian blood is remarkable. One Arkansas interviewer went so far as to say he had "never talked to a Negro
who did not claim to be part Indian." An exaggeration, to be
sure, and the phenomenon is more prevalent in the Southwest
than in the Southeast. There is probably also a psychological as
well as a biological dimension to the claim of Indian blood or
identity. At any rate, Indian blood is frequently invoked to account
for cherished traits of rebelliousness, ferocity, and fortitude. "De
Indian blood in me have held me up over a hundred years," said
Louisa Daves of South Carolina, age 102.[36] White blood was
never mentioned in such connections. If black-red interbreeding
was anywhere as extensive as suggested by testimony of ex-slaves,
then the monoracial concept of slavery in America requires
revision. And if the amount of black-white interbreeding is
realistically taken into account, the true description of American
slavery would be multiracial rather than monoracial or biracial—
white and red as well as black.

It should be clear that these interviews with ex-slaves will have to be used with caution and discrimination. The historian who does use them should be posted not only on the period with which they deal but also familiar with the period in which they were taken down, especially with the nuances of race relations in the latter period. He should be sensitive to black speech patterns and to the marvelous ambiguities characteristic of them. And of course he should bring to bear all the skepticism his trade has taught him about the use of historical sources. The necessary precautions, however, are no more elaborate or burdensome than those required by many other types of sources he is accustomed to use. They are certainly not great enough to justify continued neglect of this valuable evidence on black history in America.

NOTES

1. B. A. Botkin, ed., *Lay My Burden Down: A Folk History of Slavery* (Chicago, 1945). A more extensive and valuable selection of narratives appeared later. Norman R. Yetman, ed., *Voices From Slavery* (New York, 1970).

2. Norman R. Yetman, "The Background of the Slave Narrative Collection," *American Quarterly* 19 (1967): 536n. This article provides a valuable history of the collection. One exception to the rule of neglecting these sources is Willie Lee Rose, *Rehearsal for Reconstruction: The Port Royal Experiment* (Indianapolis, 1964).

3. Ulrich B. Phillips, *Life and Labor in the Old South* (Boston, 1929), 219.

4. Yetman, "The Background of the Slave Narrative Collection," 534–35.

5. Virginia Writers Project, *The Negro in Virginia* (New York, 1940).

6. The age estimates are in Yetman, "Background of the Slave Narrative Collection," 535.

7. Bertram W. Doyle, *The Etiquette of Race Relations in the South* (Chicago, 1937); John Dollard, *Caste and Class in a Southern Town* (New Haven, 1937); Arthur R. Raper, *The Tragedy of Lynching* (Chapel Hill, 1933); Pete Daniel, *The Shadow of Slavery: Peonage in the South, 1901–1969* (Urbana, 1972); Charles S. Johnson, *Shadow of the Plantation* (Chicago, 1934).

8. See, for example, Stephen A. Richardson *et al., Interviewing: Its Forms and Functions* (New York, 1965), especially 269–327.

9. Henry Green (age ninety), in Rawick, *The American Slave,* 9, *Arkansas,* pt. 2: 96, 100.

10. *Ibid.,* 4, *Texas,* 2: 189.

11. *Ibid.,* 17, *Florida,* 252, 254.

12. *Ibid.,* 131.

13. *Ibid.,* 14, *North Carolina,* 1: 137.

14. *Ibid.,* 9, *Arkansas,* 3: 7.

15. *Ibid.,* 2, *South Carolina,* 2: 340.

16. *Ibid.,* 18, *Unwritten History,* 82.

17. *Ibid.,* 2, *South Carolina,* 1: 53–54.

18. *Ibid.,* 19, *God Struck Me Dead,* 153.

19. *Ibid.,* 8, *Arkansas,* 2: 247.

20. *Ibid.,* 260.

21. *Ibid.,* 17, *Florida,* 311–26.

22. *Ibid.,* 282–84.

23. *Ibid.,* 14, *North Carolina,* 1: 335–37.

24. *Ibid.,* 9, *Arkansas,* 3: 78–79.

25. *Ibid.,* 7, *Oklahoma and Mississippi,* 187.

26. *Ibid.,* 8, *Arkansas,* 2: 41.

27. *Ibid.,* 1: 113.

28. *Ibid.,* 2: 42.

29. *Ibid.,* 15, *North Carolina,* 2: 106–108. Tempie evaded the law against interracial marriage by drinking blood from her lover's veins and swearing she was of mixed blood.

30. *Ibid.*, 1: 233–35.
31. *Ibid.*, 7, *Oklahoma and Mississippi*, 18.
32. *Ibid.*, 2, *South Carolina*, 2: 235.
33. *Ibid.*, 9, *Arkansas*, 3: 293.
34. *Ibid.*, 15, *North Carolina*, 2: 319.
35. *Ibid.*, 7, *Oklahoma and Mississippi*, 347.
36. *Ibid.*, 2, *South Carolina*, 1: 302.

Sambos and Rebels

THE CHARACTER OF THE SOUTHERN SLAVE

John W. Blassingame

It is one of the ironies of American historiography that scholars have generally based their characterization of slaves more on literary stereotypes than on research. Sambo, combining in his character the behavior generally ascribed to Uncle Remus, Jim Crow, and Uncle Tom, was the most pervasive and long-lasting of the literary stereotypes of the slave in antebellum Southern novels, plays, and essays. Indolent, faithful, humorous, loyal, dishonest, superstitious, improvident, and musical, Sambo was inevitably a clown and congenitally docile. Characteristically a house servant, Sambo had so much love and affection for his master that he was almost filiopietistic; his loyalty was all-consuming and self-immolating. In the Southern novel, Sambo was the epitome of devotion; he often fought and died heroically while trying to save his master's life. Yet Sambo had no thought of freedom; that was an empty boon compared to serving his master. As improbable as it may seem, many white historians accept this stereotype as a true characterization of most slaves. Was Sambo real or a figment of the white man's imagination? If he was not real, why was the slave described so often in such terms by antebellum Southern whites? While the problem is complex, we can give brief answers to these questions.

The slaves played a significant role in creating the Sambo stereotype because they frequently wore the mask of humility and

submissiveness when interacting with whites. But it was the kind
of mask about which Paul Laurence Dunbar wrote:

> We wear the mask that grins and lies,
> It hides our cheeks and shades our eyes,—
> This debt we pay to human guile;
> With torn and bleeding hearts we smile,
> And mouth with myriad subtleties.
> Why should the world be overwise,
> In counting all our tears and sighs?
> Nay, let them only see us, while
>   We wear the mask.

Most slaves carefully hid their true personality traits from
whites while adopting "sham" characteristics when interacting
with them.

According to Lucy Ann Delaney, slaves lived behind an
"impenetrable mask . . . how much of joy, of sorrow, of misery
and anguish have they hidden from their tormentors!" On innumerable occasions the slaves' public behavior contradicted their
private attitudes. For instance, they frequently pretended to love
their cruel masters. Lewis Clarke argued that this was "the hardest
work that slaves have to do. When any stranger is present we
have to love them very much . . . [but when masters were sick
or dying] Then they all look glad, and go to the cabin with a
merry heart." Austin Steward discovered the same practice among
his fellow slaves when his mistress died: "The slaves were all
deeply affected by the scene; some doubtless truly lamented the
death of their mistress; others rejoiced that she was no more . . .
One of them I remember went to the pump and wet his face, so
as to appear to weep with the rest." Similarly, when Jacob
Stroyer's cruel master died, the slaves shed false tears: "Of course
the most of them were glad that he was dead," and some said,
"Thank God, massa gone home to hell."

The slaves dissembled, they feigned ignorance and humility. If
their masters expected them to be fools, they would play the
fool's role. The slave frequently pretended to be much more
humble than he actually was. When Jermain Loguen returned

after an absence of several months to his rather despicable master, for example, he pretended to be happy. He wrote that he "went through the ceremony of servile bows and counterfeit smiles to his master and mistress and other false expressions of gladness." Later, Loguen fought with his master.

Along with the slave's play-acting, there were several other compelling factors which caused Southern writers to portray blacks as Sambos. Few of them had any relation to the slave's actual behavior. Instead, the slave was stereotyped as Sambo because he allegedly belonged to an inferior race with immutable characteristics and to a subordinate caste. Then, too, facing the withering attack of the abolitionists, the Southern writer had to prove that slavery was not an unmitigated evil. The loyal, contented slave was a *sine qua non* in Southern literary propaganda. Whether he existed, in fact, was irrelevant to the Southern writer. Without Sambo, it was impossible to prove the essential goodness of Southern society.

However pervasive Sambo was in Southern literature, this is no reason for historians to accept the portrait as representative of most slaves. This is especially true since there was another stereotyped figure—let us call him Nat, the rebel—who rivaled Sambo in the universality and continuity of his literary image. Revengeful, bloodthirsty, cunning, treacherous, and savage, Nat was the incorrigible runaway, the poisoner of white men, the ravager of white women, who defied all the rules of plantation society. Subdued and punished only when overcome by superior numbers or firepower, Nat retaliated when attacked by whites, killed overseers and planters, or burned plantation buildings when he was abused. Nat's customary obedience often hid his true feelings, self-concept, unquenchable thirst for freedom, hatred of whites, discontent, and manhood, until he violently demonstrated these traits.

James McCune Smith described the slave symbolized by Nat perfectly in 1855. Smith asserted:

Blows and insults he bore, at the moment, without resentment; deep but suppressed emotion, rendered him insensible to their sting; but it was afterward, when the memory of them went seething through his brain, breeding a fiery indignation at his injured self-hood, that the resolve came to resist, and the time fixed to resist, and the time fixed when to resist, and the plot laid, how to resist; and he always kept his self-pledged word. In what he undertook, in this line, he looked fate in the face, and had a cool, keen look at the relation of means to ends.

Southern whites often thought of their slaves in the same way as Smith. From an analysis of the constantly recurring rumors of insurrections, it is obvious that many whites considered black slaves dangerous, insubordinate, bold, evil, restless, turbulent, vengeful, barbarous, and malicious. The white man's fear and anxiety over the slave was so deep and pervasive that it was sometimes pathological. A group of whispering slaves, mysterious fires, or almost any suspicious event caused alarm, apprehension, and a deepening sense of paranoia among whites. It is clear that many whites did not believe the slaves were innately docile. Too many governors received requests for arms and troops from thousands of whites, the United States Army marched and countermarched too often, too many panic-stricken whites spent their nights guarding their neighborhoods to believe that most Southern whites equated the Sambo stereotype with the dominant slave personality.

There is overwhelming evidence that the whites had good reason to be paranoid. The slave's undying love for freedom, his intractability, and his resistance to bondage can be documented easily. The resistance began in Africa. Often, kidnapped Africans tried to escape on the long march to the coast and committed suicide by drowning or refusing food or medicine, rather than be enslaved. They often mutinied while being transported to the New World and killed their white captors. In spite of their chains and lack of arms, the Africans rebelled so frequently that a number of ship owners took out insurance to cover losses from mutinies. In their study of the slave trade, historians Mannix and Cowley uncovered "fairly detailed accounts of fifty-five mutinies on slavers from 1699 to 1845, not to mention passing references to more than a hundred others. The list of ships 'cut off' by the natives— often in revenge for the kidnapping of freemen—is almost as long. On the record it does not seem that Africans submitted tamely to being carried across the Atlantic like chained beasts."

Early records indicate that the Africans continued to resist even after they landed in the New World. Many eighteenth-century travel accounts, memoirs, and slave notices show that a number of the newly imported Africans almost literally ran away as soon as their feet touched American soil. Even when they did not run away, the Africans were often obstinate, sullen, and uncooperative laborers. An English traveler observed in 1746 that the African captive, "if he must be broke, either from Obstinacy, or, which I am more apt to suppose, from Greatness of Soul, will require . . . hard Discipline . . . you would really be supriz'd at their Perseverance . . . they often die before they can be conquer'd."

American-born slaves had as much "Greatness of Soul" as their African ancestors. The yearning for freedom came with the first realization of the finality, of the fact of slavery. Lunsford Lane claimed that his first realization that he was a chattel, a thing for the use of others, caused him deep anxiety: "I saw no prospect that my condition would ever be changed. Yet I used to plan in my mind from day to day, and from night to night, how I might be free." In spite of all the floggings, there were hopes and dreams.

While it is impossible to measure exactly the extent of the slave's desire for freedom and dissatisfaction with his lot, it appears that the relationship between master and slave was one continual tug of war. According to the Louisiana slave Allen Parker, "There was always a kind of strife between master and slave, the master on the one hand trying to get all the work he possibly could out of the slaves . . . and the slaves . . . trying to get out of all the work they could, and to take every possible advantage of their master. . . . " As a result of this strife, most slaves grudgingly labored for their masters and tried to repress their anger.

Strong-willed blacks often repressed their anger, but they were not broken by the lash. William H. Heard declared that in spite of the cruel treatment meted out to the slaves, "many of them were never conquered." Rather than cower before the overseer's lash, the slaves often cursed the man who inflicted the pain on them. Frederick Douglass reported that one slave woman, after being flogged severely, "was not subdued, for she continued to denounce the overseer, and to call him every vile name. He had bruised her flesh, but had left her invincible spirit undaunted." On many occasions the slaves proved their indomitability by refusing to cry out under the lash. Elizabeth Keckley, for instance, initially resisted the effort of her master to flog her, and when he succeeded in doing so, she recalled that it was agonizing but did not break her spirit: "Oh, God! I can feel the torture now—the terrible, excruciating agony of those moments. I did not scream; I was too proud to let my tormentor know what I was suffering."

Many of the strongest, most industrious, and intelligent slaves refused to submit passively to floggings. William Wells Brown recalled that there was one strong and valuable slave on his plantation who had never been flogged and often declared "that no white man should ever whip him—that he would die first."

The relationship of the planters and overseers to the recalcitrant slave was a strange one. They feared the unruly slave, particularly if he was noted for his strength and vindictiveness. Inevitably, the unruly slave forced the master to be wary. There were certainly many masters who were cautious with slaves like Louis Manigault's Jack Savage, who was, he wrote, "the only Negro ever in our possession who I considered capable of murdering me or burning my dwelling at night or capable of committing any act." Then, there were slaves like the black woman who told a group of Virginia whites that "If old mistress did not leave her alone and quit calling her a bitch and a strumpet, she would take an iron and split her brain. . . ." On innumerable occasions planters refused to punish such slaves unless they could get them drunk, surprise them, or get other slaves or whites to overpower them. In most cases the masters tried to avoid trouble with the intractable slave because of his value as a worker. Realizing this, many slaves parlayed it into better treatment: they threatened to run away, to fight, or to stop work if they were abused. For instance, William Green, after fighting his master to a standstill when the latter tried to flog him for disobedience, declared that no man would whip him and that if he were flogged, he would cease work. His master relented, Green declared, and "after this we made up and got along very well for almost a year." Similarly, James Mars asserted that he refused to permit his master to flog him when he was sixteen, and from that time until he was twenty-one he had no more trouble with his master: "I do not remember that he ever gave me an unpleasant word or look."

One of the most significant ways of resisting bondage was to run away. The slave who decided to follow the North Star to freedom, however, faced almost insurmountable obstacles. The most formidable obstacle he had to overcome was the psychological barrier of having to leave a home, friends, and family he loved. Mothers and wives argued passionately against it. Frederick Douglass felt that "thousands would escape from slavery . . . but for the strong cords of affection that bind them to their families, relatives, and friends." Considering the likelihood of punishment and a harder life in case of failure, ridicule from the other slaves, the slave's ignorance of the world and of geography, his penniless condition, his viewing every white man as his enemy, and his memory of his master's tales of the horrible fate which befell fugitives who succeeded in reaching the North, a slave had to think a long time before he took the first step to permanent freedom. William Green and his friends often talked about escaping to Canada, but he declared that "it requires all the nerve and energy that a poor slave can bring to his support to enable him to make up his mind to leave in this precarious manner." On the eve of his escape from bondage, Frederick Douglass expressed what most slaves probably felt upon contemplating escape from slavery: "I was making a leap in the dark. . . . I was like one going to war without weapons—ten chances of defeat to one of victory."

One of the most objective and revealing sources of information on the character of the fugitives appears in the runaway slave notices in antebellum Southern newspapers. Unbiased attempts of owners to recover property worth hundreds of dollars, the notices were carefully composed, dispassionate descriptions of the fugitives, indicating their character, clothing, motives, and identifying marks. Most of the fugitives were young, robust men. In

Louisiana most of them were between the ages of sixteen and twenty-five. Similarly, in a collection of 134 runaway slave notices from eighteenth-century newspapers, 76 percent of the fugitives were under thirty-five, and 89 percent of them were men.

Most state studies of slavery indicate that there was no uniformity of personality types among the fugitives. For instance, Orville W. Taylor systematically examined notices in Arkansas newspapers and asserted that they showed "among other things, that slaves were as individualistic as white people, despite the regimentation of slavery." The major thing to remember about the slave notices is that they contained information which would help to distinguish the fugitive from the mass of slaves. It would appear from the notices that most fugitives had no readily identifiable behavioral patterns which set them apart from their fellows.

Those fugitives who were different in character from most slaves fell into two relatively broad categories. One group was composed of what Southerners called Sambo, the slave who allegedly viewed his master as his father and identified with his interest. The fugitive Sambo as described in the notices often stuttered, whined, laughed, grinned, trembled, was "easily frightened or scared," "rather stupid," "addicted to lying," or had a "sly," "down guilty" look, or "shuffled", and had a "low voice" or "a small impediment in speech when frightened" in the presence of whites.

The Sambo of the notices was a very complex fellow. Frequently, in the same sentence in which the terms cited above appeared, the planters observed that the slave was artful, could read and write, and had probably forged a pass and stolen money, horses, and clothes. A Virginia planter asserted in 1784 that the runaway Dick had "a very roguish down look . . . is artful and plausible. . . ."

The fugitive Sambo was a bundle of contradictions. On the one hand, he was the epitome of loyalty and docility, and completely trusted by his master. On the other, in spite of his sham "loyalty," he ran away. A South Carolina master in 1786 indicated how much of an enigma Sambo was when he observed that one of his fugitive slaves was sensible and artful, speaks quick, and sometimes stutters a little; HE MAY POSSIBLY HAVE A TICKET THAT I GAVE HIM TWO DAYS BEFORE HE WENT AWAY, DATED THE 6TH OF APRIL, MENTIONING HE WAS IN QUEST OF A RUN-AWAY, AS I DID NOT MENTION WHEN HE WAS TO RETURN, HE MAY ENDEAVOR TO PASS BY THAT. . . .

How could a slave so completely gain the confidence of his master that he would be sent out to look for a runaway slave and then become a fugitive himself?

Did Sambo grin and look down all the while that he was "artfully" and "ingeniously" planning to escape? Was he only play-acting when he grinned? Did he reveal his true character when he stepped out of the Sambo role or did the master misperceive his character, read too much into his "down look," while being selectively inattentive to his artfulness and roguish behavior?

The other character type which appears in the notices is the rebellious slave. The rebellious fugitive was very artful, cunning, a "well set, hardy villain," "of good sense, and much ingenuity," "saucy," "very surly," a "very great rogue," "sober and intelligent," "bold," "fights like the Devil when arrested," and often stole large sums of money and took along a "nice short shot gun." Many of these fugitives were habitual runaways and quick to try to get revenge when punished. The archetype of the rebellious fugitive was "Sarah" whom a Kentucky planter described in 1822 as

> the biggest devil that ever lived, having poisoned a stud horse and set a stable on fire, also burnt Gen. R. Williams stable and stock yard with seven horses and other property to value of $1500. She was handcuffed and got away at Ruddles Mills on her way down the river, which is the fifth time she escaped when about to be sent out of the country.

When slaves lived near swamps, impenetrable forests, or frontier areas, they often banded together in mass efforts to escape from bondage. After a Spanish decree welcomed English slaves to Florida in 1733, often as many as twenty South Carolina slaves marched in a body to the colony, sometimes killing whites along the way. The most impressive of the South Carolina incidents

began at Stono in September, 1739, when a group of slaves sacked
and burned the armory. Then they began marching toward a
Spanish fort in Florida which contained a colony of runaway
slaves and was manned by a black militia company. Beating a
drum as they marched, the slaves attacked all of the plantations
along the way, and killed twenty or thirty whites before a militia
company killed or captured most of them.

For the most part, the possibility of a large body of slaves
marching undetected to a free state was remote. Realizing this,
many runaways built "free" or maroon communities in the
swamps and mountains in the South. The maroon communities
represented one of the gravest threats to the planters. In the first
place, these communities undermined the master's authority and
emboldened other slaves to join them. For example, a group of
North Carolina planters complained in December, 1830 that "their
slaves are become almost uncontrollable. They go and come when
and where they please, and if an attempt is made to stop them
they immediately fly to the woods and there continue for months
and years committing depredations on our Cattle hogs and Sheep
. . . patrols are of no use on account of the danger they subject
themselves to. . . ." Second, and perhaps more important, the
maroons often engaged in guerrilla-like activities, plundering and
burning plantations, stealing stock, and attacking, robbing, and
murdering whites. If the maroons obtained enough arms or allied
themselves with poor whites and Indians, they could terrorize
almost any isolated white community.

A maroon was a resourceful black man who, once having
obtained his freedom, challenged any white man to take it away
from him. If his hide-out was discovered, he was willing to die
defending it. For instance, when a group of North Carolina whites
attacked a maroon camp in August, 1856, the slaves fought back
and killed one of them. Then, the "negroes ran off cursing and
swearing and telling them to come on they were ready for them
again."

The largest semi-permanent maroon communities grew up in
areas where there was international rivalry over borders or near
sympathetic Indian tribes. In this regard, the closest relations

between red and black men developed in Florida when a branch of the Creek tribe, the Seminoles, moved into the Spanish territory. Some of the Seminoles owned black slaves who were almost indistinguishable from freemen. These blacks were joined by groups of runaway slaves from South Carolina and Georgia who accepted the Spanish invitation to desert their Protestant masters. By 1836 there were probably about twelve hundred maroons living in the Seminole towns. Better acquainted with whites than the Indians, the black maroons and slaves often acted as interpreters for their red masters. By the mid-nineteenth century so many of the Indians and blacks had intermarried that they were almost indistinguishable.

Aided by Indian wars and Spanish and British intrigues on the Georgia-Alabama border with Florida, large numbers of slaves escaped and joined the maroons. A special inducement was held out to runaways when, during the War of 1812, the British built a fort on the eastern side of the Appalachicola River for themselves and their black and red allies. Abandoning the fort in 1816 but leaving behind guns and cannon for their allies, the British inadvertently incited the First Seminole War. Three hundred runaway slaves immediately took over the fort. Led by the maroon Garcon, the runaways attacked a group of sailors from a U.S. gunboat in July and scalped most of them. After a short artillery duel the gunboat was successful in blowing up the fort's magazine, killing most of the blacks. The survivors were recaptured and returned to their owners.

Seeking revenge for their fallen comrades, the Negroes and Indians began drilling in separate units under their officers. In 1817 and 1818 between four hundred and six hundred runaways joined with the Seminoles in raiding plantations in Georgia, killing the whites and liberating slaves. On April 16, 1818, Andrew Jackson captured one of the Seminole towns in which the blacks, after their initial retreat, fought valiantly. Unable to follow the survivors into the trackless swamps, Jackson unilaterally ended what he called "this savage and negro war."

The presence of hundreds of runaway slaves plagued every effort to make a permanent peace with the Seminoles before 1865.

The immediate cause of the Second Seminole War was intimately related to the problem of the maroons. The war can be traced to the kidnapping and the return to slavery of a daughter of a Negro fugitive who was the wife of the Seminole chief, Osceola. As a result of this, in December, 1835 the Indians, after being informed of the route of a company of American soldiers by a Negro guide, massacred about one hundred of the troops. Negro warriors fought in most of the battles during the next seven years and were so numerous in some of them that on one occasion General Thomas Jesup declared: "This, you may be assured, is a negro, not an Indian war. . . ."

The character of the black maroons emerges clearly from the official records. In a typical report, an army officer asserted that "The Negroes, from the commencement of the Florida war, have, for their numbers, been the most formidable foe, more blood-thirsty, active and revengeful than the Indian. . . . Ten resolute negroes, with a knowledge of the country, are sufficient to desolate the frontier, from one extent to the other." The war ended in 1842 only after Zachary Taylor guaranteed the black maroons that they would be removed to the Southwest.

In spite of widespread maroon activity and individual resistance among slaves in the South, there were considerably fewer large-scale slave rebellions in the United States than in Latin America. The explanation for this lies in the differences between conditions in Latin America and in the South. A chronic shortage of military forces and a high slave to white population ratio (seven to one in the British West Indies, eleven to one in Haiti, twenty to one in Surinam) severely limited the ability of Latin Americans to control plantation blacks. Faced with an underdeveloped communication and transportation network, along with the propinquity of plan-tations to jungles, swamps, and mountains, Latin American masters found it difficult to prevent slaves from rebelling or escaping to the "trackless wilderness." When the slaves did escape to the almost impenetrable forest, they were able to form free communities in relative security. The military forces were so weak that it once took a Cuban army two months to dislodge seven hundred slaves from a mountain stronghold, while a colonial

Mexican army took months to reach the site of a slave rebellion in the mining region and then could not defeat the rebels. Although an ignorant slave may not have known in advance that the army was weak, the existence of the slave communities was public knowledge. The communities stood, moreover, as an open invitation for the slave to escape and a monument to the weakness of the master class. Besides, he had before him the knowledge and tradition of successful slave resistance. Of overriding importance in the apparent greater inclination of Latin American slaves to rebel was the constant importation of Africans and a slave population composed of from 60 to 70 percent males.

Having the advantage over their Latin American counterparts in practically every respect, Southern planters were able to crush every slave rebellion with relative ease, and more important, to prevent the development of a tradition of successful revolt in the quarters. Unless he was totally blind, a slave could not fail to perceive how hopeless revolt was, given the size and undeniably superior firepower of the whites. In this regard, the few revolts which did occur in the United States are convincing evidence of the indomitability of the slave. After all, he had far less chance of success than his Latin American brother.

There has been so much controversy surrounding the whole question of slave rebellions that one has to apply a very strict definition to the word "revolt." A revolt is defined in this study as any concerted effort by a group of slaves to destroy the lives and property of local whites which led public officials to call out the militia. Applying this rigid definition, there were nine slave revolts in America between 1691 and 1865. Although most of the large-scale conspiracies occurred in cities, most of the actual rebellions took place in plantation counties.

A few of these revolts must be analyzed in order to understand the full range of the black man's reaction to slavery. In 1712 several Africans formed a plot in New York City to burn the town, destroy all whites "for some hard usage they apprehended to have received from their masters," and to obtain their freedom. Sealing an oath of secrecy by sucking each other's blood and rubbing powder prepared by a black conjurer on their bodies to make them invincible, the conspirators armed themselves with guns, pistols, swords, daggers, knives, and hatchets. On the night of April 6, they set fire to several buildings and then murdered and wounded at least sixteen whites who came to put out the blaze. When the alarm was sounded and troops called out, the rebels retreated. They were later captured and convicted. Some were either burned alive, hanged, or broken on the wheel.

A larger uprising occurred in Louisiana's St. Charles and St. John the Baptist parishes in 1811. Led by a free Negro, Charles Deslondes, four hundred slaves killed two whites and burned several plantations in St. John early in January. Gaining adherents along the Mississippi River, the insurgents formed into units of as many as five hundred slaves and began marching the thirty-one miles to New Orleans. Before they reached the city, U.S. troops attacked and killed sixty-six slaves in open battle. Later, sixteen leaders were executed in New Orleans, and their heads were placed on poles on roads leading from the city.

The most destructive of all the slave revolts occurred near Jerusalem, Southampton County, Virginia, in 1831. Fortunately, a white lawyer, Thomas R. Gray, recorded the confession of "the leader of this ferocious band" and "the origin and progress of this dreadful conspiracy." According to Gray, the rebellion "was not instigated by motives of revenge or sudden anger, but the results of long deliberation and a settled purpose of mind." Nat Turner, the arch-rebel, was a precocious child who was strongly influenced by his parents and especially his father, who had escaped from slavery. After a series of mystical experiences and visions, Nat and his co-conspirators led a rebellion which left a bloody trail of battered heads across Southampton before they were captured.

A short, coal-black man, Turner was fearless, honest, temperate, religious, and extremely intelligent. Gray asserted that Turner, "for natural intelligence and quickness of apprehension, is surpassed by few man I have ever seen." He knew a great deal about military tactics, and had a "mind capable of attaining any-thing. . . ." Feeling no remorse for the fifty-five whites killed during the rebellion, Turner calmly contemplated his execution. Gray gave the best characterization of him when he wrote:

He is a complete fanatic, or plays his part most admirably. . . . The calm, deliberate composure with which he spoke of his late deeds and intentions, the expression of his fiend-like face when excited by enthusiasm, still bearing the stains of blood of helpless innocence about him; clothed with rags and covered with chains; yet daring to raise his manacled hands to heaven, with a spirit soaring above the attributes of man; I look on him and my blood curdled in my veins.

The black slaves "curdled" the blood of many Southern whites. The ubiquitous runaway was the "bogey man" for young whites, "troublesome property" for his master, and a hero in the quarters. In light of the record of slave resistance, it is a criminal libel against history for such men as Stanley Elkins to assert that most slaves were Sambos. Instead of the childlike and submissive Sambo being the dominant slave personality, there was great diversity in slave character. A former Missouri slave, Henry Clay Bruce, gave the most accurate portrayal of the captive blacks and the best summary for this lecture long ago:

There were different kinds of slaves, the lazy fellow, who would not work at all unless forced to do so, and required to be watched, the good man, who patiently submitted to everything. . . . Then there was the unruly slave, whom no master particularly wanted for several reasons: first, he would not submit to any kind of corporal punishment; second, it was hard to determine which was the master or which the slave; third, he worked when he pleased to do so. . . . This class of slaves were usually industrious, but very impudent. There were thousands of that class, who spent their lives in their master's service doing his work undisturbed, because the master understood the slave . . . there were thousands of high-toned and high spirited slaves, who had as much self-respect as their masters. . . . These slaves knew their own helpless condition. . . . But . . . they did not give up in abject servility. . . .

NOTE

For a full development of ideas presented in this lecture and a discussion of Professor Blassingame's more recent research on slave personalities, see "Sambos and Rebels: The Character of the Southern Slave," *The Slave Community: Plantation Life in the Antebellum South*, rev. ed. (New York, 1979).

Military Policy Origins
of the Thirteenth Amendment and
the Civil Rights Act of 1866

Mary Frances Berry

The notion that one of the indicators and obligations of citizenship status was a requirement for service in the military defense of the nation influenced decisions concerning the use of blacks as soldiers throughout the antebellum period. Blacks were used reluctantly and in limited numbers in the colonial wars, the Revolutionary War, the War of 1812, and the Mexican War. The pre-Civil War experience indicated that improvement in the legal status of blacks generally, or citizenship status for black soldiers and veterans was not a required result of the military use of blacks, at least when their efforts were not regarded as absolutely necessary for victory. But in the Civil War, the large-scale use of black soldiers was regarded by President Lincoln, the War Department, and a majority in Congress as absolutely essential to defeat the Confederacy. As a result of the enlistment of about two hundred thousand blacks in the military service, not only was it necessary for the national government to abolish slavery, but to settle the legal status of blacks generally by recognizing them as citizens.

Historians of Reconstruction have elaborated a number of reasons for the adoption of the Thirteenth Amendment, abolishing slavery, including the use of black soldiers. They have also described a number of reasons for the enactment of citizenship status for blacks in the Civil Rights Act of 1866 and the Fourteenth Amendment, and the negative suffrage guarantee in the Fifteenth

Amendment. John Hope Franklin, Kenneth M. Stampp, and Lawanda and John Cox have emphasized the concern of Republicans who worked for humanitarian, legal, and political equality for the freedmen. Eric L. McKitrick has suggested that the Fourteenth Amendment was a moderate civil rights measure and not radical at all. William Brock, David Donald, and Charles Fairman have described the disputes over Congressional Reconstruction as a compromise between groups of Republicans, and Michael Les Benedict has described the legislation as evolving from an uneasy alliance between radical and conservative Republicans, with a compromise of principle on race, which persisted until 1869. This essay suggests that an additional basis for the enactment of the civil rights measures of Reconstruction had its origins in miliary enlistment policy and citizenship status determinations developed in the period before and during the Civil War.

When Lyman Trumbull, Republican from Illinois, introduced in the Senate in March 1864, his amendment abolishing slavery, the Union still required the use of large numbers of black soldiers in combat in order to defeat the Confederacy. Trumbull's bill was passed in the Senate by a vote of 38 to 6 on April 8, 1864, but was tabled in the House, by a vote of 95 to 65, in mid-June. In January, 1865, when the bill came up for reconsideration, black regiments were involved daily in efforts to end the war, then in its final campaigns. The Democratic opposition again, as in the previous June, held the power to deny the abolition amendment two-thirds approval. Partly through the efforts of William Seward, secretary of war, and his lobby of moderate Democrats, a few Democrats did not vote, but sixteen Democrats voted for it, and the amendment was passed. A Republican two-thirds majority in the next Congress guaranteed its eventual passage. In addition to the possible use of money and patronage, the Seward lobby promised recalcitrant Democrats generous peace terms to the South, speedy full reinstatement of the South in the Union, and continued cooperation between conservative Republicans and moderate Democrats. The administration argued that passage of the amendment would hasten peace and ensure its permanency.

Democrats and moderate Republicans saw the amendment as settling the slavery question and permitting the formation of new conservative political alliances of Republicans and Democrats on other issues. By early 1866 most Republicans and the public were committed to the idea that a civil rights bill was necessary in order that the Thirteenth Amendment would not be a sham. Equal rights without suffrage was their position. Johnson and Seward, in the interest of creating a new party and isolating the radicals, opposed what turned out to be the majority.[1]

In fact, the Republicans were solidly together on the race issue. Some Republicans wanted equal suffrage for blacks (men like Ohio's John A Bingham, Charles Sumner of Massachusetts, Thaddeus Stevens of Pennsylvania, and Jacob Howard of Michigan), but they submerged their concerns to mesh with the party position in 1865 and 1866 of equal rights up to suffrage. Also the issue of the basis of representation in Congress after abolition, even without black suffrage, occupied the Joint Committee of Fifteen on Reconstruction all during early 1866. Republicans were concerned about maintaining control of politics, about public hostility to increasing the power of the South, about providing legal protection for Republicans in the South, and about national safety as well as what measures would enable blacks to protect themselves from re-enslavement. But first came the adoption of the Thirteenth Amendment and the Civil Rights Act of 1866 as the first enacted legal means for ensuring black protection. In addition to such factors as humanitarianism, interest in black freedom, and anger toward the South, which in seceding had caused the shedding of blood to maintain the Union, one of the important political reasons for the adoption of the Thirteenth Amendment and the Civil Rights Act of 1866 was Republican military policy during the war. The work of the Seward lobby more easily bore fruit because the tug of military expediency, which required the emancipation and the recruitment of black soldiers, moved the national government ever closer to a requirement that legal rights, including suffrage, had to be provided for blacks.[2]

Republicans, in early 1865, expressed continued awareness of the connection between military policy and the black equality problem in debates on abolition issues. In the Senate in January, Republican James R. Doolittle of Wisconsin, opposing a bill to free the families of slave soldiers in the border slave states, objected that the bill was unnecessary because adoption of the Thirteenth Amendment would free all slaves. Since by that time even Jefferson Davis in the Confederacy proposed limited abolition as a war measure, Senator Doolittle did not see how the House could fail again to adopt abolition as they had the previous June. Henry Wilson, Republican of Massachusetts, responded that the blacks against whom "outrages" were being committed could not wait for the passage of the Thirteenth Amendment. But still with an eye on military needs and the war powers as a constitutional basis for legislation, he said the bill was necessary because ". . . we owe it to the course of the country, to liberty, to justice, and to patriotism to offer every inducement to every black man who can fight the battle of the country to join our armies." Willard Saulsbury, Democrat from Delaware, still embittered by the continued failure of the states' rightist argument against military use of blacks, argued that the modern doctrine of "military necessity" could not be extended to mean that in a state of war "whatever the Congress of the United States shall decree, is constitutionally decreed." Sumner responded that slaves had been used and freed and now "intrinsic justice and humanity" dictated freedom for the families of slave soldiers.[3]

In early 1865, when the House discussed the president's annual message including strong support of abolition, John A. J. Creswell, Republican from Maryland, squarely faced up to the race question. He said that "the stern necessity of self-defense" lent support to the Emancipation Proclamation. After two years' time, the people, in the November, 1864 elections, made it clear that they desired to "dispel all legal doubts; and to make that proclamation good for all time, and universal in its application by amendment of the Constitution. If there was a governmental obligation to protect slavery before the war, "that obligation has been forfeited." Creswell had heard that even the Confederacy wanted to use black soldiers. If so, they would learn like the Union that: "Men who have handled muskets do not willingly become slaves."

Blacks would have to remain free or be forcibly returned to bondage. Glenn W. Scofield, a Pennsylvania Republican, in supporting him, stated that he did not see why slavery should "linger in party warfare through a quarter or half of a century of monotonous debate, patchwork legislation, and conflicting adjudication." They should be done with it, in conformity with the will of the people.[4]

When the abolition amendment itself was debated in the House on January 9, 1865, George H. Yeaman, Union Party representative from Kentucky, expressed the view that the Democrats should get on the right side politically in order to exercise power in the future by "cutting loose from a dead carcass." He thought that everyone would recognize that compensation, giving lands to blacks or giving them citizenship, was not really the issue. If anyone suggested continuing the war one hour "for such fruitless and malignant ends" they would be silenced. He believed that "schemes" directed toward compensation, giving land or citizenship and suffrage to blacks and the like would be universally "abandoned" once the abolition amendment was passed. Furthermore, he thought that slavery was at an end no matter what they did and even if the South won the war. There would be, under arms, former slaves "who have been *contracted* with, been armed and drilled, and have seen the force of combination." Not only would they not be returned to slavery, they would "leaven the whole mass" of slaves who had not been in the military. ". . . their mere presence, the idea, if their mouths were padlocked would soon have this effect."[5] Yeaman's efforts in support of the amendment, stimulated in part by the direct influence of Lincoln, was apparently rewarded; he was appointed minister to Denmark in 1865.

Robert Mallory, a Kentucky Democrat who opposed Yeaman, argued that the abolition amendment would create the further difficulty of deciding what to do with the blacks. Mallory predicted that the Republicans would use blacks as voters in the South for the purpose of keeping control of the national government and the Southern states. He got little support for his argument in the debate that day.[6]

On January 11 and 12, as the debate continued in the House,

the Democrats focused on constitutional arguments. Democrat William S. Holman of Indiana sought to frighten supporters of the amendment by raising the spectre of suffrage. He explained that abolition was the "entering wedge" for a bill that gave civil rights to blacks on the theory that they would not be secure unless they were citizens who could vote. Indiana Democrat James A. Cravens suggested that since Northerners were opposed to an influx of black immigrants into their states, and colonization was apparently not in the cards, abolition would mean domination by black majorities over whites in the South. Massachusetts Republican George S. Boutwell and Ohio Democrat George H. Pendleton, asserting that the amendment was unconstitutional, insisted that slavery had been an initial condition of ratification to the Constitution. The Constitution would itself become illegal if a basic unamendable particular of it concerning slavery was discarded. Illinois Republican John F. Farnsworth reminded Pendleton that he had voted in 1861 to add an amendment which prohibited abolishing slavery. If it was possible to amend the Constitution on the slavery question in 1861, it should be possible to amend it in 1865. Pendleton responded weakly that an amendment to keep slavery forever was legal but not one to get rid of it.[7]

On January 12, 1865, after Green Clay Smith, Union representative from Kentucky, explained that he would vote for the amendment because after the war the black soldiers could be marched into Mexico to drive out Napoleon, Samuel S. Cox, Ohio Democrat, electrified the House by supporting the Republicans on the issue of constitutionality. Cox, who had been approached by the Seward lobby and was wavering, although he finally voted against the amendment, entered the continuing dispute between Pendleton and James M. Ashley, Ohio Republican, over whether slavery was a non-amendable, pre-existing condition of the Constitution. According to Cox, his fellow Democrats were just using the Constitutional arguments in order to support their objectives. He thought that it was of course constitutional to amend the Constitution but that a supportable reason for Democratic opposition was that abolition was "inexpedient" and "anarchical."[8]

On January 31, the House passed the amendment, after the final plea against it by William H. Miller, Democrat of Pennsylvania, who thought they "should not pull down the old house until we have built the new one." The vote was 119 to 56 with eight Democrats absent. The bill was returned to the Senate and sent to the president, who signed it on February 1, 1865. When the amendment passed, during the last tough months of fighting, there were some two hundred thousand blacks in the army, including the all-black XXV Army Corps of thirty-two black regiments that had been organized in the Army of the Potomac in December, 1864. In the last year of the war black troops made up large contingents in almost every successful battle in the Department of the South. The Thirteenth Amendment had been passed by the Congress, but the legal issue of freedom and equality for soldiers and the masses on whom they would act as "leaven" was not yet resolved.[9]

Aside from the reports of General Ulysses Grant, and Carl Schurz, and others on conditions in the South, politicians received information from their constituents still in the military services on the behavior of Southerners toward the freedmen. For example, a soldier in Hilton Head, South Carolina, told Lyman Trumbull, in May, 1865, that the Southerners were planning to "put the colored man who has been so true to us, way out of reach of Justice." The only remedy was a continued military presence including black soldiers. Another soldier in Meridian, Mississippi, suggested that even aside from the fact that the North was opposed to it, more than black suffrage was needed. Blacks would not be permitted to vote anyway "whatever may be the laws on the subject," if the military garrisons were removed. True, the black masses did not really have the wherewithal or knowledge to fight against oppression like revolutionaries in England or Europe but, ". . . with good leaders, they will fight to the death."[10]

By the time the next Congress met in December, 1865 and Andrew Johnson, the new president, sent his annual message to Congress, events had moved quickly to make resolution of the issue of legal rights for blacks even more crucial. Lincoln had been shot and the war was ended. A period of confusion and uncertainty about Reconstruction and the programs of the new president ensued. Democrats sought to gain Johnson's support for a new conservative coalition to oppose the Republicans. Like Lincoln, Johnson made ratification of the Thirteenth Amendment a condition of readmission in the South. But, South Carolina, Alabama, and Florida, in ratifying the Thirteenth Amendment, provided that the second section did not give Congress the power needed after the Civil War to determine the political status of slaves. This position was expected since Seward had in November written just such an interpretation to the provisional governor of South Carolina. Johnson and the administration seemed to agree with white Southerners that the Thirteenth Amendment was an end and not a beginning. Many Republicans, while not committed to suffrage, supported civil equality and opposed increasing the political power of the South while blacks were held close to slavery. Blacks themselves wanted nothing less.[11]

What to do with the blacks was still an unresolved issue. If Northern states' responses served as a guide, few gave blacks the suffrage. Congress tried to develop a procedure for protecting the rights of blacks within the framework of limiting interference with states' rights. The second section of the Thirteenth Amendment offered the opportunity for this development. The Civil Rights Act of 1866, based on the second section of the amendment, left the way open for the states to enforce civil equality without the injection of a federal presence unless necessary. The act prohibited both state and private interference with civil rights. Along with the Freedmen's Bureau bill extension, protecting army officers and blacks in contracts and in certain judicial contracts, the Civil Rights Act was a limited effort to obtain enforcement of black rights. The two bills emanated from a majority concern that freedom for blacks not be a sham but that there not be too much intrusion into state power.[12]

Still, throughout 1865 and into 1866 as Congress discussed the format of acceptable civil rights legislation, black soldiers remained an ominous presence. In July, 1865 there were 123,156 black troops in the army; 120 regiments of infantry; 12 regiments of cavalry. White men were being rapidly mustered out; they were anxious to go home and any delay was questioned. Black troops were more willing to stay in the service because their terms had not expired and most of them did not have a home or employment to which to return. Those opposed to the presence of black troops in the South, especially when they outnumbered whites, argued that blacks had not been in service as long and were less well trained and disciplined. Some whites cited cases of mutiny, resulting in many instances from the black soldier's perceptions of racist treatment on the part of white officers, as a basis for declaring black troops unsuitable. White citizens complained about the "uppity" behavior of armed blacks. Commanders tried when possible to isolate black troops by stationing them in remote garrisons.[13]

Generals protested each time they received muster-out orders from Washington if more black than white regiments remained in their areas. Generals Ord and Halleck, offering incompetency and indiscipline as reasons, removed the all-black XXV Army Corps from occupation duty in Virginia. They reported complaints that black soldiers were hostile to whites, sometimes insulting them, that they allegedly raped some white women, and that they encouraged militancy and insolence among the civilian blacks, who were expected to remain docile. A good example of the kind of complaints which the whites thought justifiable is this telling report of General Gillmore:

> I have found so many bad men among the non-commissioned officers and privates of some of my colored regiments—men, who by their false representation and seditious advice, have exercised most baleful influences upon the plantation laborers—that I have been forced to devolve upon the white troops—to a much greater degree than their numbers would justify—the obvious and delicate duties of instructing the inhabitants of the country in their rights and responsibilities as well as the ratifying and enforcing of labor contracts. In many instances nearly all the laborers on large plantations under extensive cultivation have violated their contracts and suspended their work in consequence of the permissive influence of a few bad colored soldiers, who were formerly slaves in the community.

After experiencing slavery, warfare, unequal pay and work assignments, conceivably black soldiers were militant and indeed acted as a "yeast" in developing consciousness among the civilian black population. Gillmore did not encourage the discharge of black soldiers from the service because he feared they would be free to create even more militancy and discontent among black freedmen in the local community.[14]

In September, 1865, Grant successfully urged Stanton to order the muster-out of all black regiments raised in the North. Grant assumed that those raised in the North, in volunteer regiments, were a greater source of difficulty since they were unfamiliar with Southern racial ways. During the last half of 1865, when President Johnson made the Thirteenth Amendment a condition of read-mission to the Union and the first months of 1866, when Congress enacted the Civil Rights Act and Freedmen's Bureau Bill, the proportion of black to white troops in some parts of the South was three-to-one or higher. The order to muster out numerous white volunteer regiments in August, 1865 left General Stoneman in Tennessee two batteries of white artillery and thirteen black regiments of all arms. Five of these black regiments were ordered to Alabama, where at that moment white troops were in the majority, so that General Woods could muster out five white regiments. In December, 1865, when the states formally ratified the Thirteenth Amendment, only one of twelve infantry regiments in Mississippi was white, and in the following month there were 6,550 white and 17,768 black volunteers in Texas and Louisiana. Not until November of 1866 was black military strength, after muster-out, at a low enough level to make black military presence in the South a non-threatening issue, and even then the presence of black veterans remained threatening.[15]

Black troops in the field experienced daily their influence on the attitudes of white and black populations, and even some white Northerners became concerned about the possibility of an explosion. One Ohio resident told Secretary of War Stanton in January that abolition was inevitable: "It would require a power vastly greater now to arrest them [blacks] than it will to consummate the movement," but he feared for whites in the South that "armed Africans" among the depleted population in the South would "be masters of the situation, and that scenes of San Domingo may be re-enacted." When the Fifty-fourth Massachusetts regiment marched through South Carolina in the Georgetown area on April 20, 1865, about three thousand black civilians eagerly followed them. When the soldiers arrived at Charleston where they were assigned to guard and picket duty for the next four months, large numbers of blacks surrounded them wherever they went. The commanders of the Louisiana Native Guards, assigned to guarding railroad stations at Terre Bonne in the last year of the war, ordered them not to peer into the windows of the trains or to speak to the white passengers, who felt threatened by their presence.[16]

The army and white Northerners and Southerners alike regarded black soldiers as a threat to white Southerners. At no time during the period when Congress debated endlessly the issue of abolition did information from the field indicate any feeling that slavery could be imposed, without bloodshed, on the black men in the army, or on the surrounding black population. Democrats in Congress might argue unconstitutionality, inexpediency, futility, and danger in opposition to abolition, the Republicans might seriously respond, but these debates were not echoed from soldiers and commanders in the field. The end of slavery was irrevocable. Some settlement that would maintain the peace, which would make blacks believe their rights were being acknowledged, and whites resign themselves to civil equality, was necessary. The muster-out and disarming of black troops required breathing space. In Louisiana, General Canby, deviating from long-standing army procedure, at Grant's directive, ordered that black soldiers, being discharged from the army, should not be permitted to purchase their weapons to take home. The generals hoped to disperse the influence of black soldiers more widely in order to dissipate the effect of their militancy, and to arrange for the transfer of the remainder to the West where they could be occupied with fighting the Indians and defending the frontier.[17]

Black spokesmen and soldiers made clear from the beginning that they expected military participation in the war to hasten abolition and equality for black people. Since the war came and the South unabashedly fought to maintain slavery, they supported the Union effort in the hope that the course of events would lead to abolition. In any case, given the South's defense of slavery, they had to support the Union. Depending on their circumstances, blacks focused on abolition, improved economic conditions, education or civil rights, including the right to vote, as objectives in the war. Slaves and freedmen expected the war to bring individual freedom, economic conditions of life, food, clothing, and shelter that were at least as good as they had been provided by the master before the war, and the opportunity to own land, acquire an education, and exercise political freedom, in that order. They had no reason to believe that Northern whites intended to leave them economically more deprived than they had been as slaves. They placed importance on the other items on the agenda because the culture in which they lived as slaves had placed principal emphasis on their possession. They believed the Union would grant either the provision of land and education or the wherewithal to purchase them. Of course, Southern planters hoped to depart as little as possible from antebellum conditions after the war. Northern businessmen, philanthropists, and politicians, as concerned about preserving property interests as the Southerners, generally opposed confiscation of Southern plantations and the carving of homesteads out of them for the freedmen. The position of most whites, North and South, meant that the experiments in allotting abandoned properties to freedmen during the war generally did not survive the claims of the former rebel owners, and that sharecropping and crop lien systems evolved. Instead of receiving reparation payments or forty acres and a mule outright, freedmen often found themselves as deprived economically in terms of food, clothing, and shelter as they had been before the war.

The experiments in allocating land in the Sea Islands of South Carolina in 1862 and again by Sherman's Order No. 15 in 1865 ended when after the war Johnson restored most of the land to former owners. Similarly, in Mississippi at Davis Bend on Jefferson Davis's plantation, the land leased to blacks reverted to one hundred and forty former owners or other whites after the war. Attempts by the Freedmen's Bureau to distribute the abandoned lands which Congress placed under its jurisdiction failed when

Johnson decided to return those properties to pardoned Confederates. The Southern Homestead Act, passed in February, 1866, provided for the sale of remaining federal land: nearly fifty million acres as homesteads. Most of it was timbered, swampy, or poorly drained, and lack of capital prevented most freedmen from homesteading that. The Congress defeated every attempt by freedmen to claim reparations in cash payments from the government in consideration of their slave labor.[18]

In view of the generally poor wages and the miserable working conditions imposed upon white workingmen in the North, it is easy to understand why Congress did not seriously consider the expropriation of property to be transferred to blacks or the payment of cash reparations. Poor white farmers were often just as economically deprived. Blacks successfully contributed to Northern victory in the war, but Northern capitalists were no more concerned to improve the lives of blacks than they were concerned to improve the lives of their own white workers. White workers, generally, worked long and hard for as little pay as the owner chose to distribute. Working hours, even for children, lasted as long as daylight permitted, and upward mobility was largely a figment of the imagination. In providing the unskilled labor necessary for industrialization, the massive immigration of German and Irish peasants deepened the gulf between classes. The Northern "wage slave" had his conditions of life circumscribed and had no one to take responsibility for him in infancy, old age, illness, or injury and was often clothed, housed, and fed little better than slaves. There was no reason to expect the businessmen and politicians who mouthed the rhetoric of opportunity and the work ethic while they exploited white laborers to be concerned to improve the economic conditions of life for blacks.[19]

Most white laborers on the farm or in industry had little to offer blacks even if they had overcome their prejudice in the interest of an alliance between black and white workers. Blacks fared somewhat better when it came to education. Enough philanthropists believed that providing education would not undermine their self-reliance even if reparations or land would. Additionally, by controlling the emphasis in education whites

could, in part, control the destiny of the race. Freedmen's aid
societies, black and white, and the churches as well as the
Freedmen's Bureau, helped to establish schools. The private
colleges were connected with churches, and providing education
was part of proselytization. The schools were as good and
prestigious as their backers.[20] When Military Reconstruction came
in 1867, the new constitutions provided for public education.

A number of black men, those in particular who already had
some economic wherewithal and education, led the demands for
political rights. While encouraging enlistments in 1861, Frederick
Douglass explained to blacks that "you have hitherto expressed
in various ways not only your willingness but your earnest desire
to fulfill any and every obligation which the relationship of
citizenship imposes;" military service was one such obligation.
Blacks should also enlist in order to learn the art and ability of
defense. Furthermore, he asserted, "he who fights the battles of
America may claim America as his country and have that claim
respected."[21]

As the war dragged on and black soldiers proved their mettle
in successfully aiding Union victory, black servicemen expressed
similar views of the meaning of such service. The *New Orleans
Tribune,* on September 6, 1864, declared that the war had brought
freedom and the recognition of black manhood which the black
troops "are now fighting valiantly nay heroically to maintain."
When James H. Ingraham, a black officer in one of the Native
Guard Regiments, appeared at the 1864 National Convention of
Colored Men in Syracuse, New York, all business stopped, and
he was escorted to the speaker's platform while the delgates stood
and cheered. Ingraham told the delegates that despite oppression
black men were willing to fight. "This example of magnanimity
and partiotism," he declared, "finds no parallel in the world's
history." Clearly such service would support a claim to equality
after the war.[22]

Frederick Douglass, at the same convention, asserted that
political equality, suffrage at least, should be granted after the
war. He knew that, before, whites opposed claims to the vote,
in part, because blacks were not required to perform military

duty. "Of course this was only a plausible excuse; for we were subject to any call the Government was pleased to make upon us, and we could not properly be made to suffer because the Government did not see fit to impose military duty upon us. The fault was with the Government not with us. Now this frivolous though decent apology for excluding us from the ballot box is entirely swept away." He knew that it could be argued that blacks went into the service without promise of a political reward but "the fact that, when called into the service of the country, we went forward without exacting terms or conditions, to the mind of the generous man enhances our claims." Even abolitionists asked "why blacks could not be satisfied with personal freedom, the right to testify in courts of law, the right to own, buy and sell real estate, the right to sue and be sued . . . " The answer is that "in a republican country without suffrage all other rights become mere privileges, held at the option of others."[23]

On April 15, 1865, the New Orleans *Black Republican* spoke for many blacks when it declared: "Above all, our devotion to our flag, and our manly conduct must be our last appeal and the ground of our hope." But the pleas of blacks for land, money, and the vote fell largely on non-responsive ears. After all, land and money were not even given to poor whites generally, and the vote was not given to immigrant working classes. However, legislation could be enacted, without cost, that would appear to reward the freedmen for service in the war, stabilize conditions during the demobilization of black troops, and offer a basis for maintenance of the social and economic status quo.

Congressmen understood that military necessity had brought them closer to enacting legislation providing at least paper equality for the races in the South. Some radicals knew all along where the path would lead, but understood that their fellows had to be dragged step-by-step. The Democrats understood and opposed the military policy all along, but for many congressmen, who had not seen clearly before, the civil rights issue, at the end of the war, was highlighted.

In the Congress, Democrats and Republicans continued to spar over issues related to the Thirteenth Amendment, the Freedmen's

Bureau Bill, and the civil rights bill from December through March and into April, 1866. In the House, Farnsworth introduced a resolution on December 13, 1865, which expressed the idea that simple justice demanded that black soldiers be awarded citizenship rights. He theorized that if aliens, traitors, and rebels could maintain citizenship rights, then at least blacks who had served in the military should become citizens. Trumbull, who introduced the Civil Rights Act of 1866, favored a distinction between civil rights and political rights. He meant to include the right to come and go, make contracts, rent and lease property, and the like; he did not mean the right to vote. The time was not right, and necessity did not yet in 1866 compel facing that issue. Democrats, like Sydenham E. Ancona of Pennsylvania and John W. Chanler of New York, in the House, and Saulsbury, in the Senate, over and over in December made clear their understanding that the second section of the Thirteenth Amendment did not mean giving civil, and certainly not political, rights to blacks.[24]

In January, 1866 when Congress considered the bill to grant suffrage to blacks in the District of Columbia, the same issues came up, and the lines were drawn in the same fashion. Republican James F. Wilson of Iowa argued that suffrage was a reward for blacks who gave their all to aid "the nation which had been so cruel to them." Benjamin Boyer, Pennsylvania Democrat, responded that blacks did not need to be rewarded further for military service; they had been rewarded with emancipation. If they were unfit to vote before the war, they were still unfit. To educate them and make sure contracts were enforced and labor and property protected as in the civil rights bill, were enough. But it was Scofield, who favored suffrage, who pointed directly to the problem. What would be done with the blacks? Colonization was ridiculous. "If colonization is found impracticable will you try to re-enslave them?" He did not think that would work. " . . . the blacks are now too intelligent, too self-reliant and too spirited to submit again to oppression." Andrew J. Rogers, the New Jersey Democrat, however, took a different tack. He disagreed with the policy of awarding suffrage because then women who were citizens, and, in some cases, had aided in the war effort, would also have to be given the right to vote. He was sure that the Congress agreed with him in opposing suffrage for women. Chanler, in a long speech on January 12, reminded the House that at the beginning of the war "the claim to all the privileges of an American citizen was easily to be foreseen as a consequence of the policy that made the Negro a soldier. . . ." They should not have enlisted blacks in the first place and he "for one would deny that any obligation rests against this government to do anything more for the Negro than has already been done." Chanler's views did not prevail. On January 30, 1866, Howard told the Senate that "having employed this class of persons to the number of nearly two hundred thousand, . . ." the nation would "reap the fruits of our treachery and imbecility in woes which we have not yet witnessed," even worse than the Civil War itself, if legal civil rights protection was not provided.[25]

The majority of Congress of both parties rejected suffrage for blacks but adopted Trumbull's posture of civil rights protection to remove "badges of servitude made in the interest of slavery and as a part of slavery."[26] They understood that black consciousness added to the desire of whites in the North to prevent a migration of blacks out of the South, and the continuing objection of some Republicans as far back as 1862 that the government could not use black soldiers and attempt to re-enslave them made civil paper equality the absolute minimum condition of a permanent peace. They enacted the Civil Rights Act of 1866 which guaranteed civil equality to blacks under state law as a response to the need to resolve the race question. If a black person experienced discrimination under state law he could bring a case to federal court. The protection of rights required case-by-case litigation.[27]

The Fourteenth Amendment enacted by Congress in June, 1866 was designed to resolve any doubts concerning the constitutionality of the Civil Rights Act of 1866. It was also intended to give responsibility for protection of the freedmen's rights to the state governments as a matter of fundamental law. Unlike the Civil Rights Act's positive statement of individual black rights, its provisions were stated negatively. No *state* could interfere with civil rights of persons, rather than certain civil rights *belonged* to individuals.

By the end of 1866 and even before the Fourteenth Amendment was ratified, the case-litigation approach of the Civil Rights Act was recognized as a failure by a majority in Congress. Southern recalcitrance, the enforcement of Black Codes, pogrom-like race riots in Southern cities, including disturbances involving black soldiers, offered visible evidence of white Southern intentions to maintain the antebellum status quo. In the midst of the open break between President Andrew Johnson and Congress, the will of the Northern majority that the Republican party prosper, and that the South not be readmitted on a representation basis that would guarantee the resurgence of the slave power on the backs of blacks, the enactment of Military Reconstruction was required, including a guarantee of black suffrage, as the next legal step in guaranteeing a permanent rearrangement of power relationships in the South. In terms of legality and constitutional traditions, suffrage seemed to be an appropriate solution. Articulate blacks demanded suffrage, so now, arguably, they could protect themselves against white oppression and state and local governmental inequities by voting. Many blacks, particularly those from the literate free community before the war, demanded suffrage and the right to hold office as their just due as veterans of the war.[28]

Congress provided suffrage in the Military Reconstruction Act as a means of perpetuating Republican power and out of recognition that reliance on the Fourteenth Amendment alone would require continued national intervention to protect the rights of blacks. The time gained from December, 1865 to March 2, 1867 had made it possible to phase out the black soldier problem, to reduce the tension among the black masses, and to improve the old racial order. By 1867, the threat that black soldiers might engage in violent attacks upon whites had been largely erased. The lesson of Military Reconstruction was that even when blacks were given suffrage, military protection would be required to prevent white Southerners from overthrowing the radical governments in which blacks participated. The Fifteenth Amendment, enacted in February, 1869, was a last-gasp effort to reconcile the congressional belief that some assertion of the right of suffrage for blacks should be made fundamental law with the reluctance to interfere directly in state activities. The Fifteenth Amendment was declaratory; it did not require any action militarily or otherwise on the part of the national government.[29]

Even before the Fifteenth Amendment was passed, it became clear that Republican ascendancy in the presidency could be maintained without blacks, if the South was left to become Democratic and the North and East remained Republican. Also, blacks themselves, including war veterans in those states (South Carolina and Louisiana) where they had gained some share in power, agreed with their Northern Republican supporters and extended the olive branch and supported suffrage for white Southerners. The Republican dilemma was resolved; redemption could proceed. Legal and moral responsibilities had been met; suffrage and equality had been enacted into governmental law.

Military and Black Reconstruction started to become unglued almost as soon as it came into existence. Northern holders of power did not include a long-term use of soldiers to protect blacks in the South in their plans. Even the few local "Negro" militia units, composed of whites and blacks and organized by some of the Republican state governments in 1868, proved ineffective. Radical governors did not use these militia units to protect unionists from white terrorists as extensively as they should have because of their fears of race war between blacks and whites. In some states, warring factions of Republican politicans used the militia units to engage in warfare against their Republican opponents. White vigilante bands, including the Ku Klux Klan, systematically murdered and intimidated members of the militia groups. Black regular soldiers, long since mustered out, disarmed, or transferred to the frontier, their "yeast" among the masses run out of leaven, saw the bright promises of equality come to an end. Military necessity brought blacks into the service; their efforts helped to win the war, and gained the enactment of constitutional amendments and civil rights laws. The war was over, Republican party dominance in national politics was assured, and the economic organization of land, capital, and labor proceeded, North and

South, on conventional capitalistic terms. Black people possessed a number of individual freedoms, including freedom to worship, attend school, marry and divorce, and have children.[30] Military necessity receded and even the civil rights laws enacted in its wake soon became so many dead letters, paper things, largely unenforced.

NOTES

1. Lawanda and John Cox, *Politics, Principles and Prejudice, 1865–66: Dilemma of Reconstruction in America* (New York, 1963), 30; Howard Devon Hamilton, "The Legislative and Judicial History of the Thirteenth Amendment" (Ph.D. dissertation, University of Illinois, 1950), 1–10 discusses the introduction of five unsuccessful amendments into the Congress beginning with the bill of Representative James Ashley in December, 1863; also in Charles Fairman's *Reconstruction and Reunion 1864–1888;* Oliver Wendell Holmes's *Devise History of the Supreme Court of the United States* (New York, 1971), pt. I, 1136–54. Jacobus Ten Broek, *Equal Under Law* (New York, 1965), 46, 166, 167, 173.

2. Joseph B. James, *The Framing of the Fourteenth Amendment* (Urbana, 1958), *passim*, esp. 184–85; Hamilton, "The Thirteenth Amendment," 10, 20; Cox and Cox, *Politics, Principles and Prejudice,* 32–35.

3. *Congressional Globe,* 38th Congress, 3rd Session, 113–14; Hamilton, ". . .Thirteenth Amendment," 13–16.

4. *Congressional Globe,* 39th Congress, 2nd Session, 144.

5. *Ibid.,* 170.

6. *Ibid.,* 179; Jacques Voegeli, *Free but not Equal: the Midwest and the Negro during the Civil War* (Chicago, 1967), 174–77.

7. *Congressional Globe,* 38th Congress, 3rd Session, 224; Frank L. Klement, "Midwestern Opposition to Lincoln's Emancipation Policy," *Journal of Negro History* LIX (1964): 170–71.

8. *Congressional Globe,* 38th Congress, 3rd Session, 240–41; Cox and Cox, *Politics, Principles and Prejudices,* 18.

9. *Congressional Globe,* 38th Congress, 3rd Session, 531, 588; Cox and Cox, *Politics, Principles and Prejudices,* 25.

10. M. S. Littlefield to Lyman Trumbull, May 8, 1965; C. E. Lippincott to Trumbull, August 29, 1865, Lyman Trumbull Papers, reel 16,

vol. 60, and reel 17, vol. 61; Library of Congress. See also S. Brisbane to Thaddeus Stevens, December 29, 1863; Thaddeus Stevens Papers, vol. 5, Library of Congress.

11. Hamilton, ". . . The Thirteenth Amendment," 13–20; Richard Mendales, "Republic Defectors to the Democracy During Reconstruction," paper read at the November 1973 annual meeting of the Southern Historical Association, copy in my possession.

12. Hamilton, ". . . The Thirteenth Amendment," 55–58; Robert L. Kohl, "The Civil Rights Act of 1866, Its Hour Come Around At Last, *Jones* v. *Alfred Mayer Co.*", *Virginia Law Review* LV (1969): 272.

13. *O.R.* ser. 3, vol. 5, 661; James Sefton, *The United States Army and Reconstruction, 1865–77* (Baton Rouge, 1967), 50–52; John Hope Franklin, "Reconstruction and the Negro," in Harold Hyman, ed., *New Frontiers of Reconstruction Historiography* (Urbana, 1966), 69–70; William F. Messner, "Black Violence and White Response . . ." 36–37, seems to believe that whites regarded black soldiers as non-threatening and docile by the end of the war.

14. Gillmore to Lorenzo Thomas, A.G.-U.S.A. August 20, 1865, Department of the South, 15 R.G. 98; quoted in Sefton, *Army and Reconstruction,* 52.

15. *O.R.* ser. 3, vol. 5, 48, 103–108; Grant to Stanton and Stanton to Acting Assistant Secretary of War Major Thomas Eckert, September 6, 1865, vol. 28, Edwin Stanton Papers, Library Congress.

16. Regimental Order Book, Third Louisiana Native Guard Infantry Regiment and R.G. 94, AGO, MS, NA: Letter Book, Fifty-fourth Massachusetts Infantry, Regiment, R. Marsh to Stanton, January 29, 1865, Stanton Papers, vol. 24, Library of Congress.

17. Sefton, *Army and Reconstruction,* 43–45; but cf. Cox and Cox, *Politics Principles and Prejudices,* 1, and John Hope Franklin, "Reconstruction and the Negro," 69–70.

18. Lawanda Cox, "The Promise of Land for the Freedman," *Mississippi Valley Historical Review* XLV (1958): 413–39; Louis S. Gerteis, *From Contraband to Freedman,* 186–90 and notes there cited. Mary F. Berry, "Reparations for Freedman 1890–1916: Fraudulent Practices or Justice Deferred," *Journal of Negro History* LVII (1972): 219–30.

19. Lee Soltow, "Economic Inequality in the United States in the Period from 1790–1860," *Journal of Economic History* XXXI (1971): 822–39; Norman Ware, *The Industrial Worker, 1840–1860* (New York, 1964).

20. Horace M. Bond, *The Education of the Negro in the American Social Order* (New York, 1934).

21. Philip Foner, ed., *The Life and Writings of Frederick Douglass*, 4 vols. (New York, 1952), III, 343.

22. *New Orleans Tribune*, October 25, 1864.

23. Foner, ed., *Life and Writings of Frederick Douglass*, III, 418–20.

24. *Congressional Globe*, 39th Congress, 1st Session, 47–48, 90–91; Fairman, *Reconstruction and Reunion*, 104, 113–18, 465–68; pt. 1, 1172–93; Kohl, "The Civil Rights Act of 1866," 286–87.

25. *Congressional Globe*, 39th Congress, 1st Session, 174, 178, 202–17, 504.

26. *Ibid.*, 322; Kaczorowski, "Searching for the Intent of the Framers of the Fourteenth Amendment," *Connecticut Law Review*, 368, believes that civil rights in the 1866 act was meant to include the natural rights of freemen, the rights to life, liberty and property, 379–384; but cf. Hamilton ". . . Thirteenth Amendment," 59–61, and Fairman, *Reconstruction and Reunion*, pt. 1, 1216–37 on the intent of the framers, discussed within a criticism of the Supreme Court's decision in Jones *v.* Alfred Mayer and Co., 392, U.S. 409 (1968) in which the court decided that the Civil Rights Act of 1866 barred private racial discrimination in housing and was a valid exercise of authority under the Thirteenth Amendment. They agree with a narrow interpretation of the Thirteenth Amendment and the act. For purposes of this study, the endless debate over whether the framers of the Civil Rights Act intended to provide national protection for civil rights against private discrimination is not directly at issue, but it should be pointed out that legislative history, alone, is usually ambiguous, especially when debates are long and drawn out. Lawyers and judges, often, utilize legislative history and refer to it in their opinions and briefs in order to rationalize decisions and not because they believe, except while in court, that real intent has been determined. A short analysis very similar to Fairman's may be found in Senator Sam J. Ervin, Jr. "Jones *v.* Alfred H. Mayer and Co.: Judicial Activism Run Riot," *Vanderbilt Law Review* XXII (1969): 485, and Justice Harlan's opinion in the Jones case. For a contrary view see Kohl, "The Civil Rights Act of 1866," 292–300.

27. Michael Benedict, "Preserving the Constitution: The Conservative Basis of Radical Reconstruction," *Journal of American History* LXI (1974): 65–90. Michael Perman, *Reunion Without Compromise*.

28. David C. Rankin, "The Origins of Black Leadership in New Orleans During Reconstruction," *Journal of Southern History* XL (1974): 417–40 and notes there cited. Most of the Negro leaders of New Orleans after the war had served in the army and had ties of education, family, and blood to a sophisticated and exclusive community. In

South Carolina, black Union veterans, Martin Delany, L. S. Langley, William Whipper and Stephen Swails stayed in the state and held state political offices during Reconstruction. Joel Williamson, *After Slavery: the Negro in South Carolina During Reconstruction, 1861–1877* (Chapel Hill, 1965), 28–30, 330.

29. Michael Benedict, *A Compromise of Principle: Congressional Republicans and Reconstruction, 1863–1869* (New York, 1974), 164, 170, 222, 331, and notes there cited.

30. Otis Singletary, *The Negro Militia and Reconstruction* (Austin, 1957), 9, 24, 129, 145–46.

III

Racial Ideologies
and Race Relations
in United States History

The Black Image in the White Mind

A NEW PERSPECTIVE

George M. Fredrickson

There is something wonderfully appropriate about giving this particular lecture on this occasion. Rayford W. Logan, whom we are honoring today, was the great pioneer in the study of white attitudes toward blacks. His book, *The Negro in American Life and Thought,* later expanded and re-titled *Betrayal of the Negro,* helped to arouse my interest in this subject and provided a wealth of insights to guide me in the pursuit of it.

More than ten years ago, I published my own study of white racial thought and imagery in the United States during the nineteenth and early-twentieth centuries. Since then I have been concerned with the "black image in the white mind" over a more extended period and also from a comparative perspective. Emboldened by this recent work, I will survey and analyze white attitudes toward blacks for the whole span of American history, from the early colonial period to the present. Given the time limitations, I will have to be very general and will not be able to support most of my assertions with direct evidence. I should add that some of my arguments remain speculative, little more than educated hunches. But I can tell you that the foundations for much of my thinking can be found in my more recent book— *White Supremacy: A Comparative Study in American and South African History,* which compares the evolution of white racial attitudes, ideologies, and policies in the United States and South Africa from the seventeenth century to the twentieth.

99

When we talk about "black images in white minds," we are of course referring to an aspect of race relations. In my view, and here I quote from *White Supremacy,* "race relations are not so much a fixed pattern as a changing set of relationships that can only be understood within a broader historical context that is itself constantly evolving and thus altering the terms under which blacks and whites interact." In other words, I take what might be called a socio-historical, or contextual, approach to race relations. I see no need, for most purposes at least, to resort to primordial "givens," such as an instinctive white aversion to the color black. It would seem to follow therefore that there has been no single and permanent black image influencing the thought and behavior of whites throughout American history. There have, of course, been some continuities, but there have also been substantial changes over time—changes induced by new or altered circumstances—and I will attempt to describe some of the most important of these.

The main variable has been the relative importance given to biological race or group heredity as a basis or rationale for differentiation and discrimination. An alternative stress would be on culture or class—group characteristics attributed to blacks that are thought to derive from environment, cultural background, and historical experiences. This is, of course, the classic sociological distinction between "racism and ethnocentrism," between group prejudice based on physical or genetic criteria and bias derived from cultural differences. Either emphasis can inspire and rationalize discrimination, but the first points logically to an explicit ideological racism (or doctrine of innate racial inferiority), and to firm caste-like distinctions between *all* whites and *all* blacks. The second may permit access by selected members of the minority group to most of the rights and privileges of the so-called dominant group. At first glance, the distinction may seem academic—a mere difference between *de jure* and *de facto* white supremacy. But it seems obvious to me that the absence of rigid caste-like barriers between the races—even if only a relatively small proportion of blacks are in a position to benefit from the opportunities thus provided—allows for a more open-minded situation than an official and uniform pattern of discrimination. It creates, at the very least, the possibility for a further evolution toward genuine equality, toward a society where racial or ethnic origin does not significantly affect an individual's access to power, prestige, and wealth.

Recent scholarship suggests that the earliest phase of black-white relations in the United States was characterized by relative openness and a stress on culture and class rather than on race *per se.* Although slavery was taking root in the Southern colonies during the seventeenth century, there was a class of free blacks who, until late in the century, do not appear to have been the victims of flagrant discrimination. Before the 1660s and 1670s, the legal basis for enslavement in the Chesapeake was religion rather than race. The surviving records of court cases involving manumission seem to demonstrate this fairly conclusively. Until laws were passed explicitly denying the right of all Christians to freedom, converted slaves who were able to get their suits before the courts had a chance of success. There were undoubtedly negative responses to early black immigrants, but they seem to have focused on heathenism and "savagery." As English attitudes toward the Irish in this period reveal, these characteristics were not inextricably associated with color. In the sixteenth century, English domination of Ireland was justified on the grounds that the "wild Irish" were the most savage peope on earth, and that their apparent Catholicism was only a veneer covering their essential paganism. Prejudice based on physical differences must have contributed something to feelings against Africans but, in my view, it was less central than is sometimes alleged. If a black converted to Christianity, learned English, and acquired property, he could gain the status and rights of a freeman. The property-owning black yeomen discovered by T. H. Breen and Stephen Innes on the Eastern Shore of Virginia in the mid-seventeenth century (and described in their recent book *Myne Own Ground*) exemplified this opportunity. These free blacks quarrelled with whites, sued them, and even fornicated with them without arousing a perceptible white supremacist reaction. A few black planters in Virginia apparently owned white indentured servants. The law of 1670 prohibiting such a black-master/white-servant relationship was perhaps the first significant and clear-cut indication of a trend toward racial discrimination. It roughly coincided with a shift in the legal basis of slavery from heathenism to heathen ancestry.

By this time, therefore, racial origin was just beginning to displace cultural deviance from an ethnocentric norm as the principal rationale for black subordination. As Morgan Godwyn put it in 1680, "The two words *Negro* and *Slave*" have "by custom grown homogeneous and convertible even as *Negro* and *Christian, Englishman* and *Heathen,* are by the like corrupt nature and partiality made *opposites.*" In other words, ethnicity and religion were linked in a deterministic way, and heathen ancestry, rather than heathenism, was the new basis of slavery.

The main reason for this shift was a change in the labor system. When it became more profitable to use black slaves rather than white indentured servants on the tobacco plantations of the Chesapeake—a change which occurred in the 1660s, according to Edmund Morgan—a powerful incentive was created for degrading all blacks to an inferior status. When African slaves became available in greater numbers and at lower prices around 1700— this was the time when the British became heavily involved in the Atlantic slave trade—the stage was set for the emergence of a slave society and rigid racial hierarchy. The pressures that existed elsewhere to create an intermediate group of relatively privileged mulattoes were absent, for large numbers of non-slaveholding whites were available to police the slave population and put down insurrections. They could also provide a variety of ancillary services required by a plantation economy. Color distinctions among Afro-Americans would remain important in certain times and places, but the governing tendency was toward a sharp demarcation between all whites and all those with discernible African ancestry.

We now come to the period when an explicit racism gradually came to the forefront of white consciousness. The image of the African as a benighted savage theoretically capable of being civilized and assimilated was superseded by the deterministic view of blacks as unalterably subhuman and suited only to menial roles.

But there was a long period of evasion, ambivalence, and incon-sistency—lasting from the end of the seventeenth century to the early nineteenth. Eighteenth-century blacks were, for the most part, *treated* as if they were genetically inferior, but there was no available body of thought or set of ideas that could justify such treatment in a fully persuasive way. Both the Christian doctrine of the unity of mankind, and the Enlightenment conception of physical environment as the determinant of human differences worked against the articulation of overt racism. The gap between theory and practice was no great problem so long as the legitimacy of slavery as an *institution* was not seriously challenged. Blacks were identified in the white mind with the degradation of slavery, but precisely why they—and they only—were relegated to such a status was a question best answered indirectly by drawing on the traditional view that inequality was the natural state of man and hierarchy the inevitable form of social organization. "Some are meant to be greater than the rest," as Alexander Pope put it.

This premise of universal inequality was sharply attacked from two directions late in the eighteenth century by proponents of the natural rights philosophy and by evangelical Christians committed to a more literal conception of human brotherhood. I am speaking here of Quakers and of some of the evangelicals who were aroused to millenarian fervor by the Great Awakening. The institution of slavery was inevitably denounced as an obvious and flagrant denial of the new doctrine of human equality that was enshrined in the Declaration of Independence and used to justify the American Revolution. But Southern slavery survived the revolutionary era intact. It did so partly because the planters could now appeal to entrenched racial prejudice. Slavery might be wrong in principle, they argued, but it was a *necessary* evil; for the alternative was turning loose a horde of "uncivilized" blacks and provoking a race war that, in the words of Jefferson, would result "in the extermination of one or the other race." The racial fears and phobias that first arose as a by-product of the economic and political interests associated with plantation slavery had by now taken deep root in the white consciousness and can be said to have had lives of their own.

I would distinguish my point of view here from two others. I disagree with those who see racial consciousness as a decisive factor from the time of early settlement, *and also* with those who tend to regard it as being forever and always simply a cynical smoke screen for some kind of class domination. You simply cannot enslave people for two centuries without internalizing the idea that they are unalterably different and inferior. Realizing the power of prejudice, even the most sincerely antislavery Southerners of the post-revolutionary era simply could not conceive of emancipation without some program for colonizing the freedman outside the United States. But the colonization idea was obviously a pipe dream, even if it did result in the settlement of Liberia by American freedmen; and it was eventually denounced by the new breed of Northern reformers as evasive, ineffectual, and out of harmony with the more aggressive humanitarianism emerging from the second Great Awakening.

The rise in the 1830s of a more radical antislavery movement in the North, one that denounced slaveholding as a sin and called for its immediate abolition, put the beneficiaries of black subordination on the defensive. They changed their tactics and defended enslavement as "a positive good" rather than as a "necessary evil." A core element of the new pro-slavery argument was the assertion that blacks were innately inferior to whites and that their natural or God-given role was to serve the "superior race." It was not merely intellectual inferiority that was asserted but also differences in moral character. Blacks were allegedly lacking in self-control and the capacity for disciplined endeavor. Hence they had to be ruled by whites lest they revert to their "naturally uncivilized" state. This view was endorsed by a school of nineteenth-century anthropologists which gave scientific credence to slavery and white supremacy by affirming that there were unalterable differences in character and capacity among "the types of mankind."

Emancipation and Reconstruction did not discredit the dominant nineteenth-century image of blacks as members of an immutably inferior race. Even Radical Republicans of the 1860s, with a few possible exceptions, were not convinced that blacks were biologically equal to whites. They favored political and civil equality because they did not see why differences in genetic potential should be a test of citizenship or equal opportunity in a capitalistic democracy. For the most part they qualified their racism by asserting that blacks, whatever their *intellectual* deficiencies, had the same *moral* capacities as whites. This was a tenuous and vulnerable position, especially when viewed from the vantage point of ex-slaveholders who lived in proximity to large black populations. It did not survive a Southern white-supremacist uprising against Reconstruction during the 1870s. Most Southern whites remained convinced of the validity of the pro-slavery racial argument, and they sought new ways to apply it in the post-emancipation era.

With the triumph of disfranchisement and "Jim-Crow" segregation toward the end of the century, blacks were once again relegated to the status of an inferior caste. This process set off the most violent outbreak of Negrophobia in American history—a kind of dark age of racism lasting from the 1880s to the 1920s. This was the period that Professor Logan has described as the "nadir" of American race relations. In the wake of lynchings, race riots, and a torrent of racist propaganda, the image of the "Negro as beast" gained wide currency, not only in the South but in the North as well.

A variety of frustrations and anxieties were associated with the transformation of the United States into a modern industrial society with new concentrations of power and privilege. Emerging class tensions and the cultural disorientation resulting from massive changes created the need for scapegoats, and blacks were the most available and vulnerable targets (although immigrants could play much the same role for nativists). Social Darwinism provided some refinements on the old biological arguments, and the eugenics movement promulgated a rigid concept of genetic determinism that was readily applied to racial differences.

From the 1920s on, the doctrine of biological inequality came under increasing attack from scientists and liberal reformers, but the new underlying factor in American race relations in the twentieth century was the mass migration of blacks from the rural

South to the urban North. Despite the violence and discrimination that these migrants encountered, there can be little doubt that this great population movement significantly altered the basic position of blacks in American society. For one thing, black migrants regained the right to vote. By the 1930s, the urban black voter was in a position to decide the outcome of state and municipal elections. By the 1940s and 1950s, blacks were becoming a significant segment of the organized industrial work force. At the same time, the special role of Southern blacks as dependent plantation workers was being undermined as a result of the modernization and mechanization of Southern agriculture, a change that may have been a necessary precondition for the success of the civil rights movement in the 1960s. The decline of sharecropping also meant the decline of a special subordinate role for blacks in the Southern economy. A relative gain in the power resources available to the black community, and a simultaneous decrease in the incentive for traditional forms of racial control helped inspire white opinion-makers to come out against blatant forms of racism.

This repudiation of the concept of genetic inferiority and the segregationism associated with it was also conditioned by World War II and the Cold War. Hitler gave racism a bad name, and the post-war propaganda struggle against Communism turned America's discriminatory practices into a serious international liability. How could we win "the war for the hearts and minds of men" in Africa and Asia, it was asked, if we practiced Jim Crow at home?

As a result of the partially successful civil rights movement that the new circumstances made possible, a new black image penetrated the white mind. It was an image that reflected a widespread acceptance of at least a token integration. What many whites were now willing to concede was that *some* blacks might be eligible for incorporation into the mainstream of American society. The tests were similar in some ways to those that were operative in the mid-seventeenth century. These were tests of *class* and *culture*. If blacks adopted the lifestyle of the white middle class and were successful by the standards that whites used to measure achievement, they were accorded a degree of acceptance that would have been totally unthinkable at an earlier time. But most blacks were not in a position to capitalize on the new opportunities. Black poverty and high unemployment persisted or even worsened in an economy with a declining need for unskilled and semi-skilled industrial laborers; and white prejudice survived in the form of instinctive negative reactions to the thought of blacks improving their *collective* position through special, "non-market" devices such as affirmative action, busing, and anti-poverty programs. These and other factors have combined to create a huge black underclass in our central cities. The black community is now bifurcated into a relatively successful minority that can take advantage of the new opportunities created by the civil rights movement and a majority that remains trapped in a deteriorating ghetto environment without the education, skills, and access to decent jobs that would permit upward mobility. One inevitable result of this situation is an increase of crime and social disorganization among lower-class blacks.

Because of this bifurcation of the black community, and the broader historical changes that made it possible, the white image of blacks has also become a divided one. Members of the successful middle class are treated and regarded as equals by a significant number of whites. But the black lower class is viewed in stereotypical terms as the "dangerous class" of American society. When they think of non-elite blacks, most whites automatically think of the ghetto mugger, conveniently ignoring the fact that the overwhelming majority of lower-class urban blacks are not only law abiding but are themselves the principal victims of the criminal element. It is somewhat misleading to argue, as the sociologist William Wilson has recently done, that we are witnessing a decline in "the significance of race" and that the crucial fault-lines of American society are now strictly a function of economic class. That members of the ghetto underclass are black and not white adds, in my opinion, to the anxiety or even panic that their alleged criminality generates among whites and helps explain the callous indifference to their plight that one finds among white politicians pandering to what appears to be a "conservative" mood in the country.

What has changed is that middle-class blacks are relatively immune from the disabilities traditionally associated with race in the United States. In the era of overt and comprehensive racism it was precisely such upwardly mobile blacks who would have aroused the greatest hostility. But the current acceptance of Afro-Americans in positions of power and prestige remains a conditional one. It depends on their willingness to identify with the aims and ideologies of the white-dominated institutions with which they are associated. This creates an acute dilemma for many black intellectuals and high achievers. Should they fight prejudice by beating the whites at their own game, or reject the terms of integration and identify directly with the struggles of the black masses? An effort to resolve this internal conflict was one of the main sources of the black power and black nationalist movements of the late 1960s and early 1970s. It continues to give urgency to the search of black intellectuals for an effective strategy for achieving the twin goals of group identity and full equality with whites.

But let us return to the black image in the white mind. In a sense, we have come full circle. Something like the differential incorporation of blacks that existed in the mid-seventeenth century has re-emerged in a new form. Seventeenth-century whites could apparently distinguish between heathen African slaves and Christianized black freemen. Thereafter—for more than two hundred and fifty years—blacks were, for the most part, viewed through a single lens. Racist stereotypes denied to *all* blacks the kind of esteem that was automatically accorded to whites simply by virtue of their ancestry. Once again, in our own time, there is a split image. The black cabinet officer, judge, professor, or business executive is likely to be viewed very differently from the unemployed ghetto youth. Race *per se* is no longer a definitive criterion for success or influence in American society, but this is little consolation to those who suffer simultaneously from the burdens of race and class. At best, we have to some degree "Brazilianized" American race relations. Brazilians say that "money whitens." In the United States today, money, education, and accomplishment do, in a sense, "whiten." But the very fact that this language still seems appropriate shows how far we still have to go before we can say that white supremacy is a thing of the past.

NOTE

For a full discussion of the ideas presented in this lecture, see Professor Fredrickson's book, *The Black Image in the White Mind* (New York, 1971). [Eds.]

Racism in American Legal History

A. Leon Higginbotham, Jr.

At approximately 7:17 P.M., April 4, 1968, an assassin fired a shot mortally wounding Martin Luther King, Jr.[1] Late that evening I received a call from President Lyndon Johnson who had appointed me four years earlier to the United States District Court, asking me to come to the White House early the next morning to discuss with others who were being called the national significance of Dr. King's death. Though the president acted quickly in collecting his counselors for a meeting the next morning, another section of the nation would not wait the night to express its own response to this national tragedy. Ten blocks from the White House, buildings in the largely black ghettoes of Washington, D.C. were already in flames.[2] As the painful night lingered on, news reports indicated that more and more people had taken to the streets, many striking out irrationally and in anger, in city after city, in response to the senseless death of the prophet of nonviolence.[3]

President Johnson opened the meeting at the White House the next morning with the question, "What can we do now?"

There were many thoughtful responses. Some talked of strengthening civil rights legislation, others spoke of further improving manpower programs, still others argued for additional condemnations of racism. The idea for appointing yet another presidential commission was also introduced. Although the discussion was calm and dispassionate, a deep sense of shared pain was apparent. Most of us present had known Dr. King intimately and had worked with him in the attempt to obliterate racism from American life.

As I listened and reflected on the various suggestions made from such thoughtful and well-meaning people, I kept thinking of the question Thurgood Marshall had asked the Supreme Court thirteen years earlier: "Why," he had asked, "of all the multitudinous groups of people in this country, do you have to single out Negroes and give them this separate treatment?" That morning, sitting in the White House, I knew there was an indisputable nexus between the dark shadow of repression under which, historically, most American blacks have lived and the rioting occurring within ten blocks of the White House. Why, I thought to myself, in the land of the free and the home of the brave, had even brave blacks so often failed to get free? Why had that very legal process that had been devised to protect the rights of individuals against the will of the government and the whim of the majority been often employed so malevolently against blacks? What were the options that ought to have been exercised years ago, even centuries ago, to narrow those disparities in meted-out justice that had periodically—and had now once more—kindled black hatred and white fear?

In the company of the great lawyers present at the president's meeting—Supreme Court Associate Justice Thurgood Marshall and Attorney General Ramsey Clark—as well as the other notable government and public officials—cabinet officer Robert C. Weaver, civil rights leaders Roy Wilkins, Whitney Young, Clarence Mitchell, Reverend Leon Sullivan, and Vice President Humphrey[4]—it was inevitable that I would ponder how the legal process had contributed to this malaise. For in 1968, in this nation's 192nd year, things could have been different.[5] If the legal process had been racially just, the nation in the 1960s would not have been torn asunder as it was by the unrelenting demands by blacks for dignity and equal justice under the law as they struggled against the stubborn resistance of those who had been conditioned to believe in the status quo as the ultimate expression of "liberty and justice for all."[6] The institutionalized injustice of racial apartness had first brought Martin Luther King to the forefront and now, ultimately, had brought him to his death.

Particularly during this bicentennial era, it is appropriate to assess the interrelationship of race and the American legal process.[7] This nation has just celebrated its 200th birthday in a most grandiose fashion. Conventions have been held in almost every town to reaffirm those "self-evident truths," and the oratory will continue to 1987, the 200th anniversary of the United States Constitution. As praise is heaped on the great leaders of yesterday, and as some laud 1776 as the Golden Era of liberty, it is often suggested that if only today's leaders had the integrity and character of Jefferson, Franklin, John Adams, Washington, and Madison, today's racial difficulties might be quickly resolved. Few have had the temerity to contradict this general but misdirected consensus, for it is bad bicentennial form to refer to the fact that many of America's Founding Fathers owned slaves and that most, either directly or indirectly, profited from the evil institution that enslaved black human beings only.

The bicentennial drum roll of revolutionary heroes and events, then, symbolizes one thing to white Americans but quite another to blacks. From a predominantly white perspective, the Declaration of Independence is viewed as former President Nixon described it: "the greatest achievement in the history of man. We are the beneficiaries of that achievement."[8] But who, until recently, did the "we" describe? Not black America. Frederick Douglass, a leading abolitionist who was born a slave, described Independence Day in 1852 from the perspective of blacks and slaves rather than whites and slaveholders:

> This Fourth of July is *yours*, not mine. You may rejoice, I must mourn. To drag a man in fetters to the grand illuminated temple of liberty, and call upon him to join you in joyous anthems, were inhuman mockery and sacrilegious irony. . . . I say it with a sad sense of the disparity between us. I am not included within the pale of this glorious anniversary. . . . The blessings in which you, this day, rejoice, are not enjoyed in common. The rich inheritance of justice, liberty, prosperity and independence, bequeathed by your fathers, is shared by you, not by me. The sunlight that brought light and healing to you, has brought stripes and death to me.[9]

Likewise, from a predominantly white perspective, the pledges of the Preamble to the Constitution honestly set out the largest principles for which the new American legal process would strive.

> We the people . . . in order to form a more perfect union, establish justice, . . . promote the general welfare, and secure the blessings of liberty to ourselves and our posterity. . . .

From a black perspective, however, the Constitution's references to justice, welfare, and liberty were mocked by the treatment meted out daily to blacks from the seventeenth to nineteenth centuries through the courts, in legislative statutes, and in those provisions of the Constitution that sanctioned slavery for the majority of black Americans and allowed disparate treatment for those few blacks legally "free."

Further, whatever opening there might have been for one day peacefully redefining "We the people" to include, as it should have in the first place, black Americans, was abruptly closed with the 1857 United States Supreme Court decision *Dred Scott* v. *Sandford*. When asked if the phrase "We the people" included black people and whether blacks were embraced in the egalitarian language of the Declaration of Independence, Chief Justice Roger Taney, speaking for the majority, wrote:

> [A]t the time of the Declaration of Independence, and when the Constitution of the United States was framed and adopted . . . [blacks] had no rights which the white man was bound to respect.[10]

In effect, Taney had not answered the question. Rather, he had gone back in time in an attempt to determine what the Founding Fathers had intended and, in so doing, had argued from the untenable position that the Constitution might never be any larger than the restrictive vision of eighteenth-century America.

Thus, for black Americans today—the children of all the hundreds of Kunta Kintes unjustly chained in bondage—the early failure of the nation's founders and their constitutional heirs to share the legacy of freedom with black Americans is at least one factor in America's perpetual racial tensions. Twenty years after the Civil War, over one hundred years after the Declaration of Independence, two hundred fifty years after the first black man set foot in America, Mark Twain, in a parody of white attitudes in *Huckleberry Finn,* suggested that many white Americans still failed to perceive blacks as human beings:

"Good gracious. Anybody hurt?"
"No'm. Killed a nigger."
"Well, it's lucky because sometimes people do get hurt."[11]

What should have been on the minds of all in power during the seventeenth and eighteenth centuries was the question James Otis raised in his provocative paper of 1764:

Does it follow that, tis right to enslave a man because he is black?[12]

The courts, the state legislatures, and even honest public servants vascillated in trying to decide whether blacks were people, and if so, whether they were a species apart from white humans, the difference justifying separate and different treatment.

I am aware that an analysis of cases, statutes, and legal edicts does not tell the whole story as to why and how this sordid legal tradition managed to establish itself. Nevertheless, there is merit in abolitionist William Goodell's statement: "No people were ever yet found who were better than their laws, though many have been known to be worse."[13]

While I recognize that a view of slavery from the perspective of the law does not make a complete picture,[14] I join in the conclusions of Winthrop D. Jordan when writing on the Colonial period and C. Vann Woodward when writing on the Reconstruction period. Jordan has advised us:

While statutes usually speak falsely as to actual behavior, they afford probably the best single means of ascertaining what a society thinks behavior ought to be; they sweep up the felt necessities of the day and indirectly expound the social norm of the legislators.[15]

And C. Vann Woodward has stated:

I am convinced that law has a special importance in the history of segregation, more importance than some sociologists would allow, and that the emphasis on legal history is justified.[16]

Obviously, there were several factors that contributed to the inclination of the legal process to treat blacks so differently from all others. Many have written in great detail on some of these factors.[17] For instance, in so many legal decisions, there was the powerful presence of the economics of slavery. The key question for many a righteous and learned community leader was whether it was cheaper to have blacks as slaves or to have blacks as "free" labor. Or, possibly, instead of black slaves would it have been cheaper to have had white indentured servants or white free labor.

The issue of safety and the natural fear of slave revolts were also intertwined in the chain of legal judgments. While never reluctant to protect and maximize their property rights in the slaves, many judges and legislators were reluctant to recognize that slaves had, in their own right, any basic human rights. Many feared that any judicial protection of the slave would trigger further challenges to the legitimacy of the dehumanized status of blacks and slaves. Since the plantations were often in isolated settings and there was an ever threatening possibility that the slaves might rise up and slay their oppressors, any judge whose decision criticized racial injustice might be accused of weakening the master-slave system. For instance, in a famous North Carolina decision *State* v. *Mann*[18] involving the issue of whether or not it was a criminal offense to subject a slave woman to "a cruel and unreasonable battery," the court stated that a slave was to "labor upon a principle of natural duty," to disregard "his own personal happiness," and that the purpose of the legal system was to convince each slave that he had

> no will of his own [and that he must surrender] his will in implicit obedience to that of another. Such obedience is the consequence only of uncontrolled authority over the body. There is nothing else that can operate to produce the effect. The power of the master must be absolute to render the submission of the slave perfect.[19]

The court emphasized that for the slave "there is no remedy," that "[w]e cannot allow the right of the master to be brought into discussion in the courts of justice. The slave, to remain a slave, must be made sensible that there is no appeal from his master; that his power is in no instance usurped; but is conferred by the laws of man at least, if not by the law of God." The court noted that this unlimited "dominion is essential to the value of slaves as property, and to the security of the master, and the public tranquility."[20]

The control the court sought was the *total* submission of blacks. It had incorporated into its law-made morality the psychological conceptions that Frederick Douglass subsequently described:

> Beat and cuff the slave, keep him hungry and spiritless, and he will follow the chain of his master like a dog, but feed and clothe him well, work him moderately and surround him with physical comfort, and dreams of freedom will intrude. . . . You may hurl a man so low beneath the level of his kind, that he loses all just ideas of his natural position, but elevate him a little, and the clear conception of rights rises to life and power, and leads him onward.[21]

With only sightly less paranoia, white society feared that slaves and free blacks would form an alliance with either indentured servants or poor whites to topple the plantation aristocracy, which exploited both blacks and poor whites. As the percentage of blacks, slave or free, increased, the probability of successful rebellions and revolts became greater. Thus, in examining degrees of repression one can almost correlate a rise in the black population with an increased level of legal repression.

In terms of moral and religious issues, there was the underlying question of whether or not America had the right to treat differently and more malevolently people whose skins were darker. From this perspective it became necessary to determine whether blacks were part of the human family and whether, after they had adopted your "religion," they were then entitled to be treated as equals, or at least less harshly. In a nation "under God" the moral or religious rationale that justified or rejected the institution of slavery had to have been an important factor.[22] But what tortuous moral or religious rationale had to have been devised for a religious people to have tolerated treating black human beings more like horses or dogs than white human beings?[23]

Finally, there was always the issue of whether or not blacks were inherently inferior to whites.[24] If blacks could be perceived as inferior, basically uneducable and inherently venal, it might be intellectually less self-condemnatory to relegate them because of their "lower status" to a subordinate role—either for "their own good" or, as one judge had the audacity to express it, for the good of the total society, whites and blacks alike.[25]

Thus it was that even the man many Americans see as one of the major forces for liberty and equality, Thomas Jefferson, found blacks to be "inferior to whites in the endowments both of body and mind."[26] After comparing the characteristics of the three major races in America, white, black, and red, Jefferson concluded that although the condition of slavery imposed great misery on blacks, the inferiority of the black race was caused by more than mere environmental factors:

> The improvement of the blacks in body and mind, in the first instance of their mixture with the whites, has been observed by everyone, and proves that their inferiority is not the effect merely of their condition of life. . . . This unfortunate difference of color, and perhaps of faculty, is a powerful obstacle to the emancipation of these people.[27]

Yet even during the seventeenth and eighteenth centuries, there were voices that challenged the morality and legality of slavery. As early as February, 1688 the Germantown Mennonites of Philadelphia had issued a proclamation against slavery, having found it inconsistent with Christian principles. In 1772, four years prior to our Declaration of Independence and fifteen years prior to the Constitution, Lord Mansfield, Chief Justice of the King's Bench, said in the *Sommersett* case that "the state of slavery is of such a nature that it is incapable of being introduced on any reasons moral or political, . . . It is so odious that nothing can be suffered to support it, but positive law." And with that statement, Lord Mansfield freed the slave, Sommersett, demonstrating that there was no universal view on slavery among the civilized nations of the world.

It is difficult to isolate one and only one factor as the sole explanation for the legislated, adjudicated, and upheld racial deprivation that gained the official approval of the American legal establishment. As in most things, the causal factors were multifaceted. On some occasions the economic concerns seemed the dominating influence, while in other instances a moral or religious aspect appeared to be more significant. But however tightly woven into the history of their country is the legalization of black suppression, many Americans still find it too traumatic to study the true story of racism as it has existed under the "rule of law." For many, the primary conclusion of the National Commission on Civil Disorders is still too painful to hear:

> What white Americans have never fully understood—but what the Negro can never forget—is that white society is deeply implicated in the ghetto. White institutions created it, white institutions maintain it, and white society condones it.[28]

Since the language of the law shields one's consciousness from direct involvement with the stark plight of its victims, the human tragedy of the slavery system does not surface from the mere reading of cases, statutes, and constitutional provisions. Rather, it takes a skeptical reading of most of the early cases and statutes to avoid having one's surprise and anger dulled by the casualness with which the legal process dealt with human beings who were slaves. Generally neither the courts nor the legislatures seemed to have been any more sensitive about commercial transactions involving slaves than they were about sales of corn, lumber, horses, or dogs. This casualness is reflected in a perfectly legal and acceptable advertisement of that era:

> One hundred and twenty Negroes for sale—The subscriber has just arrived from Petersburg, Virginia, with one hundred and twenty likely young Negroes of both sexes and every description, which he offers for sale on the most reasonable terms. The lot now on hand consists of plough-boys, several likely and well-qualified house servants of both sexes, several women and children, small girls suitable for nurses, and *several small boys without their mothers*. Planters and traders are earnestly requested to give the subscriber a call previously to making purchases elsewhere, as he is enabled to sell as cheap or cheaper than can be sold by any other person in the trade.[29]

The above advertisement was not unique; it was typical of thousands of advertisements posted in newspapers and on bulletin boards throughout our land. In the *New Orleans Bee* an advertisement noted:

> Negroes for sale—a Negro woman, 24 years of age, and her two

children, one eight and the other three years old. Said Negroes
will be sold separately or together, as desired. The woman is a
good seamstress. She will be sold low for cash, or exchanged for
groceries. For terms apply to Matthew Bliss and Company, 1
Front Levee.[30]

How could a legal system encourage and sanction such cruelty—
cruelty that permitted the sale, of "several small boys without
their mothers"? Was there any justice in a legal process that
permitted a mother, twenty-four years of age, to be sold in
exchange for groceries and separated from her children, only eight
and three years old? Looking past the commercial façade, one sees
the advertisement as stating that American laws encouraged the
destruction of black families and the selling of human beings. The
only criterion was the demand of the marketplace.

The Georgia and South Carolina legislatures enacted several
statutes that offered rewards to bounty hunters bringing in the
scalp and ears of runaway slaves. These statutes, subtly cast in
the language of lawyers, can make one oblivious to the fact that
the lives of human beings were involved. From one perspective,
it appears that these two legislatures were merely defining penalties
and granting rewards—just as they would do upon the recovery
of an individual's lost property or as a reward for the slaying of
a bear or wild coyote. Yet the scalps and the ears referred to in
the Georgia and South Carolina statutes were *not* those of wild
animals. They were not those of murderers or traitors. They were
the scalps and ears of human beings, persons who had committed
no crime other than that of seeking that same freedom the colonists
declared to be the birthright of all whites.

While we recognize today how inhumane and how immoral
this legal process was, it seems that Americans would rather
distort their history than face the extraordinary brutality to which
these advertisements attest and the inadequacy of a system of laws
that promoted and sanctioned such brutality.

The legal process has never been devoid of values, preferences,
or policy positions. By the very nature of its pronouncements,
when the legal process establishes a right of one particular person,
group, or institution, it simultaneously imposes a restraint on

those whose preferences impinge on the right established. Ultimately, the legal process has always acted as an expression of social control. Professor Vilhelm Aubert has argued that "beneath the veneer of consensus on legal principles, a struggle of interest is going on, and the law is seen as a weapon in the hands of those who possess the power to use it for their own ends.[31]

The mechanisms of control through judicial decisions and statutes span the sanctioning of slavery and the special limitations imposed on free blacks, to the prohibitions against interracial marriage and sexual relations, to the elimination of the legal significance of black "conversions to Christianity," to general restriction of any activities or aspirations of blacks that might threaten the groups in control.

The law is usually perceived as a normative system, founded on a society's custom and convention. Charles Warren, one of the most distinguished scholars on the history of the Supreme Court, observed:

> The Court is not an organism dissociated from the conditions and history of the times in which it exists. It does not formulate and deliver its opinions in a legal vacuum. Its Judges are not abstract and impersonal oracles, but are men whose views are necessarily, though by no conscious intent, affected by inheritance, education and environment and by the impact of history past and present.[32]

Oliver Wendell Holmes shared this perception:

> The life of the law has not been logic: it has been experience. The felt necessities of the time, the prevalent moral and political theories, intuitions of public policy, avowed or unconscious, even the prejudices which judges share with their fellow-men, have had a good deal more to do than the syllogism in determining the rules by which men should be governed.[33]

During the first two hundred years of black presence in America, the entire legal apparatus was used by those with the power to do so to establish a solid legal tradition for the absolute enslavement of blacks. If one examines this history, it becomes clear that our laws sanctioned and tolerated the racist practices that caused one group of human beings to receive special, harsh and disparate treatment.

Some might suggest that when probing any pattern of man's inhumanity to man the proper place to start ought to be at the beginning of human history. Be that as it may, a special lesson lies in tracing and trying to understand exactly how the American legal process was able to set its conscience aside and, by pragmatic toadying to economic "needs," rationalize a regression of human rights for blacks. I submit that if we can determine how it came to do so during the very period it was displaying such compassion, courage, and even genius in extending and reinforcing as never before the freedom of whites, we might then better understand what many blacks see so clearly—a direct lineage of contemptuous law from the wasteland centuries of slavery, through the hundred years of false equality since the Emancipation Proclamation, to the "confrontation street politics" of the sixties.

NOTES

1. Coretta Scott King, *My Life With Martin Luther King, Jr.* (New York, 1969), 317.
2. Ben W. Gilbert and the staff of the *Washington Post, Ten Blocks from the White House* (New York, 1968).
3. *New York Times* articles: Earl Caldwell, "Guard Called Out Curfew Is Ordered in Memphis but Fires and Looting Erupt" (April 5, 1968); Thomas A. Johnson, "Scattered Violence Occurs in Harlem and Brooklyn" (April 5, 1968); "Army Troops in Capital as Negroes Riot; Guard Sent Into Chicago, Detroit, Boston; Johnson Asks a Joint Session of Congress" (April 6, 1968).
4. Others present were: Richard Hatcher, mayor of Gary, Indiana; Walter Washington, mayor of Washington, D.C.; Joseph Califano, special assistant to President Johnson; and Harry McPherson, counsel to the president.
5. This theme has been further developed by A. Leon Higginbotham, Jr., in the articles: "Racism and the Early American Legal Process, 1619–1896," *The Annals of the American Academy of Political and Social Science* 407 (May, 1973); and "To the Scale and Standing of Men," *The Journal of Negro History* 60 (July, 1975); and in chapters in several books, including: "Double Standards for Black Judges" and "Labor Union: Racial Violence" in Gilbert Ware, ed., *From the Black Bar: Voices for Equal Justice* (New York, 1976), 61–72 and 255–61; "The

Black Prisoner: America's Caged Canary," in Hugh Davis Graham, ed., *Violence: The Crisis of American Confidence* (Baltimore, Md., 1971), chap. 7.

6. See generally, *Report of the National Advisory Commission on Civil Disorders,* "Why Did It Happen?," pt. 2 (Washington, D.C., 1968), 91–145.

7. See articles by A. Leon Higginbotham, Jr.: "Racism and the American Legal Process: Many Deeds Cry Out to be Done," *Progress in Africa and America,* Scholars-Statesmen Lecture Series, Number Three, Dillard University, New Orleans, La., 1971, 1972; "Race, Racism and American Law," *University of Pennsylvania Law Review* 122 (April, 1974); "Civil Rights Litigation in the Federal Courts: The Constitutional and Statutory Prerequisites," paper presented at the Regional Meeting of The Judicial Council of the National Bar Association, Philadelphia, Pa., April 5, 1975; "The Impact of the Declaration of Independence?," *The Crisis* (November, 1975): 360, reprinted in Marr and Ward, eds., *Minorities and the American Dream: A Bicentennial Perspective* (New York, 1976), 35; "The Priority of Human Rights in Court Reform," paper presented at the National Conference on The Causes of Popular Dissatisfaction with the Administration of Justice, sponsored by the Judicial Conference of the United States, the Conference of Chief Justices and the American Bar Association, St. Paul, Minn., April 8, 1976, 70 F.R.D. 134, republished in *The Judges' Journal* 15: 34; "Race in American Law," paper presented at the Bicentennial Conference on American Law: The Third Century, sponsored by New York University School of Law, New York, April 27, 1976, reprinted in Schwartz, ed., *American Law: The Third Century* (South Hackensack, N.J., 1976), 45.

8. Recorded message of President Richard M. Nixon on July 4, 1970 at the Honor America Day Celebration in Washington, D.C., from *Weekly Compilation of Presidential Documents* 6 (July 13, 1970): 892.

9. "The Meaning of July Fourth to the Negro," 1852, in Philip S. Foner, ed., *The Life and Writings of Frederick Douglass* (New York, 1950) II, 189.

10. 60 U.S. 393, 407 (1857).

11. Mark Twain, *The Adventures of Huckleberry Finn* (New York, 1884), 306–307.

12. James Otis, "The Rights of the British Colonies Asserted and Proved," in Bailyn, *Pamphlets,* I, 437.

13. William Goodell, *The American Slave Code in Theory and Practice* (1853; reprint ed., New York, 1969), 17. William Goodell attributes this statement to Dr. Priestly.

14. My views differ from those apologists who have implied that as an institution slavery was not severely harsh. See Ulrich Phillips, *American Negro Slavery* (1918; reprint ed., Baton Rouge, 1966). Illustrative of the views which are far too complimentary of the Southern justice system are the series of articles by A. E. Kier Nash: "Fairness and Formalism In the Trials of Blacks in the State Supreme Courts of the Old South," *Virginia Law Review* 56 (1970): 63; "A More Equitable Past? Southern Supreme Courts and the Protection of the Antebellum Negro," *North Carolinia Law Review* 48 (1970): 197; "Negro Rights, Unionism and Greatness on the South Carolina Court of Appeals: The Extraordinary Chief Justice John Belton O'Neil," *South Carolina Law Review* 21 (1969): 141.

15. Winthrop Jordan, *White Over Black* (Chapel Hill, North Carolina, 1968), 588.

16. C. Vann Woodward, *The Strange Career of Jim Crow,* 3rd. rev. ed. (New York, 1974), xiii.

17. For general background, see A. Leon Higginbotham, Jr., *In the Matter of Color* (New York, 1978), 397–403.

18. 13 N.C. at 263 (1829).

19. 13 N.C. at 266.

20. *Ibid.* at 266–67.

21. Frederick Douglass, *Life and Times of Frederick Douglass* (New York, 1962), 150.

22. See Cotton Mather, *The Negro Christianized: An Essay to Encite and Assist that Good Work the Instruction of Negro Servants in Christianity* (Boston, 1706), 18–27; Thomas Bacon, *Sermons Addressed to Masters and Servants and Published in the Year 1743* . . . (Winchester, Va., 1813?), 104–11; Theodore D. Weld, *The Bible Against Slavery: An Inquiry into the Patriarchal and Mosaic Systems on the Subject of Human Rights,* 4th ed. (New York, 1838).

23. Angelina Grimké Weld, daughter of Judge Grimké of South Carolina, stated: "Slaveholders regard their slaves as *property,* the mere instruments of their convenience and pleasure. One who is a slave holder at heart, *never recognizes a human being in a slave."* Mr. L. Turner, "a regular and respectable member of the Second Presbyterian Church in Springfield," said: "Slaves are neither considered or treated as human beings." Mr. Gnolson, of the Virginia legislature, when opposing persons who had proposed abolition, said: "Why, I really have been under the impression that I *owned* my slaves. I lately purchased *four women* and ten children, in whom I thought I obtained a great bargain, for I really supposed they were *my property,*

as were my *brood mares."* Goodell, *The American Slave Code,* 36, 38, 39.

24. G. Fredrickson, *The Black Image in the White Mind* (New York, 1971), 71–96; William R. Stanton, *The Leopards' Spots: Scientific Attitudes Toward Race in America 1815–1859* (Chicago, 1960), 3–14.

25. State *v.* Mann, 13, N.C. 263 (1829); also, when speaking to the State Agricultural Society of North Carolina in 1855, Judge Ruffin said: Slavery "has a beneficial influence on the prosperity of the country and the physical and moral state of both races, rendering both better and happier than either would be here, without the other." *Publications of the North Carolina Historical Commission,* 8 vols. "The Papers of Thomas Ruffin," IV, 329.

26. Thomas Jefferson, *Notes on the State of Virginia* (New York, 1964), 138; see also John Hope Franklin, *Racial Equality in America* (Chicago, 1976), 12–20.

27. *Ibid.,* 136, 138.

28. *Report of the National Advisory Commission on Civil Disorders* (Washington, D.C., 1968), 1.

29. Goodell, *The American Slave Code,* 54–55.

30. *Ibid.*

31. Vilhelm Aubert, ed., *Sociology of Law* (Baltimore, Md., 1969), 11.

32. Charles Warren, *The Supreme Court in United States History* (Boston, 1926), I, 2.

33. Oliver Wendell Holmes, *The Common Law* (Boston, 1881), 1.

Twenty Years with
Booker T. Washington

Louis R. Harlan

Booker T. Washington, the subject of my essay, had a close affiliation with Howard University. He was a trustee of Howard University from 1907 until his death in 1915 and a trustee of Fisk during the same period. There is a certain irony in Washington, the leading advocate of industrial education, being the trustee of the leading black universities. But it was not really inconsistent with Washington's long career as a black political boss and go-between with whites. A white Methodist minister, Wilbur P. Thirkield, became president of Howard in 1906 and immediately had a conference with Washington and the head of Hampton Institute. Soon afterward, he wrote Washington that he had drastically revised the Howard curriculum. "Manual work is required of all our students and the course for the A.B. can be completed with honor without either Greek or Latin,"[1] and he then brought up the other half of what seems to have been a tacit bargain: "I trust that you have borne in mind my suggestion, in which you concurred, that you write to Mr. Carnegie with reference to a library for Howard University."[2]

Washington did get Andrew Carnegie to give Howard a library and was unanimously elected a trustee. Washington accepted the position, as he said, as an opportunity to "build up a great Negro university."[3] But Washington saw all this typically as a chance to do a surreptitious favor for his son-in-law, a Washington D.C. architect. "I suppose you have seen by the papers that Mr.

Carnegie is likely to give Howard University a building for a library," he wrote his son-in-law. "Perhaps you might see President Thirkield regarding the plans for the building. Do not mention my name in connection with this information."[4]

Despite President Thirkield's private gestures toward industrial education, in his inaugural address he said that "industrial training alone is not sufficient for the rounded and complete life of any people," and that "there must be a body of elect men and women trained to large knowledge" to play the roles of leaders. In short, he endorsed W. E. B. Du Bois's concept of the Talented Tenth.[5] There is no evidence that Washington as a trustee succeeded or even seriously tried to change the character of Howard in the direction of industrial education. He did, however, manage to aid Howard in fund raising and, in turn, used Howard to serve his own purposes. He not only helped Howard get its Carnegie library but helped it get money from the General Education Board and the United States Congress. During the Woodrow Wilson presidency, in 1915, a Southern congressman removed the entire Howard University appropriation from a congressional funding bill, an appropriation that Howard regularly received from the previous quarter-century.[6] Booker T. Washington got his Tuskegee trustees to write an appeal to President Wilson and key members of Congress to restore the cut. The White House interceded with Congress and got the cut restored.

The most important reciprocal benefit that Washington derived from his trusteeship of Howard University came when his longtime enemy W. E. B. Du Bois planned to leave Atlanta University to join the National Association for the Advancement of Colored People (NAACP) staff and to edit its magazine, *The Crisis*. Du Bois was reluctant to leave the academic world entirely, and his friends on the Howard faculty, led by Kelly Miller, joined forces with trustees, led by John R. Francis, to try to offer Du Bois a professorship of sociology. The idea had considerable support and considerable chance of success. President Thirkield asked Washington privately for his opinion. Washington advised against it, as did two other trustees. Thirkield then put the quietus on the appointment on the ground that Washington objected to it. The last thing in the world Washington wanted was to be exposed as exercising a veto on Du Bois, so he hastily sent a letter to Thirkield stating his own version of their interview. He conceded that he had opposed Du Bois as more a hindrance than a help to Howard, and as unlikely to come anyhow at the salary Howard could offer, but said that he had promised to stand by Thirkield if he decided in favor of the appointment. "In the last analysis," he wrote, the president should decide, for "he bears the burden and should have the credit or censure for success or failure."[7] As Washington's secretary put it more bluntly in private, Thirkield should have the backbone to decide for himself and not "take refuge behind somebody else." Francis tried to save the appointment by getting Du Bois to state that the NAACP was not "an organization for personal abuse,"[8] and Francis even urged Washington himself to sponsor Du Bois's appointment.[9] It would be "a good way to squelch" Du Bois, one trustee slyly suggested.[10] But Washington stood firmly against it. The offer was not made, but, in view of Washington's letter to Thirkield, it could not quite be said that Washington had vetoed the appointment. Thirkield did not make the offer, and who knows how the history of Howard or the life of Du Bois might have been different if Washington had not been a trustee at that moment.

I have spent almost as long studying the life of Booker T. Washington as he did living it. If I had to put my subject in the form of a question, therefore, it would probably be, "why twenty years with the wrong man?" That is somewhat a parody of the old popular song, "Twenty Years with the Wrong Woman," and it is also a question my friends and skeptical colleagues have often asked in one way or another over the years. Why twenty years? Why so long a study of a less-than-heroic black man? Why biography in an era when the whole trend of historical research is toward the demographic, the computerized, the anonymous? I hope that my writings on Washington can now answer such questions for me, but for many years the only answer I found to that line of questioning was the old Marx brothers line, "Why a duck?"

Why Booker T. Washington? I suppose it began with the white

Southerner's obsession with race—race as a way of dividing up mankind, race as the key to Southern exceptionalism, race as a way of scapegoating, maybe even race as a Freudian symbol. I like to believe that I stood that obsession with race on its head, but it took many years to do so. I grew up in a suburb of Atlanta, which of course bore little resemblance to the rural South that Booker T. Washington knew. At least, I did not think so until recently, until I met a black woman in Berkeley, California. When she asked where I was from, I said, "I'm from Atlanta, but that is not really the South." She said, "Even Atlanta has its Decatur." "Lady," I said, "you're talking about my home town." I attended Emory University, Vanderbilt, and Johns Hopkins, all Southern and all-white institutions at that time. But while I was at Vanderbilt I married a Peabody College student, from a little West Virginia coal mining town where you could not tell black from white until the Saturday night bath. She taught me a racial liberalism that they do not teach in school, that had nothing to do with abstractions but a lot to do with common humanity.

After a master's degree at Vanderbilt, I went to Johns Hopkins to study under C. Vann Woodward, already famous for his biography of Tom Watson, and soon to be the outstanding scholar in Southern history, the author of *Origins of the New South, The Strange Career of Jim Crow,* and other works. Woodward was a great role model because he combined the historian's craft and the writer's art, and like many other Southerners, he, too, was obsessed with the subject of race. He taught us graduate students little directly; in fact, we used to say that he believed the lecture method had been made obsolete by the invention of printing. But he taught us by example—the example of history as literature, the ironic approach to Southern history, and his personal example, as when he brought a young professor at Howard University, John Hope Franklin, to visit our seminar. It was the first time I had seen a black man in a role of distinction and authority. That is a sign of how much has changed since the 1940s.

It was about 1950 that I first saw the huge mountain of the Booker T. Washington Papers, about a million items. The Library of Congress had acquired them in 1943 from Tuskegee Institute for free. Washington's historical reputation was at that time so low, at Tuskegee as well as elsewhere, that the institute was willing to let them go, and the Library of Congress did not bother to catalog and arrange them for use for about a decade. When I first saw them they were stacked in confusion in unlabeled boxes deep in the recesses of the library's Manuscript Division. In those easygoing days before tight security regulations, the library let me go into the stacks and sit on the floor to poke around in the boxes. I was then a graduate student working on my doctoral dissertation on racial inequality in Southern education during Washington's day, commuting daily from Baltimore to the Library of Congress on old Highway One, and I only had time to sample his papers for any references to my subject.

What I found was like discovering a new world, the private world of the black middle class early in the twentieth century. It was completely different from what a Southern white person would expect, after seeing it only through the mask and veil. Washington's faithful private secretary had decided Washington was a great man whose life work, even his dirty tricks, would be vindicated if every scrap of his correspondence was saved. The jury is still out on the question of Washington's greatness, but there is no doubt that his papers are the largest and richest in the whole field of black history, with the possible exception of the NAACP archives. I decided then and there that I had found the subject of my next book.

It was twelve years before I got back to Booker T. Washington. That is another story, but the crux of it is that it was another five years before I got my degree; I spent nine years as a cultural missionary in the boonies of East Texas, where I had my first sustained experience in the real, rural South; and meanwhile a distinguished biographer, Marquis James, had begun work with three or four research assistants on a biography of Washington. He died just after starting to write, however, and I returned to the subject. I had moved, meanwhile, to the University of Cincinnati, but I took a vow of poverty never to teach summer school and, dragging my wife along as a typist, I spent every summer and finally a whole year digging into the huge mound of the Washington Papers until I had disappeared underground like a miner.

As I dug away at the evidence and came to know the man I was studying, my view of Washington began to change. I had begun thinking of him entirely in terms of the Uncle Tom stereotype—a stereotype, I should add, not without its elements of truth. I concluded that Washington's Atlanta Compromise Speech in 1895 was a Faustian bargain in which he sold his black soul to the Southern white racists and the Northern millionaires in exchange for power for himself and time to try a new strategy for black advancement. This speech was the beginning of his twenty-year rule over black America with white backing. He acquiesced in disfranchisement and segregation, at least for the time being, if whites would place no impediments in the way of black economic and educational opportunity. But the evidence of his private papers showed him to be a much more complex character, with a multilayered private or secret life that seemed at cross-purposes with the racial settlement he publicly accepted and that cast him in roles that contradicted his bland and compromising public persona. In the first place, he clandestinely financed and directed court suits challenging disfranchisement, exclusion of blacks from juries, Jim Crow railroad cars, peonage, and other forms of black subordination that he publicly accepted. Then there was also a less attractive, more feral side to Washington's secret life. While most of his public utterances were collections of Sunday-school platitudes, in secret he used Machiavellian methods against his white and black critics, hiring spies to infiltrate all the organizations of his opponents to forewarn him of their actions and also to act as provocateurs and saboteurs of their plans. He bought black newspapers to sing his song and publicly lied about it. He secretly hounded some of his more vulnerable critics until they sought safety in obscurity.

As I grew more aware of Washington's complexity and contradictions, I began to think that, in addition to the biography, one way to tell the whole truth about the man would be an edition of his papers, presenting the documentary evidence rather than merely citing the evidence. At that moment in 1966, Dr. Oliver

W. Holmes of the National Historical Publications Commission (NHPC) approached me with an invitation to do just that. He had his own reasons for the suggestion, stemming at least partly from a growing criticism of his federal agency by scholars who called for history "from the bottom up" and decried the elitism of the NHPC's almost exclusive focus on the Founding Fathers. Bottoms-up history has been more often demanded than supplied in the past twenty years, and Booker T. Washington, despite being black, was another elite character, one of the founding fathers of black history. Maybe I did not sufficiently clarify that fact for Dr. Holmes, for I was already, as I said, beginning to see a selected edition of the Washington Papers as a solution of my dilemmas as a biographer.

It probably would have been harder to edit Washington's Papers *after* completing a biography, because then the temptation would be simply to select the documents that illustrated the interpretation and themes of the biography. I published the first volume of the biography simultaneously with the first two volumes of the papers, and I deliberately avoided in that first volume any effort to say the final word on Washington's personality and character. The editing project undoubtedly slowed the pace of the biography. Editing is endless, laborious, and sometimes downright boring, mind-numbing work. My co-editor, Raymond W. Smock, and I took turns reading aloud the photocopies against the typescript of each volume, and then did it all over again, this time with four or five people reading the galleys against the photocopy. We called it galley-slavery. It was impossible after a day of that to go home and write.

So it took me ten years to write the first volume of the biography, and ten more years to write the second volume. It was easier to edit every day than to write every day, and it was also more necessary. The editing project was done on released time from teaching duties and involved an obligation to staff members, to the university, and to outside funding agencies. I felt somehow more of an obligation to put out an edited volume every year than I felt an obligation to "do my own thing." I confess that I always thought of the editing as "ours" and the biography as "mine." What the editing did for me as a biographer was allow me a leisurely second look at all the evidence, and a chance to see what each bit of evidence signified not only to me but to my fellow editors. Every interpretive theme could be tried out on an informed and critical audience before it found its way into print in the biography.

The editing of thirteen volumes of Washington's Papers certainly dragged out the process of writing his biography, but it also helped me to avoid the main pitfalls of biography, its Scylla and Charybdis. Biographers fail to understand their subjects if they see them only from the outside, always at arm's length, treating them ironically or satirically without any effort to understand their motivation. On the other side, biographers fail when they become so sympathetic that they lose perspective and treat their subjects uncritically as faultless heroes and men of destiny around whom the rest of the world revolves. I think the sustained contact with the documentary evidence, which my editing work required, helped me to avoid the pitfalls on either side and to maintain a balance between sympathy and detachment.

No doubt, there are flaws in both the biography and the edited volumes, flaws that time will inexorably uncover. I can only claim that it was a major effort of a white man to get inside a black man's head. It challenges the simplified picture of his life that Washington presented in his autobiography, *Up from Slavery*, in which the events of his life were strung together as illustrations of a succession of Sunday-school platitudes. In my biography he appears as a much more complex, clever, devious, and self-assertive character, who threaded his way through the thicket of American race relations with the skill of a Brer Rabbit moving through the briar patch. My biography discusses his pioneer role as a black educator and his social philosophy, attuned only too well to the age of racial segregation. But I portray him essentially as a minority-group political boss. He became the dominant black figure of his time because of his political skill, what I call his wizardry, his ability to read other people's thoughts and bend their purposes to his own. Washington's lifelong rival, the great black intellectual W. E. B. Du Bois, said of Washington decades after his death: "Oh, Washington was a politician. . . . He had no faith in white people, not the slightest, and he was most popular among them, because if he was talking with a white man he sat there and found out what the white man wanted him to say, and then as soon as possible he said it."[11] What struck Du Bois as a lack in Washington, a lack of principles or vision, however, was also paradoxically Washington's unique gift as a political leader, his intuitive ability to see through the masks of others to their true selves and then to manipulate them to accomplish his own ends.

Washington was a political genius, but if you combine that gift with the corruption of great power you have a political boss. Washington was a sort of early twentieth-century Mayor Daley. He dealt effectively with problems immediately before him, but in the manner of bosses, he gradually assumed the view that what was good for Booker T. Washington was good for blacks in general. More and more of his energy went into securing and protecting his own power. By the time of his death in 1915, blacks might have been slightly better off economically than when he assumed power in 1895, but in many important respects they were worse off, as measured by the loss of voting rights, the spread of segregation into every avenue of life, a wider gap between white and black educational opportunity, and a rising tide of racial violence and hostility. About the best that could be said for Washington's leadership is that without his promotion of black self-help and his soothing syrup for whites, things might have been even worse.

NOTES

1. Manual work was not required of all students at Howard University. The "modernization" of the curriculum of the College of Arts and Sciences included the addition of the social sciences and expansion of the natural sciences. [Eds.]

2. Wilbur P. Thirkield to Booker T. Washington (hereafter cited as BTW), March 9, 1907, Container 814, Booker T. Washington

Papers, Library of Congress (hereafter cited as BTW Papers, with container number in parentheses).

3. BTW to Thirkield, June 1, 1907 (362), BTW Papers.

4. BTW to William Sidney Pittman, December 12, 1907, quoted in Louis R. Harlan, *Booker T. Washington: The Wizard of Tuskegee, 1901–1915* (New York, 1983), 119. Booker T. Washington's son-in-law was not the architect for the Carnegie Library at Howard. [Eds.]

5. Wilbur P. Thirkield, "The Meaning and Mission of Education," typescript of inaugural address, November 15, 1907 (362), BTW Papers.

6. The first federal funds in support of Howard were a part of the War Department appropriation designated for the Bureau of Refugees, Freedmen and Abandoned Lands, thus dating from the institution's founding in 1867. The first direct appropriation to the university from the United States Congress was enacted in 1879. [Eds.]

7. BTW to Thirkield, August 15, 1909, in Louis R. Harlan and Raymond W. Smock, eds., *The Booker T. Washington Papers* (14 vols., Urbana, Ill., 1972–88), X, 156–57.

8. W. E. B. Du Bois to John R. Francis, August 31, 1909, copy (390), BTW Papers.

9. John R. Francis to BTW, September 11, 1909 (390), BTW Papers.

10. James A. Cobb to BTW, September 11, 1909, reporting a conversation with Kelly Miller (389), BTW Papers.

11. W. E. B. Du Bois, oral history memoir, 1961, Oral History Collection, Columbia University.

Parallels and Divergences

ASSIMILATIONIST STRATEGIES
OF AFRO-AMERICAN AND JEWISH ELITES
FROM 1910 TO THE EARLY 1930S

David Levering Lewis

If, as most behavioral scientists maintain, the dynamics of minority group acculturation and assimilation are crucially influenced by the assimilationist aversions of majority groups, the fact remains that historically most Afro-Americans and Jews in the United States have themselves insisted that acculturation must not lead to assimilation. Indeed, both Jews and Afro-Americans have tended to cling to reinforcing ideologies to conceal or to deny the assimilative process whenever it begins to operate with great efficacy. As a fact of social life, acculturation invariably *tends* to lead to assimilation, but it is not *inevitable* that the former process end in the latter—in self-denial and the disappearance of ethnic group identity through dispersion and intermarriage.[1] Most Afro-Americans and Jews have not wanted to disappear; this essay is concerned with those who did.

The argument, simply stated, is that there was a time when a small number of socially powerful and politically privileged Jews and Afro-Americans embraced an ideology of extreme cultural assimilationism; that, although this ideology was emphatically not without paradox and illogic, its ultimate consequence entailed the abandonment of identity; and that these two elites—one, wealthy and of primarily German-Jewish descent; the other, largely Northern, college-trained Afro-American—reacting to threats to their hegemony both from within and from outside their ethnic universes, decided to concert many of their undertakings in the belief that group assimilation could be accelerated through strategies of overt and covert mutual assistance. Influential Jews and "Talented Tenth" Afro-Americans feared that within a short span of time they would be powerless to promote their social and political programs because of recrudescent nativism and racism set off among old-stock Americans by uncontrolled migration from Eastern Europe and the Deep South, triggering in turn divisive and strident cultural and political nationalisms among the unabsorbed, increasingly despised newcomers. The passage of their people—certainly the celerity of that passage—into the mainstream was believed to be at risk.[2]

One of the nation's most brilliant jurists and its outstanding anthropologist, both Jews, and two of the leading civil rights advocates, both Afro-Americans, publicly and privately expressed extreme assimilationist views that were, if controversial and increasingly unrepresentative of some younger leadership opinion, typical of established Jewish and Afro-American leadership until well into the 1930s. "Habits of living or of thought which tend to keep alive difference of origin or classify men according to their beliefs," Louis D. Brandeis admonished in a 1910 interview, "are inconsistent with the American ideal of brotherhood, and are disloyal." "It would seem," Franz Boas wrote in 1921, "that man being what he is, the negro problem will not disappear in America until the negro blood has been so much diluted that it will no longer be recognized just as anti-Semitism will not disappear until the last vestige of the Jew as a Jew has disappeared." Four years later Walter F. White of the National Association for the Advancement of Colored People (NAACP) expressed the view that the "greatest handicap [the Negro] experiences is that he is not permitted to forget that he is a Negro. . . . The economic and social strictures do not play, in my opinion, so large a part." In 1928 James Weldon Johnson, dean of Afro-American letters and executive secretary of the NAACP, foresaw the promised land of racial invisibility when he wrote that the " 'race problem' is fast reaching the stage of being more a question of national mental attitudes toward the Negro than a question of his actual condition." Think of us as being just like you, he was urging, and there would be no more American dilemma. In the same year he described the alleged marital preferences of Afro-American professional men for light-skinned women as a positive example of racial natural selection.[3]

Not everyone spoke so candidly or saw solutions so clearly. Indeed, the same spokespersons could and, frequently enough, did endorse opposite convictions. Abruptly, in 1914, Brandeis became the country's leading Zionist. James Weldon Johnson startled a 1917 socialist conference at Belleport, New York, with the declaration that the "only things artistic in America that have sprung from American soil, permeated American life, and been universally acknowledged as distinctively American" were the creations of the Afro-American. Psychological and situational marginality led to ambiguity and ambivalence among many of the upper-crust Jews and Afro-Americans. Many, in their personal lives and public utterances, held to acculturationist ideals, only subconsciously aware of their acts of omission and commission, small and large, that served the cause of assimilation. Jacob H. Schiff would never have considered personal religious conversion, and W. E. B. Du Bois never ceased to extol African cultural attributes in contradistinction to those of mainstream America. Ethnic pride, both men believed, could be sublimated in the dogma of unexceptionable public conformity to the best ideals and behavior of white Anglo-Saxon Protestant (WASP) America— the better to guarantee private space for retention of what was most precious in minority culture.[4] Yet the desire for retention of minority culture was clearly eroded by complex feelings about the prospects for ultimate Americanization. The suspicion that many of those men and women were prepared to see a higher price paid for full acceptance than they admitted for the record does not seem at all unwarranted.

Despite their objectively similar historical situations and per- haps, a certain psychological affinity, the two elites were fairly slow to discover mutual interests.[5] Before 1915 there was little to distinguish Jewish "friends of the Negro" from their WASP counterparts. A quickening of Jewish interest had occurred in the wake of the Springfield, Illinois, riot of August, 1908. Appalled by racial violence against Afro-Americans in the urban North, the well-born socialist William English Walling and his Russian-Jewish wife, Anna Strunsky, assisted by pedigreed New England socialists and neoabolitionists (namely, Oswald Garrison Villard, Moorfield Storey, Mary White Ovington, and Charles Edward Russell), founded the NAACP. Most of the first whites prominent in the NAACP were gentiles, but at its organizing conference in 1910, the so-called Russian Revolution (condemning Czarist expulsion of Kievan Jews) reflected the planning-committee labors of Rabbi Stephen S. Wise, Columbia University economics professor Edwin R. A. Seligman, and social worker Henry Moskowitz. In 1911 a similar rescue operation for the Afro-American—this one also comprised mainly of white Protestants (slightly more moderate than those of the NAACP), led to the incorporation of the National Urban League (NUL). Again, Seligman's chairmanship and the presence on the board of Felix Adler, founder of the Ethical Culture Society, Lillian Wald, Fabian Socialist founder of the Henry Street Settlement on the Lower East Side of New York City, Abraham Lefkowitz, educator, and, shortly thereafter, Julius Rosenwald of Sears, Roebuck forecast significant Jewish contributions to the NUL. During the first years of both civil rights organizations, however, not only did WASP influence prevail, but also there was no discernible Jewish inclination to play a larger role.[6]

The early motives of Jewish philanthropists and social workers were varied. There were Talmudic prescriptions of charity, reinforced, for many, by the status-enhancing affiliations with Carnegie and Rockefeller interests that philanthropy among Afro-Americans afforded. There was abstract affinity for another race torn from its homeland and long persecuted. "I belong to an ancient race which has had even longer experience of oppression than you have," the outstanding jurist Louis Marshall told the 1926 annual convention of the NAACP. "We were subjected to indignities in comparison with which to sit in a 'Jim Crow' car is to occupy a palace." There were individual personality factors ranging, undoubtedly, from the noble to the clinical. Affecting all of these motives, of course, was the steady erosion of the professional and social gains of the small Sephardic and the larger Ashkenazic American Jewish communities as anti-Semitism spread throughout much of the nation. In 1898 the financial leader Schiff made his famous public protest against stated policies and the "tacit understanding" barring Jews from "trustee rooms of Columbia College, of the public museums, the public library, and many similar institutions." "The wealthy Jewish businessman and the successful members of established professions were brought face to face with a high social barrier," the standard history of Jewish leadership records. Eight years later Schiff, Julius Rosenwald, Louis Marshall, and Oscar Straus, the department-store owner, helped to establish the American Jewish Committee (AJC) and, in 1908, the New York Kehillah to mobilize influential Jews in quiet work within and outside their communities in order to counteract anti-Semitism.[7]

What the familiar details of the beginnings of American anti-Semitism do not adequately explain is why Jewish involvement with Afro-Americans greatly intensified after 1915, taking on the urgency of a special mission; why Jews of influence and wealth rapidly moved from a racial altruism barely distinguishable from that of neoabolitionist and parlor socialist WASPs to virtual management of Afro-American civil rights organizations. The predisposing factors of a vaguely kindred past and a similarly persecuted present lack the force of inevitability. They suggest, in fact, a more compelling rationale for avoidance by Jews of a special relationship with Afro-Americans. Old-stock American Jews might well have concluded that bad matters could only worsen if they were perceived as special friends of the nation's most visible pariah population. The available literature is silent about pre-1915 debate on this issue, but it is a safe presumption that the pro's and con's were explored. Nor does it seem wildly speculative to suppose that a majority of Jewish leaders, given their conservatism and caginess, would have favored continuing the policy of aloof philanthropy complementing that of liberal WASP donors to Afro-American causes.

What debate there was, was abruptly resolved by the August 17, 1915, lynching of Leo Frank in Marietta, Georgia. Frank, a Cornell University graduate whose grandfather had been a decorated Confederate officer, was a leading Atlanta businessman, his match factory a cynosure of Henry W. Grady's New South philosophy. Accused of the murder-rape of a white female employee, he was the first white in the postbellum South to be convicted of a capital offense on the testimony of an Afro-American. The incendiary speeches of Tom Watson, the nearly demented Georgia Populist leader, and the barbarism of the Marietta mob made it clear that the victim's punishment had been determined by race and class rather than by regard for evidence. The Frank case also briefly threatened Afro-American–Jewish goodwill when the Jewish-owned New York Times demanded that Georgia authorities try the Afro-American janitor, sole witness to the crime, as the guilty party. The case, one historian has observed, "escalated Jewish involvement in civil rights."[8]

What made the Frank case so alarming to the Jewish leaders was that even in the South, where Jews were numerically insignificant, an established Jewish merchant could be more vulnerable than a black janitor. Rather than mount a sustained, frontal attack on racial and religious injustices, which they believed would only aggravate matters, German-Jewish leaders in the United States preferred to concentrate on the victims of intolerance. Nurtured in the flexibility of Reform Judaism, possessing wealth and, many of them, great culture, the descendants of Bavarian, Baden, and Württemburg Jews had placed their bets on assimilation. The long German migration beginning about 1830, was over by 1880, and families such as the Schiffs, Rosenwalds, Adlers, Flexners, Lehmans, Gruenings, and Spingarns had become decade by decade less distinguishable from other white Americans. "Their main concern," Yonathan Shapiro states, "was to facilitate the assimilation of their brethren. They were, to use a distinction made by Gunnar Myrdal in connection with the Negro community, leaders of accommodation rather than of protest." Israel Zangwill's The

Melting Pot informed their credo, but the newer migrants were not "melting." The wealthy Uptown Jews of New York City were "ashamed of the appearance, the language, and the manners of the Russian Jews," Lucy Dawidowicz reports, "aghast at their political ideologies, and terrified lest the world crumble by the mad act of a Jewish radical." Too many—1.5 million between 1900 and 1914—and too different, the new immigrants were playing havoc with the assimilationist vision and timetable.[9]

Afro-American leadership in the North found itself in a similar predicament in 1915, with D. W. Griffith's *The Birth of a Nation*. The enormous passion and effort expended by the NAACP to suppress the film was the first attempt by the rising new Afro-American leadership to mobilize interracial support from coast to coast for a specific issue.[10]

During the ascendancy of Booker T. Washington, militant Afro-American spokespersons in the North had commanded little of the loyalty of the masses of their own people nor the attention of most of white philanthropy—to say nothing of the heed of politicians. The death of the Great Accommodator in November, 1915 opened a crisis in race leadership. It had already become apparent that the Bookerite philosophy of Afro-American development through subordinate agriculture and trades was far more suited to the rural South. By 1917 perhaps as many as 250,000 Southern Afro-Americans were resettling in the urban North and East, and Bookerites had few answers to the socioeconomic crises raised by the Great Migration. Consequently, many of the great industrial philanthropists turned from Tuskegee Institute and Hampton Institute political cadres to the urban, mostly Northern men and women who had never forsworn faith in full civil and social equality and for whom the NAACP's Du Bois, Boston's William Monroe Trotter, Washington's Francis J. Grimké and Kelly Miller, and Chicago's Ida B. Wells-Barnett were heroes.[11] Those were the racially radical men and women with whom the socially conservative Jewish elite would form an alliance.

Many of those Talented Tenth Afro-Americans were stamped in what E. Franklin Frazier describes as the "genteel tradition of the small group of mulattoes who assimilated the morals and manners of the slaveholding aristocracy." But the nucleus was the free black, descended from tiny colonial populations concentrated in Boston, Brooklyn, Philadelphia, and Providence, Rhode Island, gradually augmented by Underground Railroad fugitives and, after the Civil War, by Southerners with some or all of the endowments of pedigree, professional distinction, good morals, and acceptable racial admixture (that is, derived from antebellum liaisons). A few names—Forten, Herndon, Purvis, Syphax, Trotter, Whipper, Downey—represented moderate fortunes from real estate, insurance, publishing, medicine, hosteling, and construction, but most had depended for generations on solid, middle-class incomes from service occupations historically monopolized by free blacks: barbering, catering, draying, carpentry, tailoring, and preaching.[12] The Talented Tenth typology was exemplified in the NUL leadership of the early 1920s: executive co-secretaries Eugene Kinckle Jones and George Edmund Haynes; *Opportunity* editor Charles S. Johnson; Chicago Urban League director T. Arnold Hill—all of whom were sons of professional fathers, second-generation college products (graduates—with the exception of Fisk University man Haynes—of Virginia Union University), polished by advanced studies at prestigious Northern universities, at ease in the world of white power, and usually registered Republicans. The NAACP Afro-Americans were superlative: Du Bois (intellectual and formulator of the Talented Tenth concept); James Weldon Johnson (ultracosmopolite); White ("voluntary Negro"); and Jessie R. Fauset (one of the first female graduates of Cornell University and of the University of Pennsylvania). Notwithstanding debates over tactics, those NUL and NAACP leaders fully shared the same cultural values.[13]

Just as established Jewish leaders were separated from the post-1880s migrants by geographic provenance, religion, culture, and wealth, so, too, were the Northern Afro-American leaders of a radically different mold from the folk of the Great Migration. The members of the Talented Tenth also believed themselves (despite episodic race riots) well along toward full citizenship through circumspect politics and ostentatious patriotism, by good manners, education, and industry, and by quiet cultivation of influential WASPs. Public transportation had been accessible to them without discrimination; department stores had politely encouraged their patronage; most public schools had accepted their children; and a handful had even been elected municipal and state officials in Massachusetts and Illinois. But the relatively privileged status of the Northern Afro-Americans began to deteriorate during the first years of the twentieth century. The combined migrations from Europe and from the Deep South created economic competition and residential confrontation that had already poisoned race relations in the North well before the 1916 commencement of the Great Migration. In the first truly modern novella by an Afro-American, *The Sport of the Gods,* Paul Laurence Dunbar poses the dilemma starkly: " 'Oh, is there no way to keep these people from rushing away from the small villages and country districts of the South up to the cities, where they cannot battle with the terrible force of a strange and unusual environment?' " The leading Afro-American historian, Carter G. Woodson, would later predict that "the maltreatment of the Negroes will be nationalized by this exodus. The poor whites of both sections will strike at this race."[14]

Without exception, studies of Northern urban Afro-America report the nostalgia for the supposedly golden days before the Great Migration. "There was no discrimination in Chicago during my early childhood days," a matron told St. Clair Drake and Horace R. Cayton, typically, "but as the Negroes began coming . . . in numbers it seems they brought discrimination with them." An Afro-American student of pre-migration Philadelphia reported that, with the arrival of a "group of generally uneducated and untrained persons," opportunities that had been enjoyed by cultured Afro-Americans in Philadelphia "were withdrawn." Furthermore, when Philadelphia pastors risked welcoming the migrant, "many of the congregation made him know that he was not wanted. In some cases the church split over the matter, the migrants and their sympathizers withdrawing and forming a church for themselves." A longtime woman resident of Harlem lamented the physical deterioration wrought by the migration and could but wonder, "Are we responsible for at least some of the race prejudice which has developed since the entry of Negroes in Harlem?" And even the young Frazier characterized the migrants as "ignorant and unsophisticated peasant people without experience [in] urban living."[15]

Like New York City's Uptown Jews who lived in terror of the Hester Street anarchist's mad act, Talented Tenth leaders complained, "We all suffer for what one fool will do." Churches and benevolent orders temporarily housed and fed the migrants; the NUL located jobs for them and studied their condition; the NAACP watched over their uncertain civil rights and collected membership dues—all amid a chorus of grief about "ignorant and rough-mannered" newcomers, "inefficient, groping seekers for something better." Like Schiff and his associates who had backed the 1906 Galveston plan for dispersal and resettlement in the Southwest of the East European Jews, Jones entreated "right-thinking Negroes . . . to discourage the wholesale migration of shiftless people." By early 1919 the Chicago Urban League was deeply divided over a recommendation by some of its members that the organization take an official stand against further migration from the South. Opposition to such a policy on the part of the organization's industrialist contributors (many of whom used the migrants as strikebreakers) led to a temporary adjournment of the debate. The race riots in late summer of that year caused the Chicago Urban League and the NUL officially to endorse continued migration; the NUL would have lost credibility with rank-and-file Afro-Americans had it not done so, although its business supporters were now increasingly wary of the dangers of all imported labor.[16]

Just as Schiff had pleaded with Lower East Side leaders to urge immigrant parents not to speak Yiddish to their children, NUL workers delivered lectures on proper English, boisterousness, proper dress, and soap and toothbrushes. NUL officials spoke of "civilizing" and "Americanizing" the migrant with the same patronizing authority as Irving Howe cites from the *Jewish Messenger:* "[Jewish migrants] must be Americanized in spite of themselves, in the mode prescribed by their friends and benefactors." The *Chicago Defender* editorialized about "habits of life little better than [those of] hottentots," and Thomas Lee Philpott's study of Chicago neighborhoods details heroic efforts to maintain standards and to transform migrants: "As migrants fresh from the cottonfields down South crowded into their neighborhoods, [old settlers] imposed their standards on the newcomers"—for a time. Leaders such as James Weldon Johnson and Haynes believed that Southern migrants, because of their greater familiarity with the language and culture, would move into mainstream America more quickly than their European counterparts. With a little help and proper guidance, Haynes explained, the peasant would readily "embrace American advantages." He conceded that the migrant was "lacking in the regularity demanded by the routine of industry day by day" but counted on character improvements to come from membership in the "Dress Well Club" and from "lectures on food and dress . . . supplied by the churches." Like most NUL officials, Haynes was committed to what James Weldon Johnson's biographer calls the social-psychological, rather than the political or economic, solution to racial discrimination—a mental-states formula. In his classic study of Detroit, Haynes remonstrated that "every individual Negro needs to have it brought home to him by constant reminder that all the Negro workmen are on trial in the face of unusual industrial opportunities and that individually they must make good for the sake of all their fellow workmen." Membership in a labor union was not recommended. "Get a job," the brochure issued by the St. Louis Urban League enjoined, "get there on time, be regular, master it, dignify it, do better than the other man; this breaks down prejudice."[17]

By the early 1920s assimilationist Jews and Afro-Americans needed each other more than ever. The Palmer raids and the Red Scare of 1919 were source and symptom of exacerbated anti-Semitism, while the riots and lynchings of the Red Summer of 1919 announced the halt and, in many cases, reversal of wartime socio-economic gains by Afro-Americans. The Anglo-Saxon leagues, various eugenics groups, and the reconstituted Ku Klux Klan gave priority to the so-called Jewish threat, as did Henry Ford's wacky *Dearborn Independent*. Harvard University and Columbia imposed admissions quotas on Jews and residential segregation on Afro-Americans. Restrictive immigration bills (opposed by Jewish organizations but, secretly, not utterly repugnant to some), which over the years had failed to become law by narrowing congressional margins, were now enacted. It was to be expected that the foreign-born, many of them Jews, would play prominent roles in the deep and widespread labor unrest of the postwar years. The Uptown Jews also knew that the spread of "radical" ideas among black workers would be blamed on their people. In reality Marxism's appeal for Afro-Americans was negligible, but the *Dearborn Independent,* intentionally mistaking the racial egalitarian radicalism of the Talented Tenth for Marxism, was a reminder of Jewish vulnerability to farfetched charges. "Let the man of color distrust those false friends who mingle with him to get his money, who seek an alliance with him on the alleged common ground of 'oppression,' " Henry Ford's paper warned in late 1923, "and who expose their whole hand when they urge him to that kind of Bolshevism found only in Moscow and on the East Side of New York." The prognosis for the virus of American anti-Semitism in the early 1920s was far from encouraging.[18]

Meanwhile, no matter to what lengths the "better classes" of Northern Afro-Americans went to prove to whites that they were "capable of living in 'respectable' communities without depreciating property," the reality was one of slums and high rents. Residential covenants fell with about equal severity on both races, a factor of considerable weight in rallying Jews to support the NAACP's successful 1917 effort before the United States Supreme Court in *Buchanan* v. *Warley* to outlaw municipally enforced residential apartheid.[19] By 1920 the NAACP relied heavily on its Jewish connection, both for fund raising and for administration. The brothers Joel E. Spingarn and Arthur B. Spingarn served as board chairman and *pro bono* legal counsel, respectively. Herbert Lehman served on the executive committee. Arthur Sachs succeeded Wald on the board. Herbert J. Seligmann directed public relations; assertive Martha Gruening was his assistant. A Du Bois interview of the period in the *Jewish Daily Forward* is fittingly captioned, "The Negro Race Looks to Jews for Sympathy and Understanding." It is hardly surprising, then, that a newly arrived, bewildered Marcus Garvey had stormed out of the NAACP's headquarters in 1917 "dumbfounded" by the apparent domination there of whites.[20]

As the melting pot turned into a skillet for the two races, controversial new theories and ideologies of Jewish and Afro-American cultures arose to challenge the social meliorism of upper-class leaders. The Jewish pluralists Isaac B. Berkson, Julius Drachsler, and Judah L. Magnes had called at the turn of the century for educational and social progams that would maintain and enrich the traditions of Jewish life. The philosopher Horace M. Kallen rejected assimilationism and proposed instead that Jews retain their "racial" uniqueness, the better to enrich American society. By the early 1910s, in addition to Kallen, intellectuals such as Du Bois (Pan-Africanism), Randolph Bourne (transnationalism), the brothers Norman Hapgood and Hutchins Hapgood (variety), and Robert E. Park (racial temperaments) were modifying or abjuring the once sacrosanct paradigm of "Anglo-conformity"—the Wilsonian dogma that a "hyphenated" American was an impossibility. That the United States ought to reflect and to preserve the variegated traditions of its peoples was a novel enough intellectual proposition in the early twentieth century, far from broadly subscribed to and seemingly of little political moment. Yet even as an intellectual proposition, cultural pluralism was a source of malaise among elite Jews because of its potential to raise the dual loyalty charge. "To be good Americans," Brandeis declared in 1915, "we must be better Jews, and to be better Jews we must become Zionists."[21] The Kallen and Brandeis heterodoxies distressed old-stock Jews somewhat more than similar ideas worried the Talented Tenth, but neither leadership group was equipped to deal with the new, dynamic, mass-based ideologies of white and black Zionism.

The great majority of the Jews closely associated with the NAACP and the NUL—Louis Marshall, Jacob Billikopf, a lawyer and Louis Marshall's son-in-law, Boas, Melville J. Herskovits, and the Altmans, Lehmans, Rosenwalds, and Spingarns—opposed Zionism, in both its secular and its cultural manifestations and had fully endorsed the opposition of the *New York Times* to the

Balfour Declaration. Although Magnes, leader of the New York Kehillah and Louis Marshall's brother-in-law, Julian W. Mack, prominent Chicago jurist and Rosenwald intimate, and Felix Frankfurter, Brandeis's protégé, were significant Zionist exceptions among the civil rights forces, theirs was a very German-Jewish Zionism—politically cautious and emotionally cool. Brandeisian Zionism was characterized by the slogan "Silence in America; service in Palestine." For the great majority, nonetheless, there could be no such thing as circumspect Zionism. During the fierce internal debate in early 1916 over the wisdom of founding the American Jewish Congress, Schiff complained to a friend about the noisy militancy of East European backers of the congress: "Thanks to the preaching and machinations of Jewish nationalists we are gradually being forced into a class by ourselves and if this continues, it will not be many years before we shall be looked upon by our fellow citizens as an entirely separate class, whose interests are different than those of the grass [roots] of American people."[22] Zionism was not the solution to a problem, the German Jews asserted, but a deadly manifestation of the problem itself—a failure to assimilate. According to them, the correct approach—more urgent than ever, they felt—was to defuse American racism and extreme nativism by reassuring the gentile majority that it was mistaken in believing that Jews in America were different.

Such an approach would be most effective, the Jewish elite believed, if it were pursued with minimum visibility and vulnerability. When Julius Rosenwald told a friend that he was not "in the least anxious to see many Jews in politics or even on the bench," he spoke for most of his class, for whom high public profile *as Jews* was anathema. Support of and participation in the Afro-American civil rights movement was seen, after 1915, as a stratagem exactly meeting Jewish needs. Where barely ten years earlier they had supported those Afro-American forces—the Bookerites—equally averse to agitation and publicity in race relations, upper-class Jews in the aftermath of the Frank case increasingly encouraged the new Afro-American leadership—the Talented Tenth—which employed agitation and publicity as principal weapons to force the glacial pace of civil rights. By establishing a presence at the center of the civil rights movement with intelligence, money, and influence, elite Jews and their delegates could fight against anti-Semitism by remote control. "By helping the colored people in this country," the *American Hebrew* editorialized, "Mr. Rosenwald doubtless also serves Judaism." The Jewish civil rights role also relieved du Ponts, Fords, Mellons, Rockefellers, and other gentile capitalists of the burden of more than infrequent, ceremonial contact with Afro-American leaders and organizations, which in turn somewhat vaguely obligated those capitalists to closer ties with Jewish financiers and philanthropists. "I have never appealed to them for aid for the Negro . . . and been rebuffed," Villard averred, speaking for his gentile associates.[23]

Julius Rosenwald became a trustee of the Rockefeller Foundation in 1922, after disbursing more than $4,000,000 more or less out of pocket to build schools for Southern blacks. Six years later the reorganized Rosenwald Fund, patterned on the Rockefeller Foundation, was launched to upgrade higher education in the South, particularly for Afro-Americans. Between 1928 and 1948 the Rosenwald Fund allocated monies toward endowment and construction to the major private Afro-American institutions of higher learning: $1,037,000 to Dillard University; $668,175 to Fisk; $542,258 to the Atlanta University Center, most of these granted in the early years of the Rosenwald Fund's existence. Fellowships to artists, educators, and scholars advanced the careers of Afro-America's most gifted or enterprising: future college presidents such as Charles S. Johnson of Fisk, Mordecai W. Johnson of Howard University, Horace Mann Bond of Lincoln University, Dwight O. W. Holmes of Morgan State College; humanists and social scientists such as Adelaide Cromwell Hill, Frazier, Kenneth Clark, Allison Davis, Drake, Ira De A. Reid, Abram L. Harris, and Lorenzo Turner; and artists and writers such as James Weldon Johnson (the first grantee), Sterling Brown, Langston Hughes, Claude McKay, and Arna Bontemps, Richmond Barthé, Selma Burke, Augusta Savage, Hale Woodruff, and Jacob Lawrence.[24]

Significantly, Jewish educational philanthropy accelerated shortly after Fisk, Howard, Hampton, and several other Afro-American institutions of higher learning had sustained vigorous protests in the mid-1920s against policies and curricula that a new generation of students considered racially demeaning. A crucial, if not always apparent, difference between Jewish and WASP benefaction to Afro-American higher education was the insistence of the former (notwithstanding the insuperable fact of segregation) on education of competitive quality. The erstwhile similar commitment of WASP philanthropy had become increasingly compromised after the turn of the century because of Southern white pressures to supplant liberal arts and white-collar professional training with vocational instruction, reinforced by an ethic of subservient separateness.

Ever mindful of what they believed were the perils of marked cultural distinctions and anchored in a tradition in which learning was revered, the Jewish elite wished to see Afro-American college graduates able to make their way in the larger society, even able to compel that society gradually to recognize their varied competences. Billikopf, chairman of the trustee executive committee of Howard, and Abraham Flexner, chairman of the board of trustees of Howard, pushed for excellence unrelated to race. "There is no such thing as a university especially created for any race or denomination," Flexner told his fellow trustees in 1933. "The university is devoted to teaching competent young men and women."[25] Constructive charity, profound influence, and contribution to the formation of a kindred elite flowed quietly from the policies of Jewish leadership. An additional benefit deriving from Afro-American philanthropy, or so Alfred Stern, Julius Rosenwald's son-in-law, hoped, was the undermining of the stereotype of Jews as predatory merchants and exploiters of real estate. Rosenwald millions went to build the model Michigan Boulevard Garden Apartments ("The Rosenwald") and a medical facility in Chicago and would have underwritten a medical center in New York had not middle-class opposition in Harlem to a segregated facility defeated the proposal.[26]

For the Talented Tenth, heightened Jewish collaboration was extremely beneficial, for it, too, was caught unprepared by what the novelist and poet Claude McKay called the "African Zionism" of Garvey's Universal Negro Improvement Association (UNIA).

The Garvey movement's leadership was largely West Indian, as was the majority of its true believers, but its growing appeal among Afro-Americans extended from coast to coast and deep into the South.[27] Charisma and pageantry, exotic titles and emoluments, phalanxes of uniformed cadres, the daunting cry of "Africa for the Africans!" and a strident doctrine of unique, racially purified destiny in renascent Mother Africa exploded upon the American scene after 1917. With its stress on separate development, entrepreneurship, and self-help, UNIA ideology appealed to thousands who felt the void created by Booker T. Washington's death; and Garvey, of course, professed to be a modernizing, internationalizing disciple of Washington. Although there were several significant defections to Garveyism, the overwhelming majority of Talented Tenth leadership was stunned, defensive, and resentful. Even Du Bois, who could claim to be the originator of Pan-Africanism in the United States, recoiled from Garveyism after a brief period of probing uncertainty. "Why then does he sneer at the work of the powerful group of his race in the United States where he finds asylum and sympathy?" *The Crisis* editor wondered. Du Boisian Pan-Africanism was strikingly similar to the intellectual Zionism of Brandeis, and Brandeisian Zionism was already in temporary retreat before the onslaught of militant cultural and political Jewish nationalists. Du Bois foresaw the same threat unleashed by the forces of Garveyism.[28]

From the perspective of the Talented Tenth, then, the more Garvey succeeded, the greater the dangers of racial polarization and, finally, of repression. "American Negro leaders are not jealous of Garvey," *The Crisis* protested (not entirely truthfully), "they are not envious of his success; they are simply afraid of his failure, for his failure would be theirs." But, despite Du Bois's disclaimer, the Talented Tenth was envious and afraid of having to share, and perhaps even to yield, its pretensions to leadership of the Afro-American masses. Garvey was only partly blustering when he charged that "the Negro who has had the benefit of an education of forty, thirty, and twenty years ago, is the greatest fraud and stumbling block to the real progress of the race." Nor was he guilty, as some pretended to believe, of applying an inappropriate West Indian color-status theorem to Afro-American leadership in the United States. If it was vicious to call attention publicly to the light complexions of the Talented Tenth (the perennial Afro-American taboo), it was also extremely effective against Du Bois, Jesse Moorland of the Young Men's Christian Association, White, and their kind. The charge drew from Du Bois the immediate warning: "American Negroes recognize no color line in or out of the race, and they will in the end punish the man who attempts to establish it." Just as Uptown Jews tried to outflank the Zionists by combining with Lower East Side socialists, upper-crust Afro-Americans readily joined with the Harlem socialists led by the African Blood Brotherhood's Cyril Briggs to defeat the Garveyites.[29] With Garvey's imprisonment for mail fraud in 1925, black Zionism rapidly lost momentum.

The deflation of Garveyism presented the Talented Tenth leaders with an acute credibility crisis, however, for now they had to prove that Garvey's extreme pessimism about the future of the race in the United States was unjustified and that, by helping to scuttle the fervent mass movement, they had not consigned eleven million Afro-Americans to perpetual economic and social misery. But the evidence and trends supported the Garveyite predictions. Louise Venable Kennedy found that the proportion of Northern Afro-Americans in manufacturing had steadily declined during the 1920s, and that "numbers of them have gone back into . . . domestic and personal service, while many of the Negro women who had given up outside employment have been forced to return to work." Talented Tenth anxieties about that dilemma permeated the writings of Alain L. Locke. Cannily observing the analogous embarrassment of older Jewish leadership, Afro-America's first Rhodes Scholar knew what a close call Garveyism had represented: "We have for the present, in spite of Mr. Garvey's hectic efforts, no Zionistic hope or intention." But what *Opportunity* called the "dark, dumb masses" were urgently in need of a new opiate, for, as Locke well understood, Garveyism had shown how much "more ready and ripe for action than the minds of the leaders and the educated few" the masses were.[30]

In his introductory essays in the special 1925 issue of *Survey*, devoted to the "New Negro," Locke spelled out the problem and the solution. "The migrant masses" were stirring, he wrote. "The only safeguard for mass relations in the future must be provided in the carefully maintained contacts of the enlightened minorities of both race groups." But time was running out, Locke warned. "There is an increasing group who affiliate with radical and liberal movements. . . . Harlem's quixotic radicalisms call for their ounce of democracy today lest tomorrow they be beyond cure." Hence, the race's leaders must be clearly seen to have influence among the movers and shakers in the white world, a role-legitimating requirement that, despite Garvey's example, Myrdal found to be a fundamental race feature. Interracial undertakings as dazzlingly mounted and as publicized as those of the UNIA were called for; promotion and celebration of symbolic racial breakthroughs were indispensable. Given the near total political and economic post-war impasse, however, Talented Tenth options were limited. Two strategies were adopted: The first and most obvious was that of redoubled advocacy of elemental civil rights before the courts and in Congress. The second, a surprisingly novel strategy, was that of harnessing art and literature for civil rights.[31]

Court victories afforded Talented Tenth leadership maximal publicity with minimal potential to overturn the real world of race relations (which would have frightened away numbers of white philanthropists). Given the shabby record of evasion and nonenforcement of court decisions on the state and local levels, civil rights advocates could claim important victories, and civil rights opponents could ignore them. A personnel problem had to be solved before going to court, however: There were no more than eleven hundred Afro-American lawyers in the entire country in 1920, few of them really well trained. The vacuum was filled by Arthur B. Spingarn and his partner, Charles Studin; Louis Marshall and his son, James Marshall; Nathan Margold, the first salaried NAACP counsel; and Frankfurter as valuable advisor. Protestants Moorfield Storey and Clarence Darrow handled a limited number of appellate cases. Jewish support, legal and financial, afforded a string of significant court challenges and several victories. Storey, a former American Bar Association president, presented the winning 1923 Supreme Court argument, in *Moore* v. *Dempsey,* that "mob spirit" had denied militant Arkansas sharecroppers a fair trial, a decision that drew Louis Marshall into NAACP work, as Louis Marshall had unsuccessfully used the same argument before the Supreme Court in the Frank appeal.[32]

James Weldon Johnson, himself a lawyer, exploited every opportunity to draw parallels between Jewish and Afro-American disabilities and to urge Louis Marshall in the unsuccessful 1926 restrictive covenant case, *Corrigan* v. *Buckley,* "that you might be willing to make a statement on the case calling its importance to the attention of Jewish people." Jewish assistance was also valuable in the NAACP's lobbying for the unsuccessful Dyer and Costigan-Wagner federal antilynching bills. Important Jewish support also went to A. Philip Randolph's Brotherhood of Sleeping Car Porters battle with the Pullman Company for union recognition and with the American Federation of Labor for full admission. There is less exaggeration than truth in an American Jewish Congress lawyer's assertion that legal briefs, local ordinances, and federal laws beneficial to Afro-Americans "were actually written in the offices of Jewish agencies, by Jewish staff people, introduced by Jewish legislators and pressured into being by Jewish voters."[33]

By the end of the 1920s, the Talented Tenth spoke warmly of the "special relationship" with Jews. James Weldon Johnson and White routinely scrutinized obituary columns for Jewish legacies that the NAACP might tap and listed prospective contributors, a disproportionate number of whom were Jews. "The clue to Pierre duPont [is] that his wife is a Jewess," White wrote crudely, and mistakenly, of that potential donor (du Pont's mother was Jewish). Faith in Jewish largesse was generally rewarded. During the Depression William Rosenwald made a three-year grant to the NAACP, on condition of being matched by three others. Lehman, Mary Fels, and Felix Warburg—and, also, Edsel Ford—matched the grant. The second largest NUL funding source from 1924 to 1931 was the Altman Foundation. That Jews were extremely careful not to abuse the influence flowing from their contributions is evident from the one notable instance in which circumspection was abandoned. James Weldon Johnson's correspondence confirms the contemporary impression that Stern was arrogant and impolitic. After Julius Rosenwald's death in 1932, Stern interfered directly in NUL administrative matters in Chicago, expressed his dislike of Jones, the national secretary, and even notified the NUL and the NAACP that Rosenwald funds would be drastically reduced unless both organizations agreed to his plans for a merger, a scheme civil rights officials managed to bury, though not without reduction in Rosenwald revenues.[34]

The Talented Tenth's primary answer to black Zionism was the literary and artistic industry that manufactured the so-called Harlem Renaissance. The half-dozen or so Afro-American orchestrators of the Harlem Renaissance—Charles S. Johnson, James Weldon Johnson, White, Fauset, Locke, West Indian bibliophile Arthur A. Schomburg, and West Indian numbers king Casper Holstein—conceived of it as serious racial politics—art for politics' sake, or civil rights by copyright. Students of American culture have seen the Harlem Renaissance as another predictable, creative bubble in the melting pot, a savory ingredient in a New England, Knickerbocker, Hoosier, and Yiddish concoction. "The Negro writers were caught up [in] the spirit of the artistic yearnings of the time," S. P. Fullinwider argues.[35] That was true of the writers Langston Hughes and Jean Toomer, but it was not typical of most of the other artists and writers. Nothing could have seemed to most educated Afro-Americans more impractical as a means of improving racial standing in the 1920s than writing poetry and novels or painting. Art and literature were artificially created through glamorous ceremony (NAACP- and NUL-sponsored banquets and galas), prizes and fellowships (Guggenheim and Rosenwald grants, Spingarn medals, *Opportunity* literary prizes funded by Holstein), traveling art shows and well-advertised fiction and poetry (published by the Harmon Foundation, Boni and Liveright, Alfred A. Knopf), and national recruitment of talent by Fauset and Charles S. Johnson.[36]

Charles S. Johnson's staff at *Opportunity* culled the Afro-American press, kept files on promising artists and poets in remote towns, and arranged for temporary billeting and employment for them once they had accepted Charles S. Johnson's risky invitation to relocate in Harlem from, say, Topeka, Kansas. Fauset discovered Toomer and Hughes for *The Crisis*. White boasted that he had persuaded Paul Robeson to foresake law for the concert stage, as he also had encouraged the singing career of Julius Bledsoe, a Columbia medical student, and the writing career of Rudolf Fisher, a Harlem physician. Upwardly mobile Afro-Americans were at least a generation away from the special cultural aliena-tion—the insider-as-outsider syndrome—of which the contem-porary "Lost Generation" was the well-publicized example. But with the decisive infusion of white philanthropy (much of it Jewish), the entrepreneurs of the Harlem Renaissance were able to mount a generation-skipping movement, diverting to its ranks men and women who, in the natural course of events, would have devoted their exclusive energies to teaching, lawyering, doctoring, fixing teeth, and burying. The degree to which the use of arts and letters for broad political purposes was premeditated and programmatic is cogently expressed in White's voluminous correspondence. An indefatigable dispatcher of notes, letters, and telegrams about the arts movement, White's enthusiasm led him to plan for an arts institute to support black drama, dance, and music; and in Europe, a bureau for disseminating scholarly and literary attacks on racism in America.[37]

By the early 1930s the influence of White in Algonquin Hotel circles, of Locke at the Harmon Foundation, of James Weldon Johnson as trustee of the Garland and the Rosenwald funds, and of Charles S. Johnson as all-purpose advisor to foundations had made the Harlem Renaissance a well-oiled machine turning out a total of twenty-six novels, ten volumes of poetry, five Broadway plays, innumerable essays and short stories, two or three performed ballets and concerti, and a large amount of painting and sculpture. "We must admit our debt to these foster agencies," Locke wrote in acknowledgment of *The Crisis, Opportunity,* and the *Messenger.* "The three journals which have been vehicles of most of our artistic expression have been the avowed organs of social move-ments and organized social programs." The Southern white literary critic Robert T. Kerlin evaluated the social impact of the arts and letters program more bluntly: "Here, unsegregated, the Negro poet appears on his merit by the side of the white poet, competitor with him for the same honors. The fact is immensely significant. It is hostile to lynching, and to jimcrowing." James Weldon Johnson enthusiastically concurred, writing in 1928 that it was not "too much to say that through artistic achievement the Negro has found a means of getting at the very core of the prejudice against him, by challenging the Nordic superiority complex."[38]

Not everyone agreed. Although his own magazine had helped promote the movement, Du Bois came to disapprove of a racial program offering poetry in the place of politics and Broadway musicals in the place of jobs. In time, a few of the more gifted lights of the Harlem Renaissance came to resist the mixture of art and propaganda and applauded Wallace Thurman's Pollyannaish burlesque of Locke in *Infants of the Spring:* " 'Because of your concerted storming up Parnassus, new vistas will be spread open to the entire race. The Negro in the South will no more know peonage, Jim Crowism, or the loss of the ballot, and the Negro everywhere in America will know complete freedom and equality.'" Reviewing the civil rights policies of those times for his work on the Carnegie-Myrdal project, Ralph J. Bunche concluded that "the truth of the matter is that in the thinking of the Negro elite there is a tremendous gap between it and the black mass."[39]

Although it does not appear that the Jewish leaders were the first to encourage the civil-rights-through-art program, they were not unsympathetic to it, as the special influence of Joel E. Spingarn at Harcourt, Brace and the special relationship with Alfred A. Knopf indicate. Moreover, Jewish success in Tin Pan Alley and in Hollywood, in publishing and on Broadway was exemplary proof of the power of art and entertainment to alter ethnic images. The fact that so many successful Jewish talents used modified Afro-American materials—Al Jolsen, George Gershwin, Jimmy Durante, Benny Goodman, Artie Shaw, Sophie Tucker—was not lost on Harlem Renaissance enthusiasts.[40] But Afro-American leadership was far more influenced by analogies of history and intellect and prone to describe itself, in the manner of Jews, as an ancient, special people, achieving superiority through suffering. "The Jew has been made international by persecution and forced dispersion," Locke declared, "and so, potentially, have we." When Kelly Miller, the highly respected former dean at Howard, appealed to Afro-America's most distinguished and powerful figures to meet in Chicago in early 1924 to plan for the race's future, he called his well-publicized but unsuccessful convocation the "Negro Sanhedrin." Fauset's novels depict her class as superior to privileged whites by virtue of culture and attainments that had been infinitely harder to acquire because of racism. James Weldon Johnson called on his race to emulate the Jews in measuring up "brain for brain" with mainstream Americans. When wealthy or influential Jewish leaders such as Louis Marshall or Julius Rosenwald told Afro-American audiences that, by comparison with the historic suffering of Jews, the black diaspora had been less destructive, the Talented Tenth was greatly encouraged by the prospect of analogous overcoming of prejudice and attainment of affluence and influence.[41]

Unlike their Jewish models, however, the Afro-American leaders tended to minimize or to ignore the grimy aspects of migrant Jewish business success as a basic condition for the perpetuation of collective achievement. Hence, the Harlem Renaissance literally took place in rented space—in a Harlem they did not own. Racial aristocrats steeped in liberal arts educations, they missed the significance of the butcher and tailor shops, the sweatshops, the pawn shops, and the liquor stores—and, despite some mid-1930s rhetoric, the paramount importance of organized labor. On the latter institution, Miller's pronouncement continued to elicit approval: "Logic aligns the Negro with labor, but good sense arrays him with capital." The leaders overstressed the psychosocial and juridical at the expense of economic and political approaches. In 1928 Charles S. Johnson was elated to record that "the University of North Carolina has entertained at least three Negro lectures. The conference at Vassar, and the admission this year of a Negro girl at Bryn Mawr, are flashes of the new spirit of youth in race relations."[42]

It is not surprising, then, that on those few occasions in the early 1930s when the Talented Tenth mobilized the masses to protest economic discrimination, its specific demands were usually for middle-class advancement. "Perhaps there is nothing more significant in the social history of the United States," McKay wrote, "than the spectacle of the common black folk in overalls and sweaters agitating and parading for jobs for apathetic white-collar Negroes." Not until the controversial 1933 Amenia Conference (virtually forced on them by Du Bois and such Young Turks as Bunche, the poet Sterling Brown, and the economist Abram L. Harris) did Talented Tenth leaders begin to appreciate some of the limitations of litigation and literature and the potential of alliances with the liberal wing of the Democratic party and of the more racially progressive labor unions.[43]

It seems evident that what Jewish and Afro-American elites principally shared was not a similar history but an identical adversary—a species of white gentile. Theirs was a politically determined kinship, a defensive alliance, cemented more from the outside than from within. Believing themselves at the threshold of full acceptance by mainstream America, then knocked off balance by an unwelcome population infusion, becoming frightened and dismayed by the eruption from below of nationalisms, the privileged Ashkenazim reached for the Afro-American leadership and even helped to create it, hoping, as Louis Marshall remarked in 1924, that the success of Afro-American civil rights organizations "may incidentally benefit Jews."[44] Determined to find themselves one day also at the same threshold of acceptance, embarrassed and alarmed by a similar explosion from below, the Talented Tenth welcomed the Jewish embrace and made Jewish success, as it was understood, a paradigm for its own. At least in the short term, the collaboration was beneficial for the Afro-Americans. Their leadership position was secured and would remain so for another forty years. The Harlem Renaissance bubble would soon go flat, but the basic assimilationist values and goals of the Talented Tenth would be perpetuated in civil rights strategies in which the emphasis remained on court cases, contracts, contacts, and culture. For the Jews, the collaboration was extremely beneficial. By assisting in the crusade to prove that Afro-Americans could be decent, conformist, cultured human beings, the civil rights Jews were, in a sense, spared some of the necessity of directly rebutting anti-Semitic stereotypes; for if blacks could make good citizens, clearly, most white Americans believed, all other groups could make better ones.

NOTES

1. Melford E. Spiro, "The Acculturation of American Ethnic Groups," *American Anthropologist* 57 (Dec. 1955): 1244; John Higham, "American Anti-Semitism Historically Reconsidered," in Charles Herbert Stember et al., *Jews in the Mind of America* (New York, 1966), 243–53; Deborah Dash Moore, "Defining American Jewish Ethnicity," *Prospects* 6 (1981), 387–409; Marshall Sklare, *America's Jews* (New York, 1971), 4–5; W. E. B. Du Bois, "The Conservation of Races," in *The Seventh Son: The Thought and Writings of W. E. B. Du Bois,* ed. Julius Lester (2 vols., New York, 1971), I, 182–83; S. P. Fullinwider, *The Mind and Mood of Black America: 20th Century Thought* (Homewood, Ill., 1969), 55; Milton M. Gordon, *Assimilation in American Life: The Role of Race, Religion, and National Origins* (New York, 1964), esp. 81–101; W. Lloyd Warner, Buford H. Junker, and Walter A. Davis, *Color and Human Nature: Negro Personality Development in a Northern City* (Washington, 1941), esp. 15.

2. Yonathan Shapiro, *Leadership of the American Zionist Organization, 1897–1930* (Urbana, 1971), esp. 12–15; Irving Howe, *World of Our Fathers* (New York, 1976), esp. 229–30; Ronald Steel, *Walter Lippman and the American Century* (Boston, 1980), 6–11; Lucy S. Dawidowicz, *The Jewish Presence: Essays on Identity and History* (New York, 1977), esp. 127; *Harvard Encyclopedia of American Ethnic Groups,* s.v. "Jews"; James Weldon Johnson, *Negro Americans, What Now?* (New York, 1938), esp. 12–15; E. Franklin Frazier, *Black Bourgeoisie* (Glencoe, Ill., 1957), 112–29.

3. Shapiro, *Leadership of the American Zionist Organization,* 61–62; Franz Boas, "The Problem of the American Negro," *Yale Review* 10 (Jan. 1921): 395; Walter F. White to L. M. Hussey, Jan. 19, 1925, box 92, Walter F. White Collection (Library of Congress); James Weldon Johnson, "Race Prejudice and the Negro Artist," *Harper's* 157 (Nov. 1928): 775; James Weldon Johnson, "A Negro Looks at Race Prejudice," *American Mercury* 14 (May 1928): 52; G. Franklin Ed-

wards, *The Negro Professional Class* (Glencoe, Ill., 1959), esp. 17–75.

4. James Weldon Johnson, *Along This Way: The Autobiography of James Weldon Johnson* (New York, 1954), 326–27; Edwin R. Embree and Julia Waxman, *Investment in People: The Story of the Julius Rosenwald Fund* (New York, 1949), 11. On W. E. B. Du Bois's complex racial chauvinism, see W. E. Burghardt Du Bois, *The Gift of Black Folk: The Negroes in the Making of America* (Boston, 1924), esp. 287–340; W. E. Burghardt Du Bois, *Darkwater: Voices from within the Veil* (New York, 1920), 9; and Fullinwider, *Mind and Mood of Black America*, 47–71.

5. On early contacts between Jewish and Afro-American leaders, see Louis R. Harlan, *Booker T. Washington: The Wizard of Tuskegee, 1905–1915* (New York, 1983), 140–41; August Meier, *Negro Thought in America, 1880–1915: Racial Ideologies in the Age of Booker T. Washington* (Ann Arbor, 1966), 105; Hasia R. Diner, *In the Almost Promised Land: American Jews and Blacks, 1915–1935* (Westport, Conn., 1977), 171; and Lenora E. Berson, *The Negroes and the Jews* (New York, 1971), 70–71.

6. Charles Flint Kellogg, *NAACP: A History of the National Association for the Advancement of Colored People, 1909–1920* (Baltimore, 1967), 9–30; B. Joyce Ross, *J. E. Spingarn and the Rise of the NAACP, 1911–1939* (New York, 1972), esp. 116–17; Guichard Parris and Lester Brooks, *Blacks in the City: A History of the National Urban League* (Boston, 1971), 32–65; Nancy J. Weiss, *The National Urban League, 1910–1940* (New York, 1974), esp. 53–54.

7. Diner, *In the Almost Promised Land*, 151–52; *Harvard Encyclopedia of American Ethnic Groups*, s.v. "Jews"; John Higham, *Strangers in the Land: Patterns of American Nativism, 1860–1925* (New Brunswick, N.J., 1955), 92–94, 160–61; Herbert L. Feingold, *Zion in America: The Jewish Experience from Colonial Times to the Present* (New York, 1974), 142–50; Robert K. Murray, *Red Scare: A Study of National Hysteria, 1919–1920* (New York, 1964); Howard M. Sachar, *The Course of Modern Jewish History* (Cleveland, 1958), 311–13; E. Digby Baltzell, *The Protestant Establishment: Aristocracy and Caste in America* (New York, 1964), esp. 60–120; Michael N. Dobkowski, *The Tarnished Dream: The Basis of American Anti-Semitism* (Westport, Conn., 1979), esp. 123.

8. Berson, *Negroes and the Jews*, 44; Leonard Dinnerstein, *The Leo Frank Case* (New York, 1968); Steven Bloom "Interaction between Blacks and Jews in New York City, 1900–1930, as Reflected in the Black Press" (Ph.D. diss., New York University, 1973), 20, 30,

32–33; Eugene Levy, *James Weldon Johnson: Black Leader, Black Voice* (Chicago, 1973), 158–59; Ronald Sanders, *The Downtown Jews: Portraits of an Immigrant Generation* (New York, 1969), 427–28. On the probable guilt of the black janitor, Jim Conely, see Berson, *Negroes and the Jews,* 38, 43–44.

9. Shapiro, *Leadership of the American Zionist Organization,* 60; Israel Zangwill, *The Melting Pot* (New York, 1909); Moses Rischin, *The Promised City: New York's Jews, 1870–1914* (Cambridge, Mass., 1962), 97–98; Dawidowicz, *Jewish Presence, 127;* Howe, *World of Our Fathers, 229; Harvard Encyclopedia of American Ethnic Groups,* s.v. "Jews."

10. Thomas Cripps, *Slow Fade to Black: The Negro in American Film, 1900–1942* (New York, 1977), esp. 41–61; Kellogg, *NAACP,* 142–45.

11. On the "New Negro" personalities and their affiliations, see W. E. B. Du Bois, *The Autobiography of W. E. B. Du Bois: A Soliloquy on Viewing My Life from the Last Decade of Its First Century* (New York, 1968), 236–76; Elliott M. Rudwick, *W. E. B. Du Bois: Propagandist of the Negro Protest* (Philadelphia, 1968), 94–149; Stephen R. Fox, *The Guardian of Boston: William Monroe Trotter* (New York, 1970), 31–80; Alfreda M. Duster, ed., *Crusade for Justice: The Autobiography of Ida B. Wells* (Chicago, 1970), 323–28; Harlan, *Booker T. Washington, 359–78,* Kellogg, *NAACP,* 67–115; Meier, *Negro Thought in America,* 207–78; and Weiss, *National Urban League,* 47–70.

12. Frazier, *Black Bourgeoisie,* 113; E. Franklin Frazier, *The Free Negro Family: A Study of Family Origins before the Civil War* (Nashville, 1932); Lorenzo Johnston Greene, *The Negro in Colonial New England, 1620–1776* (New York, 1942), 72–99, 290–315; Edgar J. McManus, *Black Bondage in the North* (Syracuse, 1973), 160–98; David A. Gerber, *Black Ohio and the Color Line, 1860–1915* (Urbana, 1976), 60–92; Leon F. Litwack, *North of Slavery: The Negro in the Free States, 1790–1860* (Chicago, 1961), 178, 180.

13. Edwin R. Embree, *13 against the Odds* (New York, 1944), 47–70, 71–96, 153–74, 175–96; Mary White Ovington, *The Walls Came Tumbling Down* (New York, 1947), 78–91, 104–17; Patrick J. Gilpin, "Charles S. Johnson: Entrepreneur of the Harlem Renaissance," in *The Harlem Renaissance Remembered,* ed. Arna Bontemps (New York, 1972), 215–46; David Levering Lewis, "Dr. Johnson's Friends: Civil Rights by Copyright during Harlem's Mid-Twenties," *Massachusetts Review* 20 (Autumn 1979): 501–19; David Levering Lewis, *When Harlem Was in Vogue* (New York, 1981), 119–55; Mary White Ovington, *Portraits in Color* (New York, 1927), 78–91, 104–17;

Kellogg, *NAACP*, 47–65; Rudwick, *W. E. B. Du Bois*, 120–50; Weiss, *National Urban League*, 47–70; Levy, *James Weldon Johnson*, 49–74; Thomas C. Holt, "The Lonely Warrior: Ida B. Wells-Barnett and the Struggle for Black Leadership," in *Black Leaders of the Twentieth Century*, ed. John Hope Franklin and August Meier (Urbana, 1982), 39–61; Walter White, *A Man Called White: The Autobiography of Walter White* (New York, 1948), 39–80; Edward E. Waldron, *Walter White and the Harlem Renaissance* (Port Washington, N.Y., 1978), 3–22.

14. Paul Laurence Dunbar, *The Sport of the Gods* (New York, 1902), 212; Carter G. Woodson, *A Century of Negro Migration* (Washington, 1918), 180.

15. St. Clair Drake and Horace R. Cayton, *Black Metropolis: A Study of Negro Life in a Northern City* (2 vols., New York, 1970), I, 73; Sadie Tanner Mossell, "The Standard of Living Among One Hundred Negro Migrant Families in Philadelphia" (Ph.D. diss., University of Pennsylvania, 1921), 9; Gilbert Osofsky, *Harlem: The Making of a Ghetto: Negro New York, 1890–1930* (New York, 1966), 139–40; Thomas Lee Philpott, *The Slum and the Ghetto: Neighborhood Deterioration and Middle-Class Reform, Chicago, 1800–1930* New York, 1978), esp. 148–65, 169; Allan H. Spear, *Black Chicago: The Making of a Negro Ghetto, 1890–1920* (Chicago, 1967), esp. 51–56; George Edmund Haynes, *Negro New-Comers in Detroit, Michigan: A Challenge to Christian Statesmanship: A Preliminary Survey* (New York, 1918); Kenneth L. Kusmer, *A Ghetto Takes Shape: Black Cleveland, 1870–1930* (Urbana, 1976), esp. 35–76.

16. Drake and Cayton, *Black Metropolis*, I, 74; Weiss, *National Urban League*, 109–11, 121; Arvarh E. Strickland, *History of the Chicago Urban League* (Urbana, 1966, 56–72; Feingold, *Zion in America*, 155.

17. Howe, *World of Our Fathers*, 230; Philpott, *Slum and the Ghetto*, 165; James Weldon Johnson, "Harlem: The Culture Capital," in *The New Negro: An Interpretation*, ed. Alain Locke (New York, 1925), 309–10; Weiss, *National Urban League*, 123; Haynes, *Negro New-Comers in Detroit*, 18, 20. Raymond Wolters observes that, among students, "most blacks felt that their problem was more manageable than that of the Jews." Raymond Wolters, *The New Negro on Campus: Black College Rebellions of the 1920s* (Princeton, 1975), 326.

18. Albert Lee, *Henry Ford and the Jews* (New York, 1980), 1–47; Higham, "American Anti-Semitism Historically Reconsidered," 237–58; Arthur Liebman, "The Ties That Bind: The Jewish Support for the Left in the United States," *American Jewish Historical Quarterly* 66 (Dec. 1976): 301–302; August Meier and Elliott Rudwick, *Black*

Detroit and the Rise of the UAW (New York, 1979), 14. On Communism and the Afro-American, see Harold Cruse, *The Crisis of the Negro Intellectual* (New York, 1967), 115–80; Theodore Draper, *American Communism and Soviet Russia: The Formative Period* (New York, 1960), 315–56; Nathan Glazer, *The Social Basis of American Communism* (New York, 1961), 169–84; and Mark Naison, *Communists in Harlem during the Depression* (Urbana, 1983), esp. 3–30.

19. Philpott, *Slum and the Ghetto*, 164–65; Osofsky, *Harlem*, 139–40; Diner, *In the Almost Promised Land*, 129–31; Richard Kluger, *Simple Justice: The History of* Brown *v.* Board of Education *and Black America's Struggle for Equality* (New York, 1976), 105–25; John Hope Franklin, *From Slavery to Freedom: A History of Negro Americans* (New York, 1980), 350; White, *Man Called White*, 73–79; Ira De A. Reid, *The Negro Immigrant: His Background, Characteristics and Social Adjustment, 1899–1937* (New York, 1939), esp. 25–29; Louise Venable Kennedy, *The Negro Peasant Turns Cityward: Effects of Recent Migrations to Northern Centers* (New York, 1930), 143–69; Levy, *James Weldon Johnson*, 282–83.

20. Kellogg, *NAACP*, 47–65; Weiss, *National Urban League*, 29–70; Diner, *In the Almost Promised Land*, 151, 164–91; Berson, *Negroes and the Jews*, 81–82; Amy Jacques Garvey, comp., *Philosophy and Opinions of Marcus Garvey, or Africa for the Africans* (London, 1967), 57; Tony Martin, *Race First: The Ideological and Organizational Struggles of Marcus Garvey and the Universal Negro Improvement Association* (Westport, Conn., 1976), 300.

21. Horace M. Kallen, *Culture and Democracy in the United States* (New York, 1924); Horace M. Kallen, "Democracy versus the Melting Pot: A Study of American Nationality," *The Nation* (Feb. 18, 1915): 190–94; *ibid.* (Feb. 25, 1915): 217–20; *Harvard Encyclopedia of American Ethnic Groups*, s.v. "Jews"; Gordon, *Assimilation in American Life*, 140–50; Melvin I. Urofsky, *American Zionism from Herzl to the Holocaust* (Garden City, N.Y., 1975), 129; Shapiro, *Leadership of the American Zionist Organization*, 67–68.

22. Feingold, *Zion in America*, 219; Shapiro, *Leadership of the American Zionist Organization*, 82, 114, 167; Urofsky, *American Zionism*, 179, 318.

23. Diner, *In the Almost Promised Land*, 189, 190; Oswald Garrison Villard, *Fighting Years: Memoirs of a Liberal Editor* (New York, 1939), 529.

24. Embree and Waxman, *Investment in People*, 28–32, 101, 135–37, 143.

25. Diner, *In the Almost Promised Land*, 173. On Julius Rosenwald and the Rosenwald Fund, see Embree and Waxman, *Investment in People,*

31–33, 101–37. On white philanthropy and Afro-American education in general, see Horace Mann Bond, *The Education of the Negro in the American Social Order* (New York, 1934), 127–50; Henry Allen Bullock, *A History of Negro Education in the South: From 1619 to the Present* (Cambridge, Mass., 1967), 117–46; Louis R. Harlan, *Separate and Unequal: Public School Campaigns and Racism in the Southern Seaboard States, 1901–1915* (Chapel Hill, 1958); Kenneth R. Manning, *Black Apollo of Science: The Life of Ernest Everett Just* (New York, 1983), 115–63; David W. Southern, *The Malignant Heritage: Yankee Progressives and the Negro Question, 1901–1914* (Chicago, 1968); and John H. Stanfield, "Dollars for the Silent South: Southern White Liberalism and the Julius Rosenwald Fund, 1928–1948," *Perspectives on the American South* 2 (1984): 117–38.

26. Myrtle Evangeline Pollard, "Harlem As Is: Sociological Notes on Harlem Social Life" (2 vols., B.B.A. thesis, City College of New York, 1936), II, 55–56; Lewis, *When Harlem Was in Vogue*, 256; Philpott, *Slum and the Ghetto*, 263–69.

27. Claude McKay, *Harlem: Negro Metropolis* (New York, 1940), 143–80; Martin, *Race First*, 343; E. David Cronon, *Black Leaders of the Twentieth Century*, ed. Franklin and Meier, 105–38; Robert A. Hill, "General Introduction," in *The Marcus Garvey and Universal Negro Improvement Association Papers*, ed. Robert A. Hill (2 vols., Berkeley, 1983—), I, xxxv–xc.

28. Robert A. Hill, "The First England Years and After, 1912–1916," in *Marcus Garvey and the Vision of Africa*, ed. John Henrik Clarke and Amy Jacques Garvey (New York, 1974), 52, 65–67; W. E. B. Du Bois, "Marcus Garvey," in *ibid.*, 207; Cronon, *Black Moses*, 16–18, 19; Shapiro, *Leadership of the American Zionist Organization*, 83, 136–47; Urofsky, *American Zionism*, 250–58. For illuminating analyses of Du Boisian Pan-Africanism, see Wilson Jeremiah Moses, *The Golden Age of Black Nationalism, 1850–1925* (Hamden, Conn., 1978), 141–43; and Theodore Draper, *The Rediscovery of Black Nationalism* (New York, 1970), 48–56.

29. Du Bois, "Marcus Garvey," 207, 209; Cronon, *Black Moses*, 99–100, 106–109, 110–11; Tony Martin, "Some Aspects of the Political Ideas of Marcus Garvey," in *Marcus Garvey and the Vision of Africa*, ed. Clarke and Garvey, 434–35; Weiss, *National Urban League*, 152; Jervis Anderson, *A. Philip Randolph: A Biographical Portrait* (New York, 1973), 132–34; Martin, *Race First*, 103, 316; Theodore Kornweibel, Jr., *No Crystal Stair: Black Life and the Messenger, 1917–1928* (Westport, Conn., 1975), 137–42.

30. Kennedy, *Negro Peasant Turns Cityward*, 49–50, 131; Harvard Sitkoff,

A New Deal for Blacks: The Emergence of Civil Rights as a National Issue: The Depression Decade (New York, 1978), 3–33; Strickland, *History of the Chicago Urban League,* 64; Alain Locke, "Apropos of Africa," *Opportunity* 2 (Feb. 1924): 38, 40; "The Passing of Garvey," *ibid.,* 3 (March 1925): 66.

31. Alain Locke, "Enter the New Negro," *Survey* 53 (March 1, 1925): 631, 632, 633. Gunnar Myrdal observed that "leadership conferred upon a Negro by whites raises his class status in the Negro community." Of Afro-Americans' experience with Marcus Garvey, Ralph J. Bunche wrote: "When the curtain dropped on the Garvey theatricals, the black man of America was exactly where Garvey had found him, though a little bit sadder, perhaps a bit poorer—if not wiser." It is a statement not to be taken unqualifiedly but one that is suggestive. Gunnar Myrdal, *An American Dilemma: The Negro Problem and Modern Democracy* (2 vols., New York, 1944), II, 727, 748.

32. August Meier and Elliott Rudwick, "Attorneys Black and White: A Case Study of Race Relations Within the NAACP," in August Meier and Elliott Rudwick, *Along the Color Line: Explorations in the Black Experience* (Urbana, 1976), 130; Kluger, *Simple Justice,* 113–14, 125.

33. Diner, *In the Almost Promised Land,* 131; Berson, *Negroes and the Jews,* 97.

34. Diner, *In the Almost Promised Land,* 128; Parris and Brooks, *Blacks in the City,* 39, 201–203; Weiss, *National Urban League,* 156–57. A typical Alfred Stern letter instructed James Weldon Johnson to "set aside Saturday evening, February 28, for a reading to a group of our friends. Mrs. Stern and I should be delighted to have both you and Mrs. Johnson at our home for dinner that evening." Alfred Stern to James Weldon Johnson, Jan. 14, 1931, folio 413, series 1, James Weldon Johnson Memorial Collection (Beinecke Rare Book and Manuscript Library, Yale University, New Haven, Conn.).

35. Lewis, *When Harlem Was in Vogue,* 119–97; Lewis, "Dr. Johnson's Friends"; David Levering Lewis, "The Politics of Art: The New Negro, 1920–1935," *Prospects* 3 (1977): 237–61; Fullinwider, *Mind and Mood of Black America,* 119; Van Wyck Brooks, *The Confident Years: 1855–1915* (New York, 1952), 544–51; Arthur Frank Wertheim, *The New York Little Renaissance: Iconoclasm, Modernism, and Nationalism in American Culture, 1908–1917* (New York, 1976), 3–17.

36. Charles S. Johnson, "An Opportunity for Negro Writers," *Opportunity* 2 (Sept. 1924): 258; Gilpin, "Charles S. Johnson," 238; Langston Hughes, *The Big Sea: An Autobiography* (New York, 1975),

218; Carolyn W. Sylvander, "Jessie Redmon Fauset: Black American Writer: Her Relationships, Biographical and Literary, with Black and White Writers, 1910–1935" (Ph.D. diss., University of Wisconsin, 1976), 71–73; Hiroko Sato, "Under the Harlem Shadow: A Study of Jessie Fauset and Nella Larsen," in *Harlem Renaissance Remembered*, ed. Bontemps, 108; Zora Neale Hurston, *Dust Tracks on a Road: An Autobiography* (Philadelphia, 1971), 168; "Arna Bontemps Talks about the Harlem Renaissance," in "The Harlem Renaissance Generation: An Anthology," comp. and ed. L. M. Collins, typescript, 1972, 2 vols., I, 216 (Fisk University Library, Nashville, Tenn.); "Aaron Douglas Chats about the Harlem Renaissance," in *ibid.*, 181–82, 184; Ethel Ray Nance interview by Ann A. Schockley, transcript, 43, Fisk University Oral History Program (Fisk University Library); Lewis, *When Harlem Was in Vogue*, 119–97; Lewis, "Politics of Art," 237–61; Elinor Des Verney Sinnette, "Arthur Alfonso Schomburg, Black Bibliophile and Curator: His Contribution to the Collection and Dissemination of Materials about Africans and Peoples of African Descent" (D.L.S. diss., Columbia University, 1977), 111; Charles F. Cooney, "Forgotten Philanthropy: The Amy Spingarn Prizes," typescript, 1–25 (in Lewis's possession); Darwin T. Turner, *In a Minor Chord: Three Afro-American Writers and Their Search for Identity* (Carbondale, Ill., 1971).

37. Lewis, *When Harlem Was in Vogue*, 138–40; Waldron, *Walter White and the Harlem Renaissance*, 113–66.

38. Alain Locke, "Art of Propaganda," *Harlem* 1 (Nov. 1928): 12; Robert T. Kerlin, "Conquest by Poetry," *Southern Workman* 56 (June 1927): 283; Johnson, "Race Prejudice and the Negro Artist," 776.

39. W. E. B. Du Bois, "Criteria of Negro Art," *The Crisis* 32 (Oct. 1926): 294; Wallace Thurman, *Infants of the Spring* (New York, 1932), 234; Ralph J. Bunche, "Extended Memorandum on the Programs, Ideologies, Tactics and Achievements of Negro Betterment Interracial Organizations: A Research Memorandum," (June 7, 1940): 144, Carnegie-Myrdal Study: The Negro in America, Special Collections (Schomburg Center for Research in Black Culture, New York Public Library, New York City).

40. Lewis, *When Harlem Was in Vogue*, 102–103; Willie the Lion Smith and George Hoefer, *Music on My Mind: The Memoirs of an American Pianist* (Garden City, N.Y., 1964), 131–79; Rudolph Fisher, "The Caucasian Storms Harlem," *American Mercury* 11 (Aug. 1927): 393–98; Artie Shaw, *The Trouble with Cinderella: An Outline of Identity* (New York, 1952), 223–24, Samuel B. Charters and Leonard Kunstadt, *Jazz: A History of the New York Scene* (Garden City,

N.Y., 1962), 82–238; Eileen Southern, *The Music of Black Americans: A History* (New York, 1971), 374–446; Doris E. Abramson, *Negro Playwrights in the American Theatre, 1925–1959* (New York, 1969), 22–88.

41. Locke, "Apropos of Africa," 40; Kelly Miller, "Before the Negro Becomes One with the Rest of the American People, He Must Become One with Himself," in *Black Nationalism in America*, ed. John H. Bracey, Jr., August Meier, and Elliott Rudwick (Indianapolis, 1970), 349–65; Levy, *James Weldon Johnson*, 115–16; Diner, *In the Almost Promised Land*, 153. A *Messenger* editorial declared: "Hitting the Jew is helping the Negro. Why? Negroes have large numbers and small money: Jews have small numbers and large money." Bloom, "Interaction between Blacks and Jews," 82.

42. Sitkoff, *New Deal for Blacks*, 170; Charles S. Johnson, "The Balance Sheet: Debits and Credits in Negro-White Relations," *World Tomorrow* 11 (Jan. 1928): 15.

43. McKay, *Harlem*, 184; Bunche, "Extended Memorandum on the Programs," 145–48; Ross, *J. E. Spingarn*, 182–85; Sitkoff, *New Deal for Blacks*, 250–51; John B. Kirby, *Black Americans in the Roosevelt Era: Liberalism and Race* (Knoxville, 1980), 177–78.

44. Diner, *In the Almost Promised Land*, 153.

IV

Afro-American Biography
in Historical Analysis

Uses of the Self

AFRO–AMERICAN AUTOBIOGRAPHY

Nathan I. Huggins

Let us consider the whys and wherefores of autobiography, the idea of writing the story of one's life and making it available to the public. What motivates one to make one's life (or at least some version of one's life) a matter of public record? Can one tell the truth, the whole truth about himself? Can one, in fact, know the whole truth? And, for the reader, what is it about any individual life that can make it of value?

Both biography and autobiography presume the importance of the individual either to the course of history or, at least, to an understanding of the human predicament. Historians have argued (and continue to argue) about the "great man" in history, whether or not we learn more or less by looking at history as it refracts off of dominant individual personalities. It has for many years been accepted by historians that individuals have little effect on the course of history, and that while personalities may be interesting in themselves and may help us to see or relive events, the main historical currents would remain much as they are if some of the most storied individuals had never lived. Furthermore, some have argued that subjectivity and, therefore, distortions are more likely in biography as well as autobiography. For those of us who are interested in Afro-American life and history, the problems of biography are especially acute because (given the nature of the sources and testimony) we are most dependent on the stories of individuals as told by themselves or others.[1]

Biography and autobiography are fundamentally different. The biographer is a person outside the self who has determined that a particular life is significant, that it is dramatic, that it has public interest, and that it introduces a reader into some world (or, better, some views of the world) otherwise not available. The biographer, not being the subject, may be critical and tough on his subject, but he could also be filled with awe and adulation, a hero worshipper. Whatever, the biographer has the advantage of distance and is expected to provide a somewhat objective perspective on the subject. In contrast, autobiographers—those writing about their own lives—stand within the life—privy to all there is to know, but clearly interested in a personal and subjective way about the impression the life-story will make.

Autobiography requires that a person be persuaded that his or her life is important, or that his or her views on events and circumstances are special, that a person sees events as unique and valuable to the world.

Ordinarily, we value autobiography not only for its special perspective, but for its truth and accuracy, for the authority of a first-hand account. We do not, of course, value dubious versions of life-stories, but sometimes we are willing to suspend disbelief if the story is good enough.

We know, nonetheless, that with all of us there can be versions (or various possible explanations) of the facts of our lives and experiences. We have only to discuss the same event with others who shared the experience with us—wife or husband, children or parents. Each may tell a strikingly different version of the same event. Is only one version true? Are they all true?

So it is with each of us, and so it is with the person who writes his or her life-story. Choices are made—selecting out, limiting, excluding, emphasizing—all for the purpose of meaning.

If memory were like a moving picture camera—recording, nonstop, throughout a life, capturing the whole of it—one would need herculean energies to edit the resulting film to make it concise and meaningful. The autobiographer makes exactly such choices from a less-than-perfect memory—choosing focus, highlighting, repressing, and emphasizing what he or she thinks is crucial to the meaning of the work and the life.

I would like now to direct your attention to a few choices made in certain well-known, black autobiographies. In doing so, there are two important points I want to make: (1) Autobiographers use their lives (or aspects or versions of their lives) to instruct, demonstrate, or illuminate some larger issues. Autobiographies of whites are usually of celebrities or persons who have had some crucial role in historically significant institutions or events. Usually, for Afro-American autobiography, it is race, itself, and the conditions of race in America that provide the most compelling aspect of their lives. (2) The Afro-American biography generally has a racial and social meaning larger than the particular life portrayed; the life comes to exemplify the need for reform.

Identity, of course, is the core ingredient in any biography. Because identity is a central problem of the Afro-American condition, in one way or another, "who am I, really?" persists as the essential question to be asked and answered. As with all blacks who were born in slavery, the problem of identity may have been "where was I born, and who were my parents?" In another time, the central question might have to do with the trauma of self-consciousness of race, of being black. Or, again, that trauma of self-consciousness might be at the arrival of militant commitment to the cause of racial reform (the discovery of a truth or a strategy by which one would reorder life). Central to all of the problems is the peculiar Afro-American dilemma of being both black and an American.

Autobiographies of former slaves uniformly begin with a statement about birth, place of birth, and parentage. In Frederick Douglass's *Narrative of the Life of Frederick Douglass, an American Slave* (1845) we have this opening paragraph:

> I was born in Tuckahoe, near Hillsborough, and about twelve miles from Easton, in Talbot County, Maryland. I have no accurate knowledge of my age, never having seen any authentic record containing it. By far the larger part of the slaves know as little of their ages as horses know of theirs, and it is the wish of most masters within my knowledge to keep their slaves thus ignorant.[2]

One cannot but notice the balance of detail and vagueness. The fugitive in autobiography needed the detail for sake of authenticity. So, Douglass would seem to mark the precise place of his birth.

But the fugitive has polemic points to make, and so he is vague about both the date of his birth and his exact parentage.[3] The slave is little better than the horse. In later versions of his autobiography (1855, 1880), Douglass remembered his mother and grandmother with fuller and loving detail. He knew more than he had intention of telling in his first effort, where he made his life into an abolitionist tract.[4]

Or, consider Booker T. Washington, also born in slavery. He begins his *Up From Slavery,* 1901, with these sentences:

> I was born a slave on a plantation in Franklin County, Virginia. I am not quite sure of the exact place or exact date of my birth, but at any rate I suspect I must have been born somewhere and at some time.[5]

In this we find the same pattern of detail and vagueness. With Washington, however, a tone of humor of the stage rustic is used to make light his slave origins. Neither his style, nor his strategy, nor his autobiography was angry or polemic. What is remembered and what is forgotten in the telling of his life-story serve to bury the past or personal claims because of the past. "I was born, sometime and somewhere, and I am here, and that's all that matters. I don't care to remember the pain of the past, and I give you permission also to suppress it."

The consciousness of one's self as different, as black, is revealed in many ways. We are familiar with the story W. E. B. Du Bois tells in *The Souls of Black Folk* when the white girl refuses his visiting card, causing him to see himself as if for the first time as different, as an outcast, as marginal, as removed from normal society by the "veil."[6]

Malcolm X revealed this awareness of race as if it were innate, encoded in the womb, so to speak. His story begins in violence:

> When my mother was pregnant with me, *she told me later,* a party of hooded Ku Klux Klan riders galloped up to our home in Omaha, Nebraska, one night. Surrounding the house, brandishing their shotguns and rifles, they shouted for my father to come out. . . . The Klansmen shouted threats and warnings at her that we had better get out of town because "the good Christian white people" were not going to stand for my father's "spreading trouble" among

"good" Negroes of Omaha with the "back to Africa" preachings of Marcus Garvey.[7]

For Malcolm, race consciousness came with his mother's milk, and the presumption of struggle and violence seemed to come with it.

As Eldridge Cleaver told it, the events and discussion following the *Brown* decision in 1954 were what awakened him as a black and a revolutionary:

> This controversy awakened me to my position in America and I began to form a concept of what it means to be black in white America.
>
> Of course I'd always known that I was black, but I'd never really stopped to take stock of what I was involved in. I met life as an individual and took my chances. Prior to 1954, we lived in an atmosphere of Novocain.[8]

However the black subject negotiates the problem of identity, the object of his autobiography is to present the self as exemplary. Autobiographies such as those of Douglass and Washington used the self to show the white world the humanity and potentiality of blacks. The selves they constructed in their life-stories could stand as models of manhood, achievement, and virtue. For the bulk of the black population, they could be seen as role models, and they were meant to suggest that within the black masses were others like themselves.

Douglass's qualities could include manliness (in his defeat of the overseer, Covey), an immanent sense of freedom which could not be denied, and, later, in his life, statesmanship. Similarly, Booker T. Washington used his life, through his autobiography, to be exemplary of the black man's potentialities. His work is filled with moralistic pronouncements for the benefit of blacks as well as for his image to whites. Blacks could use him and his life as a model, and whites could find in his life a reflection of their own best expectations for blacks.

Of course, exemplars are not necessarily always conventional heroic types like Douglass and Washington. In a time of revolutionary spirit, the exemplar can also be an anti-hero. Such, I believe, were Malcolm X and Eldridge Cleaver. Their lives were used to exemplify a critique and challenge of the system, and they became symbols of defiance.

W. E. B. Du Bois represents a somewhat different case. Much of his writing merges autobiography with poetry, exposition, and other styles and genres. Works like *The Souls of Black Folk* and *Dusk of Dawn* are, in fact, mixed genres. They represent a distinctly different idea of self-concept. Du Bois sees his life as a lens opening onto a world much larger than the self, as revealed in the subtitle of *Dusk of Dawn,* which is *Autobiography of a Race Concept.* From the beginning, Du Bois raises fundamental questions about self-concept. Unlike Douglass and Washington, he cannot simply assume a Negro self, as we see in this famous passage known to us all:

> After the Egyptian and Indian, the Greek and Roman, the Teuton and Mongolian, the Negro is a sort of seventh son, born with a veil and gifted with second sight in this American world—a world which yields him no true self consciousness, but only lets him see himself through the revelation of the other world. It is a peculiar sensation, this double consciousness, this sense of always looking at one's self through the eyes of others, of measuring one's soul by the tape of a world that looks on in amused contempt and pity. One ever feels his twoness,—an American, a Negro; two souls, two thoughts, two unreconciled strivings.[9]

Here, the object and the use of the self is to arrive at a better self-consciousness (a truer self-consciousness), an analysis of the fundamental problem of the Afro-American in the American world. It is set in terms of paradox and tension.

To discover the sources of this concept, we need to consider Du Bois's philosophical influence—Hegel's *Phenomenology of the Spirit*—as understood through Du Bois's teachers, Josiah Royce, George Santayana, and William James.

The central idea is the essential need of a context in which to find the self. The "veil" becomes the hindrance for the true American consciousness. The Sorrow Songs of blacks become the metaphor for the potentiality. But the dialectic needs a tension which the "veil" seems to deny.

NOTES

1. I allude here to the character of historical sources in Afro-American history, especially until the early decades of the twentieth century. Narratives, autobiographies, and biographies predominate. Recent methodological developments in social, economic, and political history which exploit quantifiable sources make the hitherto heavy reliance on historical personalities less dominant, but histories written from these sources have yet to make commanding inroads into Afro-American historical literature.

2. Frederick Douglass, *Narrative of the Life of Frederick Douglass, an American Slave* (New York, 1982), 47.

3. Douglass implies in the next paragraphs that his father was his mother's owner, and his mother remains quite a shadowy figure.

4. Dickson J. Preston in *Young Frederick Douglass* (Baltimore, 1980) is very revealing on this point.

5. Booker T. Washington, *Up From Slavery* (New York, 1965), 15.

6. W. E. B. Du Bois, *The Souls of Black Folk* (New York, 1953), 2.

7. Malcolm X, *The Autobiography of Malcolm X* (New York, 1964), 1.

8. Eldridge Cleaver, *Soul on Ice* (New York, 1968), 3. This quote is notably in a chapter entitled, "On Becoming."

9. *The Souls of Black Folk,* 3.

Beyond Amnesia

MARTIN LUTHER KING, JR.
AND THE FUTURE OF AMERICA

Vincent G. Harding

In the 1970s, as a fascinating variety of voices began to press the nation to decide where it stood concerning the memory and meaning of Martin Luther King, Jr., and as we instinctively sought an easy way to deal with the unrelenting power of this disturber of all unjust peace, a black poet perhaps best reflected our ambivalence. Carl Wendell Hines, Jr., wrote:

> Now that he is safely dead
> let us praise him
>   build monuments to his glory
>   sing hosannas to his name.
>   Dead men make
>   such convenient heroes; They
>   cannot rise
>   To challenge the images
>   we would fashion from their lives.
>   And besides,
>   it is easier to build monuments
>   than to make a better world.[1]

Then as the voices of artists and family and millions of black people (and their votes, and their nonblack allies) began to build, the sad wisdom of Hines's words seemed to sharpen and to cut deeper at every moment. For it became increasingly clear that most of those who were leading the campaign for the national holiday had chosen, consciously or unconsciously, to allow King to become a convenient hero, to try to tailor him to the shape and mood of mainstream, liberal/moderate America.

Symbolic of the direction given the campaign has been the unremitting focus on the 1963 March on Washington, the never-ending repetition of the great speech and its dream metaphor, the sometimes innocent and sometimes manipulative boxing of King into the relatively safe categories of "civil rights leader," "great orator," harmless dreamer of black and white children on the hillside. And surely nothing could be more ironic or amnesiac than having Vice President George Bush, the former head of the Central Intelligence Agency, the probable White House overseer of Contra actions, speaking words in King's honor. Or was it more ironic to watch the representatives of the Marine Corps, carrying fresh memories from the invasion of Grenada and from their training for Libya and for Nicaragua, playing "We Shall Overcome," while the bust of the prince of nonviolence was placed in the Capitol rotunda, without a word being spoken about nonviolence?

It appears as if the price for the first national holiday honoring a black man is the development of a massive case of national amnesia concerning who that black man really was. At both personal and collective levels, of course, it is often the case that amnesia is not ultimately harmful to the patient. However, in this case it is very dangerous, for the things we have chosen to forget about King (and about ourselves) constitute some of the most hopeful possibilities and resources for our magnificent and very needy nation. Indeed, I would suggest that we Americans have chosen amnesia rather than continue King's painful, uncharted, and often disruptive struggle toward a more perfect union. I would also suggest that those of us who are historians and citizens have a special responsibility to challenge the loss of memory, in ourselves and others, to allow our skills in probing the past to become resources for healing and for hope, not simply sources of pages in books or of steps in careers. In other words, if as Hines wrote, Martin King "cannot rise to challenge" those who would make him a harmless black icon, then *we* surely can—assuming that we are still alive.

Although there are many points at which our challenge to the comfortable images might be raised, I believe that the central encounters with King that begin to take us beyond the static March-on-Washington, "integrationist," "civil rights leader" image are located in Chicago and Mississippi in 1966. During the winter of that year King moved North. He was driven by the fires of Watts and the early hot summers of 1964 and 1965. Challenged and nurtured by the powerful commitment of Malcolm X to the black street forces, he was also compelled by his own deep compassion for the urban black community—whose peculiar problems were not fundamentally addressed by the civil rights laws so dearly won in the South. Under such urgent compulsion, King left his familiar Southern base and stepped out on very unfamiliar turf. For Hamlin Avenue on Chicago's blighted West Side was a long way from the marvelous, costly victories of Selma, St. Augustine, and Birmingham, and Mayor Richard Daley was a consummate professional compared with the sheriffs, mayors, and police commissioners of the South. But King had made his choice, and it is one that we dare not forget.

By 1966 King had made an essentially religious commitment to the poor, and he was prepared to say:

> I choose to identify with the underprivileged. I choose to identify with the poor. I choose to give my life for the hungry. I choose to give my life for those who have been left out of the sunlight of opportunity. I choose to live for and with those who find themselves seeing life as a long and desolate corridor with no exit sign. This is the way I'm going. If it means suffering a little bit, I'm going that way. If it means sacrificing, I'm going that way. If it means dying for them, I'm going that way, because I heard a voice saying, "Do something for others."[2]

We understand nothing about the King whose life ended in the midst of a struggle for garbage workers if we miss that earlier offering of himself to the struggle against poverty in America, to the continuing battle for the empowerment of the powerless—in this nation, in Vietnam, in South Africa, in Central America, and beyond.

In a sense, it was that commitment that took him from Chicago to Mississippi in the late spring of 1966, as he responded to the attempted assassination of James Meredith, taking up with others that enigmatic hero's "march against fear." There on the highways of the Magnolia State we have a second crucial encounter with the forgotten King. He was an embattled leader, the King who was challenged, chastened, and inspired by the courageous, foolhardy Young Turks of the Student Nonviolent Coordinating Committee. He was attentive to those veterans of the struggle who raised the cry for "Black Power," who made public the long-simmering challenge to King's leadership, who increasingly voiced their doubts about the primacy of nonviolence as a way of struggle, and who seemed prepared to read whites out of the movement. Perhaps the most important aspect of the Meredith March for King's development was the question the young people raised in many forms: "Dr. King, why do you want us to love white folks before we even love ourselves?" From then on the issues of black self-love, of black and white power, and of the need to develop a more militant form of nonviolence that could challenge and enlist the rising rage of urban black youth were never far from King's consciousness. Along with his deepening commitment to the poor, those were the subjects and questions that did much to shape the hero we have forgotten.

One of the reasons for our amnesia, of course, is the fact that the forgotten King is not easy to handle now. Indeed, he never was. In 1967, after spending two hectic weeks traveling with the impassioned black prophet, a perceptive journalist, David Halberstam, reported that

> King has decided to represent the ghettos; he will work in them and speak for them. But their voice is harsh and alienated. If King is to speak for them truly, then his voice must reflect theirs; it too must be alienated, and it is likely to be increasingly at odds with the rest of American society.[3]

Halberstam was right, but only partly so. After the Selma marches of 1965, King's voice did sound harsher in its criticism of the mainstream American way of life and its dominant values—including the assumption that the United States had the right to police the world for "free enterprise." Not only did the white mainstream object to such uncompromising criticism from a "civil rights leader" who was supposed to know his place, but respectable black people were increasingly uncomfortable as well.[4] For some of them were making use of the fragile doorways that the freedom movement had helped open. Others, after years of frustration, were finally being promoted into the positions of responsibility and higher earnings that their skills and experience should have earlier made available. Too often, King was considered a threat to them as well, especially as his commitment to the poor drove him to increasingly radical assessments of the systemic flaws in the American economic order, an order they had finally begun to enjoy.

But Halberstam, a man of words, saw only part of the picture. King did more than *speak* for the ghettos. He was committed to mobilizing and organizing them for self-liberating action. That was his deeper threat to the status quo, beyond words, beyond alienation. That was what King's friend Rabbi Abraham Heschel surely understood when he introduced King to an assembly of rabbis in these words: "Martin Luther King is a voice, a vision, and a way. I call upon every Jew to harken to his voice, to share his vision, to follow in his way. The whole future of America will depend on the impact and influence of Dr. King."[5]

Part of what we have forgotten, then, is King's vision, beyond the appealing dream of black and white children holding hands, beyond the necessary goal of "civil rights." From the outset, he held a vision for all America, often calling the black movement more than a quest for rights—a struggle "to redeem the soul of America." By the end of his life, no one who paid attention could mistake the depth and meaning of that vision. At the convention of the Southern Christian Leadership Conference (SCLC) in 1967, King announced, "We must go from this convention and say, 'America, you must be born again . . . your whole structure must be changed.' " He insisted that "the problem of racism, the problem of economic exploitation, and the problem of war are all tied together." These, King said, were "the triple evils" that the freedom movement must address as it set itself to the challenge of "restructuring the whole of American society." This was the vision behind the call he issued in his final public speech in Memphis on April 3, 1968: "Let us move on in these powerful days, these days of challenge to make America what it ought to be. We have an opportunity to make America a better nation."[6]

That final speech was delivered to a crowd of some two thousand persons, mostly black residents of Memphis who had come out in a soaking rain to hear King and to support the garbage workers' union in its struggle for justice. King's challenge to his last movement audience reminds us that he also carried a large and powerful vision concerning the role of black people and others of the "disinherited" in American society. His vision always included more than "rights" or "equal opportunity." On December 5, 1955, at the public meeting that launched the Montgomery bus boycott and Martin Luther King, Jr., into the heart of twentieth-century history, King had announced,

> We, the disinherited of this land, we who have been oppressed so long, are tired of going through the long night of captivity. And now we are reaching out for the daybreak of freedom and justice and equality.

As a result of that decision and that movement, King said,

> When the history books are written in the future somebody will have to say "There lived a race of people, of black people, fleecy locks and black complexion, a people who had the moral courage to stand up for their rights, and thereby they injected a new meaning into the veins of history and of civilization." And we're gonna do that. God grant that we will do it before it's too late.[7]

From beginning to end, the grand vision, the magnificent obsession never left him, the audacious hope for America and its disinherited. Only in the light of that dual vision can we understand his voice, especially in its increasing alienation from the mainstream, in its urgent movement beyond the black and white civil rights establishment. In his last years, the vision led him to call repeatedly for "a reconstruction of the entire society, a revolution of values."[8] Only as we recapture the wholeness of King's vision can we understand his conclusion in 1967 that "something is wrong with capitalism as it now stands in the United States." Only then can we grasp his words to his co-workers in SCLC: "We are not interested in being integrated into *this* value structure. Power must be relocated." The vision leads directly to the voice, calling for "a radical redistribution of economic and political power" as the only way to meet the real needs of the poor in America.[9]

When our memories allow us to absorb King's vision of a transformed America and a transforming force of black people and their allies, then we understand his powerful critique of the American war in Vietnam. After he struggled with his conscience about how open to make his opposition, after he endured intense pressure to be quiet from Washington and from the civil rights establishment, King's social vision and his religious faith stood him in good stead. He spoke out in a stirring series of statements and actions and declared:

> Never again will I be silent on an issue that is destroying the soul of our nation and destroying thousands and thousands of little children in Vietnam . . . the time has come for a real prophecy, and I'm willing to go that road.[10]

Of course, King knew the costly way of prophets—as did the rabbi who called us "to follow in his way." We must assume that neither the black prophet nor his Jewish brother was speaking idle words, opening up frivolous ways. Rather those were visions, voices, and ways not meant to be forgotten.

Indeed, in a nation where the gap between rich and poor continues to expand with cruel regularity, where the numbers of black and Hispanic poor vie with each other for supremacy, where farmers and industrial workers are in profound crisis, where racism continues to proclaim its ruthless American presence, who can afford to forget King's compassionate and courageous movement toward justice? When the leaders of the country spew reams of lies to Congress and the people alike, in public and private statements, when the official keepers of the nation's best hopes seem locked in what King called "paranoid anti-communism," when we make cynical mercenaries out of jobless young people, sacrificing them to a rigid militarism that threatens the future of the world, do we dare repress the memory of a man who called us to struggle bravely toward "the daybreak of freedom and justice and equality"? Dare we forget a man who told us that "a nation that continues year after year to spend more money on military defense than on programs of social uplift is approaching spiritual death"?[11]

Clearly, we serve our scholarship and our citizenship most faithfully when we move ourselves and others beyond amnesia toward encounters with the jagged leading edges of King's prophetic vision. When we do that we recognize that Martin King himself was unclear about many aspects of the "way" he had chosen. In his commitment to the poor, in his search for the redistribution of wealth and power in America, in his relentless stand against war, in his determination to help America "repent of her modern economic imperialism," he set out on a largely uncharted way. Still, several polestars pointed the way for him, and they may suggest creative directions for our personal and collective lives.

As King searched for a way for Americans to press the nation toward its best possibilities, toward its next birth of freedom and justice, he held fast to several basic assumptions. Perhaps it will help to remember them:

1. He seemed convinced that in the last part of the twentieth century, anyone who still held a vision of "a more perfect union" and worked toward that goal had to be prepared to move toward fundamental, structural changes in the mainstream values, economic and political structures, and traditional leadership of American society.

2. King believed that those who are committed to a real, renewed war against poverty in America must recognize the connections between our domestic economic and political problems and the unhealthy position that we occupy in the military, economic, and political wards of the global community. In other words, what King called "the triple evils

of racism, extreme materialism and militarism" could be effectively fought only by addressing their reality and relationships in our life at home and abroad.[12]

3. Unlike many participants in current discussions of poverty and "the underclass" in American society, King assumed that his ultimate commitment was to help find the ways by which the full energies and angers of the poor could be challenged, organized, and engaged in a revolutionary process that confronted the status quo and opened creative new possibilities for them and for the nation. Surely this was what he meant when he said

> the dispossessed of this nation—the poor, both white and Negro—live in a cruelly unjust society. They must organize a revolution against that injustice, not against the lives of . . . their fellow citizens, but against the structures through which the society is refusing to lift . . . the load of poverty.[13]

4. By the last months of his life, as King reflected on the developments in the freedom movement since its energies had turned northward and since some of its participants had begun to offer more radical challenges to the policies of the federal government at home and abroad, he reached an inescapable conclusion. The next stages of the struggle for a just American order could no longer expect even the reluctant support from the national government that the movement had received since Montgomery. Now, he said, "we must formulate a program and we must fashion the new tactics which do not count on government goodwill, but instead serve to compel unwilling authorities to yield to the mandates of justice."[14]

5. Defying most of the conventional wisdom of black and white America, King determined to hold fast to both of his fundamental, religiously based commitments: to the humanizing empowerment and transformation of the poor and of the nation, and to the way of nonviolence and creative peace making. His attempt to create a Poor People's Campaign to challenge—and, if necessary, to disrupt—the federal government on its home ground was an expression of this wild and

beautiful experiment in creating nonviolent revolution. Planning for a massive campaign of civil disobedience carried on by poor people of all races, aided by their un-poor allies, King announced, "We've got to make it known that until our problem is solved, America may have many, many days, but they will be full of trouble. There will be no rest, there will be no tranquility in this country until the nation comes to terms with [that problem]."[15]

For those who seek a gentle, non-abrasive hero whose recorded speeches can be used as inspirational resources for rocking our memories to sleep, Martin Luther King, Jr., is surely the wrong man. However, if there is even a chance that Rabbi Heschel was correct, that the untranquil King and his peace-disturbing vision, words, and deeds hold the key to the future of America, then another story unfolds, another search begins. We who are scholars and citizens then owe ourselves, our children, and our nation a far more serious exploration and comprehension of the man and the widespread movement with which he was identified.

Recently, the Afro-American liberation theologian Cornel West said of King, "As a proponent of nonviolent resistance, he holds out the only slim hope for social sanity in a violence-prone world."[16] What if both the black theologian and the Jewish scholar-mystic are correct? What if the way that King was exploring is indeed vital to the future of our nation and our world? For scholars, citizens, or celebrants to forget the real man and his deepest implications would be not only faithless, but also suicidal. For in the light of the news that inundates us every day, where else do we go from here to make a better world?

NOTES

1. Ira G. Zepp, Jr., and Melvyn D. Palmer, eds., *Drum Major for a Dream: Poetic Tributes to Martin Luther King, Jr.* (Thompson, Conn., 1977), 23.
2. David J. Garrow, *Bearing the Cross: Martin Luther King, Jr., and the Southern Christian Leadership Conference* (New York, 1986), 524.

3. David Halberstam, "The Second Coming of Martin Luther King, Jr.," *Harper's*, 235 (Aug. 1967): 46.

4. James M. Washington, ed., *A Testament of Hope: The Essential Writings of Martin Luther King, Jr.* (San Francisco, 1986), 189–94, 340–77; Garrow, *Bearing the Cross*, 539–40; Stephen B. Oates, *Let the Trumpet Sound* (New York, 1982), 367–69. For examples of such objections to King's critical stance, see Garrow, *Bearing the Cross*, 469–70, 496–97.

5. Oates, *Trumpet*, 473.

6. Washington, ed., *Testament*, 250–51, 285.

7. Martin Luther King, Jr., "Address at Holt Street Baptist Church," Dec. 5, 1955, Martin Luther King, Jr., Papers (Martin Luther King, Jr., Center for Nonviolent Social Change, Atlanta, Georgia).

8. For such language in King's speeches, articles, and sermons, see Washington, ed., *Testament*, 240–43, 250–51, 314–23. See also Oates, *Trumpet*, 441–42; and Garrow, *Bearing the Cross*, 553.

9. Garrow, *Bearing the Cross*, 581; Washington, ed., *Testament*, 314–15; Garrow, *Bearing the Cross*, 563–64.

10. For the full text of the central document, Martin Luther King, Jr., "Beyond Vietnam," Riverside Church, New York, April 4, 1967, see Washington, ed., *Testament*, 231–44. For an exploration of King's movement toward his position of radical opposition, see also Garrow, *Bearing the Cross*, 527–74.

11. In a 1968 speech, King condemned "irrational obsessive anti-communism" in America. Martin Luther King, Jr., "Honoring Dr. Du Bois," *Freedomways* 8 (Spring 1968): 109. King, "Address at Holt Street Baptist Church"; Washington, ed., *Testament*, 241.

12. For instance, see Washington, ed., *Testament*, 240, 250, 315; and Garrow, *Bearing the Cross*, 552.

13. For a summary of the debate on poverty, see *Newsweek* (Oct. 21, 1985): 84, 87. Examples of King's resolve to organize the poor for nonviolent militant challenges to the status quo are found throughout his post-1965 conversations, speeches, and writings. See, for example, Garrow, *Bearing the Cross*, 575–624; as well as Martin Luther King, Jr., *The Trumpet of Conscience* (New York, 1968), 59–64. For King's statement on the dispossessed, see *ibid.*, 59–60.

14. Garrow, *Bearing the Cross*, 581.

15. *Ibid.*, 580.

16. Cornel West, "The Religious Foundations of Martin Luther King, Jr.'s Thought," paper presented at the conference, "Martin Luther King, Jr.: The Leader and the Legacy," Washington, Oct. 16, 1986 (in Cornel West's possession).

V

*Content and Context
in Historical Interpretation*

Before Color Prejudice

BLACK-WHITE RELATIONS IN
THE ANCIENT MEDITERRANEAN WORLD

Frank M. Snowden, Jr.

Who are the blacks of this essay? They are the blacks of the oldest, reliably attested chapter in the annals of black-white encounters. We are most fully informed about the blacks who came from a region of the Nile Valley south of Egypt, designated frequently in Egyptian texts and the Old Testament as Kush, and by classical and early Christian authors most frequently as Ethiopia but sometimes as Nubia. Several other peoples described as Ethiopians are also reported to have lived in various parts of Northwest Africa. What were the physical characteristics of these African blacks? Classical authors in detailed descriptions and ancient artists in realistic portraits have provided copious information on this point. Many of these black Africans bore a close resemblance to racial types designated in the modern world as "colored," "Negro," and "black."

As early as the beginning of this century, even before the copious and widely scattered iconographic and written evidence relating to blacks in antiquity had been collected and studied, scholars were already commenting on the absence of color prejudice in the Greek and Roman world. In 1902, Lord Bryce[1] observed that in the Roman Empire we hear little of any repugnance to dark-skinned Africans. Evelyn Baring,[2] the Earl of Cromer (1910), wrote that color antipathy, by itself, formed no bar to social intercourse; and E. E. Sikes (1914)[3] noted that the ancients were quite free from the color bar. The Greeks, according to A. E. Zimmern (1931),[4] showed no trace of color prejudice, and in 1948 wrote to me that it was gratifying to know that his generalization, made in a footnote many years ago had stood the test of time and had been verified by careful scholarship. Among other early observations on the absence of anti-black bias in antiquity were those of W. L. Westermann[5] that Greek society had no color line, and of T. J. Haarhoff (1948)[6] that there had never been any color prejudice in Italy.

The first detailed study of blacks in antiquity, *The Negro in Greek and Roman Civilization: A Study of the Ethiopian Type* (1929) by G. H. Beardsley, however, made scant use of pertinent Greek sources and devoted only nineteen pages to the Negro in Roman art and literature. Further, there was a tendency in this pioneer study to see color prejudice where none existed, and to make general statements about blacks on the basis of a few lines from a single author or a few texts without considering the total image of blacks in the ancient world.

Beardsley stated, for example, that Juvenal summed up racial feeling in the words *derideat Aethiopem albus* (let the white man laugh at the Ethiopian). In the same vein, D. S. Wiesen[7] interpreted this and similar black-white contrasts in Juvenal as a "kind of insult to nature and to nature's proper product—the white man." According to Wiesen, these same black-white contrasts are proof that the satirist despised the physical being of blacks and attached "a special stigma to the physical attributes of blacks and finds in them faults that are neither of their own making nor capable of being corrected." What both Beardsley and Wiesen and a few others cite as evidence of anti-black bias in Juvenal is merely a reflection of a narcissistic canon of physical beauty, something found in all societies, black included. Even Juvenal himself recognized such an ethnocentric standard when he wrote that

Germans with blue eyes and yellow hair (greasy curls twisted into a horn) evoke no astonishment in their native land because their physical traits are common. Similarly, the satirist adds, no one would laugh at Pygmies in Africa because the whole population is no taller than one foot. There is nothing strange about a preference for a "white" type of beauty in predominantly white society or a preference for a "black" type among blacks. But what was unusual was the fact that in the predominantly white Greek and Roman societies there were those who rejected a somatic norm image of "whiteness," others who extolled the beauty of blackness, and still others with preference for blacks who had no hesitancy in saying so. In short, such passages are not proof that Juvenal and other Greeks or Romans who mentioned a somatic norm image of Mediterranean white were "racists" but that they merely accepted prevailing aesthetic canons.

In the entire corpus of Greek and Roman literature there are only a very few texts which suggest color prejudice to a few commentators or at least the germ of an anti-black bias. It can be demonstrated, however, that in all of these instances modern commentators have read a nonexistent color prejudice. An observation of Agatharchides on the reaction of Greek children to the color of the Ethiopian's skin, for example, has been interpreted by Albrecht Dihle[8] as evidence of Greek aversion to the black man's color, rooted in childhood. Ethiopians do not astonish Greeks because of their blackness, wrote Agatharchides, "such a reaction ceases at childhood." This statement was not only an accurate assessment of Greek reaction to the Ethiopian's color but a sound observation on an aspect of child behavior that has been studied by modern psychologists: it is perfectly normal for a white child living in a predominantly white society to notice the color of blacks. Furthermore, A. Dihle's theory of a widespread ancient aversion to the black man's color is untenable in the light of the total Greco-Roman image of the Ethiopian.

Even when one allows for an element of subjectivity in the interpretation of Greek and Roman art, it is obvious that there are those who have perceived the blacks of ancient artists through lenses severely distorted by racism of a much later day. Beardsley,[9] for example, saw in fifth-century depictions of the Negro-crocodile group "a keen sense of the comic interest of the Ethiopians" as the predominating element. C. T. Seltman[10] maintained that the ugliness of the Negro seems to have appealed to sculptor, engraver, and painter; A. Lane[11] found plastic heads always best when the subject, like the Negro's head, is itself grotesque. A. W. Lawrence[12] considers a black terracotta *Spinario* as a parody of the white prototype, with the head of a black imbecile substituted for the original. By far a majority of scholars, however, who have examined the extensive gallery of blacks from ancient workshops see in the Negroes an astonishing variety and vitality and penetrating depictions of popular ethnic types, and would agree that the so-called comic, ugliness, imbecility, grotesqueness, and hideousness exist in the minds of modern beholders, not in the eyes of ancient artists. Negro models presented the ancient artists with a challenge to represent the distinctive features of blacks in a variety of media and with an opportunity, by contrasting blacks with Mediterranean types, to express the infinite variety of a common human nature. The obvious aesthetic attractiveness of many Negro models to many artists, the high quality of many pieces, some the finest from ancient workshops, and numerous sympathetic portrayals have given rise to a common opinion that ancient artists were free from prejudice in their depictions of blacks.

Some of the previously mentioned interpretations of the blacks of ancient documents were made before the extensive evidence had been collected and examined. Most of the scholars who have since examined the total evidence have concluded that nothing comparable to the virulent color prejudice of modern times existed in the ancient world. W. R. Connor[13] observed that the Greek and Roman world was "a society which for all its faults and failures never made color the basis for judging a man," and adds that "the signs of bigotry which we find in studying the history of classical antiquity are almost always among the modern scholars, not among their ancient subjects."

A rapid summary of some essentials of the Greco-Roman attitude toward blacks and the reasons for the classical outlook

will, at the same time, shed light on the reasons for the absence
of virulent color prejudice and for the difference in attitudes of
whites toward blacks in ancient and modern societies. In my
survey of the ancient view of blacks, I shall look briefly at the
following: the size of the black population, the first impressions
of blacks, contemporary images of Nubia and Nubians, awareness
of color and color symbolism, the daily experience of blacks in
predominantly white societies, cultural assimilation, and blacks
and religions of the Mediterranean world.

THE SIZE OF THE BLACK POPULATION

The proportion of blacks in predominantly white societies is
often included among factors that have contributed to the development of color prejudice, and some scholars have maintained
that the small size of the black population was a factor in
minimizing racial hostility in antiquity. Although the exact ratio
of blacks to whites in various parts of the ancient world is not
known, the evidence suggests that blacks were much more
numerous than has been realized. The instances are few that
provide numbers in the hundreds or thousands, but the figures
are at least suggestive when one considers the scope of the military
operations in which blacks participated—the encounters with
blacks in Egypt in the Ptolemaic and Roman periods, the presence
of Ethiopians in the Persian and Carthaginian forces, and in other
military conflicts in Northeast and Northwest Africa. Iconographic
evidence has not been given proper weight in the assessment of
the black population. And when it is kept in mind how often it
is possible to relate the large number of Negroes portrayed by
ancient artists of every major period to specific facts or historical
events, the importance of iconography as evidence becomes
apparent.

At any rate, the population was at least large enough to satisfy
what has been considered by some modern sociologists as the
most important necessary condition for the development of racism:
" . . . the presence in sufficient numbers of two or more groups

that look different enough so that at least some of their numbers can be easily classifiable."[14] And there is no doubt that such a condition existed at least from the fifth century B.C. onward. Further, with respect to the question of "numbers," the importance of Egypt is often overlooked: peoples from three continents formed their views of blacks, to a large extent, on the basis of what they saw and heard in Egypt, where the black element in the population was obviously sizeable. Observations of Greeks and Romans who visited or who lived in Egypt show no indication of hostility toward blacks: in fact, writers like Herodotus, Diodorus, and Origen did much to further a highly favorable image of blacks.

EARLY WHITE–BLACK ENCOUNTERS

An inclination to discriminate on the basis of readily observable physical differences, it has been argued, is lessened in white societies that have always had blacks in their midst. The hypothesis that a feeling of common humanity is generated by white-black familiarity over the years merits consideration.

Populations of different pigmentation were nothing novel to ancient Mediterranean peoples. The presence of Negroes in Egypt has been documented by written and iconographic evidence as early as the Fourth Dynasty, in the middle of the third millennium B.C., as far north as Giza. Thereafter, the Egyptians knew blacks at various times as soldiers in their armies, as conquerors and rulers of their country, as allies in opposition to the Assyrians. The Negroid type was known in Crete early in the second millennium B.C. Blacks were among the first Africans whom Greek colonists and mercenaries encountered in Egypt in the sixth century B.C. And the Romans were acquainted with them as early as the Carthaginian wars, and later in the Roman provinces of Northwest Africa, and as neighbors in Egypt who apparently caused Augustus to revise his plans for territorial expansion in Nubia. In short, in the ancient Mediterranean world the black man was from earliest times seldom a strange, unknown being.

First impressions are often important in the formation of images of others. A majority of the first blacks whom Mediterranean whites encountered, both within and outside Africa, were not so-called savages or slaves, but, like the whites themselves, soldiers protecting their own territory against foreign encroachment, or pursuing their national or personal interests in other lands. Nothing in these initial contacts points to a pejorative view of blacks. On the contrary, among many Mediterraneans the first and continuing image of blacks was that of a respected ally, or often, a redoubtable foe.

Like other prisoners of war, blacks were often enslaved. But in antiquity slavery was independent of race, and by far the vast majority of the thousands of slaves was white, not black. It has often been noted that anti-black racism developed or increased in intensity *after black and slave became synonymous. The ancients, however, never developed a concept of the equivalence of slave and black; nor did they create theories to prove that blacks were especially or more suited to slavery than other peoples.*

Given the place of the Homeric epics in the Greek consciousness, another first impression of tremendous impact on ancient attitudes toward blacks was the image of Ethiopians in Homer. Echoes of Homer's Ethiopians, favorites of the gods, were heard until late in classical literature. The Ethiopian king Sabacos of Herodotus, apparently the Pharaoh Shabaka of the Twenty-fifth Ethiopian Dynasty, never put wrongdoers to death, but instead required them to perform public works, and he voluntarily left Egypt because of a fear of committing sacrilege. The king of the Macrobian Ethiopians, according to Herodotus, the tallest and most handsome men on earth, cautioned the Persian king Cambyses about his plans to invade Ethiopia and reminded him of his injustice in coveting a land not his own. Citing Homer, Diodorus presents Ethiopians as the first men to be taught to honor the gods and as blessed with internal security and free from invasion because they enjoyed divine good will by reason of their piety. The Ethiopian king Hydaspes of Heliodorus was a late example of Ethiopian wisdom and justice.

In marked contrast, however, were the accounts of the first

English voyagers to Africa in the mid-sixteenth century which described Negroes as a people of "beastly living, without a God, laws, religion, or commonwealth,"[15] obviously vastly different from the first descriptions in Homer and Herodotus. In fact, the Negro's color became in the English mind, Winthrop Jordan[16] has observed, the identification of a native of a distant continent of African peoples radically defective in religion, libidinous, bestial, and a source of slaves.

A few classical writers circulated stories about bizarre Ethiopians such as those reported to have had no heads, with their eyes attached to their chests, and others who were said to crawl instead of walk. There were also reports of some wild Ethiopian tribes and a few who believed in no gods at all. In antiquity, however, similar stories were circulated about white peoples, Scythians, for example, with one eye in the center of their foreheads, others with feet turned backward who ran through forests like wild beasts. The inhabitants of ancient Ireland, according to Strabo, were the most "savage" peoples in the ancient world, more savage than the Britons. It was distance from Greece and Italy, *not color,* that gave rise to elements of unreality in some descriptions of distant peoples. There was in antiquity, however, no tendency to limit such descriptions to blacks or to stereotype blacks as savages or primitives. In spite of accounts of a few strange Ethiopians on the southern edge of the earth, the overall Greco-Roman view of blacks was highly positive.

IMAGE OF NUBIA AND NUBIANS
IN CONTEMPORARY SOCIETIES

In the modern world the image of Africans in the minds of whites has often been considered a major factor in the development of color prejudice. Edward Shils,[17] for example, has observed that one of the most obvious reasons for the great importance which color has assumed in the self-imagery of many peoples is that it is an easy means of distinguishing "between those from the periphery and those from the center of the world society." Whites in the modern world have often seen themselves as wealthy and powerful, Africans as poor and weak; themselves as eminent in intellectual creativity, and Africans as intellectually unproductive. In the eighteenth and nineteenth centuries, for example, as a result of the differences perceived by whites of European stock between themselves and the black colonials whom they dominated, many whites associated poverty, inefficiency, and backwardness with nonwhites and attached strong emotions to physical differences. Among the ancients, on the other hand, similar associations with material poverty, military weakness, political insignificance, and cultural unproductivity did not arise.

The history of the relation between the inhabitants of Egypt and the peoples to the south was in large part the story of Egypt's efforts to exploit the human and natural resources of the south, and of Nubia's response to the commercial and imperial ambitions of its northern neighbors. The most successful Nubian venture in Egypt took place in the middle of the eighth century B.C., about the time of the traditional founding of Rome. The Nubian monarchs from Napata conquered Egypt and ruled it as the Twenty-fifth Ethiopian Dynasty for almost three-quarters of a century. The period of Ethiopian rule in Egypt—the first and only time that a country from the interior of Africa played an important role in the politics of the Mediterranean—received notice in later chronicles. In the Old Testament the Kushites, like the Assyrians, were cited among the great military powers of the day, and Isaiah described the Kushites as a people "dreaded near and far, a nation strong and proud." Reports of the Ethiopian king reached the Greeks through Herodotus, and later Strabo included Taharqa, one of the pharaohs of the Twenty-fifth Dynasty, in a catalogue of the world's great conquerors. Ethiopian military presence continued to be felt in the Ptolemaic and Roman periods. In some of the Egyptian rebellions that plagued the later Ptolemies Ethiopians played a role. A regent cautioned an unnamed youthful Ptolemy, perhaps the Fifth, as to the risks of undertaking an expedition against the Ethiopians, a formidable military force. Augustus, at the conclusion of a conflict with the Ethiopians who had defeated Roman cohorts protecting the Roman frontier in

Egypt and had enslaved the inhabitants, decided to grant the envoys of the Ethiopian queen everything they pleaded for, including remission of the tribute which the Emperor had imposed. The differences between the ancient and modern views of the black African's military and political power are obvious. In the ancient world, contemporaries, whether Egyptian, Asiatic, or European, far from regarding blacks as materially poor, or politically and militarily weak, were clearly aware of Nubia's resources and conscious of its position in the politics of the day.

Another factor perhaps responsible for the importance of color in the self-imagery of peoples, Shils observed, has been the view of blacks as culturally backward. Regarding themselves as perpetuators of the Pharaonic tradition, the Pharaohs of the Twenty-fifth Dynasty patronized Egyptian gods and shrines, restored ancient religious texts, renovated existing temples, built new structures, and led Egypt to what has been called Egypt's last age of outstanding achievement. In the third century B.C. and later, the Nubians gradually developed their own distinctive writing, worshipped their own gods, and created a style of their own in architecture, reliefs, statuary, and ceramics—some of the finest ever produced in the Nile valley. Herodotus described Meroë as a great city, the capital of the other Ethiopians. The Meroë of the late third century B.C. has been described as a "Nubian Alexandria." In the first century B.C., Diodorus described Ethiopians in his world history as the originators of several Egyptian institutions; Pliny refers to Ethiopian wisdom; and Lucian notes that Ethiopians transmitted their discoveries about the heavens to the Egyptians. Parenthetically, classical accounts of Ethiopians, even when "idealized," were important parts of the Greco-Roman image of blacks: perceptions are often as influential as reality in shaping racial attitudes and are important factors to be considered in assessing the ancient view of blacks.

In short, it is clear that Nubians, though located on the southern periphery of the ancient world, were not considered sufficiently different from contemporary Mediterranean peoples with respect to their resources, military and political power, and cultural attainments to warrant the extreme contrasts between blacks and whites which have been associated with the development of color prejudice in the modern world.

AWARENESS OF COLOR

To what extent did the ancients indicate an awareness of the black man's color, and in what way did Greek and Roman awareness of color influence their attitude toward blacks? The Greeks were the first to invent a word to describe the Nubian's color—*Aithiops*—a person with a burnt skin, a colored person. Ethiopians became the yardstick by which classical antiquity measured colored peoples—Manilius described a familiar "color scheme": Ethiopians, the blackest; Indians, less sunburned; Egyptians, mildly dark; and Moors, the lightest. The Ethiopian's color became proverbial: "to wash an Ethiopian white" was a common expression used to describe futile efforts or to illustrate the unchangeability of nature. Neither the Greeks nor the Romans and early Christians used the word "Ethiopian" in a pejorative sense. In fact, the word "Ethiopian" seems in origin to have been a reflection of a common belief that attributed the Ethiopian's color as well as his tightly coiled hair to the intense heat of the southern sun—a belief also reflected in the story of Phaethon, who, by coming close to earth in his father's chariot, blackened the skin and curled the hair of Ethiopians.

Classical anthropology in many statements of an environment theory attributed physical differences to the effects of diverse environments upon a common human nature, explained the physical characteristics of all mankind, regardless of color, in the same manner, and evolved from these differences no theory as to the inferiority of blacks or the superiority of whites. Contrasts of black-white physical characteristics were first seen in Xenophanes' contrast of Thracians and Ethiopians and in sixth-century terracottas of conjoined black-white heads. There was nothing pejorative in these first black-white juxtapositions nor in the later, very popular, contrast of Scythians and Ethiopians, who were selected as favorite northern-southern illustrations of the environment theory because, as physical and geographic extremes, they provided dramatic examples of human diversity. Ethiopian-Scythian contrasts came to be used also in statements of conviction that race is of no consequence in evaluating men and that all whom God created He created equal and alike. It makes no difference, Menander wrote, whether one is as physically different from a Greek as an Ethiopian from the distant south or a Scythian from the far north: it is individual merit, not race, that counts. Menander's statement begins with an attack on the validity of birth as a criterion for judging the worth of an individual, but the poet was not suggesting, as some have argued, the existence of a special theory about the inferiority of Ethiopians. Just as Menander had employed a traditional antithesis to exemplify the broad scale of human faculties and potentialities, Origen later used it, with appropriate extentions, for an expression of a Christian view. A man, Origen declared, may be born among Hebrews, Greeks, Ethiopians, Scythians, or Taurians, yet God created all equal and alike.

As I have already mentioned, Greeks and Romans in definitions of what constitutes beauty used their own physical traits as a yardstick. In general, lovers in classical poetry seemed to prefer their own complexion to that of the extremely fair Germans or of dark-hued Africans; their noses to those of the hooked-nosed Persians or flat-nosed Africans. About preferences of this kind there is nothing unusual. In judging beauty, most peoples employ what H. Hoetink[18] calls a "somatic norm image," which he defines as "the complex of physical (somatic) characteristics which are accepted by a group as its norm and ideal." Yet some scholars have seen an anti-black bias among Greeks and Romans because of the inclusion of "whiteness" in their somatic norm image. Such modern assessments of the Greco-Roman reactions to color overlook much of relevance for a complete picture of the classical view—statements such as those of Sextus Empiricus who emphasized the subjectivity of criteria for judging the beautiful and the numerous rejections of the norm of "whiteness."

Herodotus, the first Greek to express an opinion about the physical appearance of Ethiopians, described some of them as the most handsome men on earth. The presence of black gods or heroes in legend and their interracial amours presented no embarrassment and evoked no apologies from poets or artists. Epaphos, the child that Io, the daughter of the primeval king of Argos, bore to Zeus, was described as black and was said by Hesiod to have been the ancestor of the Libyans and Ethiopians. Seven of Danaus' fifty daughters, according to one version of the legend, were born to Danaus by an Ethiopian woman. Perseus, the son of Zeus by Danae, married the dark-skinned Andromeda, whose father was a mulatto, at least in the eyes of one fifth-century B.C. vase painter. Delphos, the eponymous founder of Delphi, the son of Poseidon or Apollo, and a woman several variants of whose name means the Black Woman, is, in my opinion, the most convincing identification of a Negro appearing on the coinage of Athens at the end of the sixth century B.C., and of Delphi in the fifth.

The number of implied or expressed preferences for white beauty in classical literature exceeds slightly those for black or dark beauty. About this there is nothing strange, but the many rejections of the conventional standard should not be overlooked. In the third century B.C., Asclepiades, the chief epigrammatic poet of the Alexandrian period, was the first to state clearly a preference for a "black beauty" when he wrote of a certain Didyme: "Gazing at her beauty I melt like wax before the fire. And if she is black, what difference to me? So are coals, but when we light them, they shine like rose-buds." As Propertius observed, a tender beauty, white or dark attracts, and the dark were inclusive, from *fusca* (dark), like Ovid's Andromeda who captivated Perseus by her exquisite beauty to *nigerrima* (very black) like Martial's preferred lady, blacker than an ant, pitch, a jackdaw or a cicada. The daughter of the dark-skinned (*fuscus*) Terence is said to have married a Roman knight. King Juba II of Mauretania, one of whose portraits has Negroid traits, was married first to Cleopatra Selene, the daughter of Antony and Cleopatra, and later to the daughter of the king of Cappadocia. Further, numerous realistic portraits of mulattoes and of various mixed black-white types provide dramatic confirmation of the many references to racial mixture noted in ancient texts. In short, in spite of a somatic norm image of "Mediterranean white," black-white sexual relations were not taboo, and many blacks were physically assimilated into predominantly white populations.

COLOR SYMBOLISM

Among the Greeks and Romans, white was generally associated with light, the day, with Olympus and victims sacrificed to the higher gods, and with good omens; black with night and darkness, with the underworld, death, chthonian deities, and with ill omens. In this the Greeks and Romans resembled people in general among whom, according to recent studies, there is a "widespread communality in feelings about black and white,"[19] and a tendency among both Negroes and whites for the color white to evoke a positive and black a negative reaction. Although the Greek and Roman association of the color black with death and the underworld had in origin nothing to do with skin color, the introduction of dark-skinned peoples into such a context was a natural development. Homer's and Vergil's underworlds were dark and murky; the god of the underworld himself was often black (*niger Jupiter* or *niger Dis*). Some writers of the early Roman Empire placed Ethiopians, Egyptians, and Garamantians in ill-omened settings. At the time of Caligula's death, according to Suetonius, a nocturnal performance was in rehearsal in which scenes from the lower world were enacted by Egyptians and Ethiopians. Events foreshadowing the death of Septimius Severus included the sight of an Ethiopian soldier carrying a garland of cypress. Research in the social sciences has raised the question of whether individuals who react negatively to the color black develop antipathy to dark-skinned people, and suggests that, though such a reaction would seem plausible in theory, the evidence is far from conclusive. In the ancient world, at least, the daily experience of blacks in predominantly white societies demonstrates that neither the existence of a black-white symbolism nor a prevailing aesthetic norm of "Mediterranean white" triggered hostile sentiments or negative reactions to blacks. Further, it should be noted that at the same time that the notion linking dark-skinned peoples and omens of disaster was being circulated, proponents of the environment theory were setting forth unprejudiced explanations of physical differences; the image of the just Ethiopian was being reinforced; and Christian authors were developing a rich black-white imagery emphasizing the black man's membership in the Christian brotherhood.

THE DAILY LIFE OF BLACKS

The experience of blacks, whether slave or free, was no different from that of other newcomers in alien lands. Numerous terracottas, bronzes, and other portrayals of Negroes point to the lives of blacks as soldiers, prisoners of war, diplomats, slaves, entertainers such as actors and musicians, athletes, and day-laborers of various kinds. Blacks in the Ptolemaic and Roman world, as earlier in the Pharaonic era, found careers in the military attractive. An over life-size Negroid head in basalt (*c.* 80–50 B.C.) probably represents some high official in the Ptolemaic army of the period. One of the elite bodyguard of Septimius Severus was a Negro, one of three soldiers depicted on a sarcophagus receiving suppliant Roman captives. Blacks also served under Septimius Severus in an auxiliary unit of Moors (*numerus Maurorum*), defending a distant Roman outpost in northern England. Like other non-Romans who served in auxiliary units, blacks discharged from service received Roman citizenship for themselves and their descendants. The popular tragic actor Glycon, freed by Nero, was one of a number of black actors admired for their art. Black athletes won the acclaim of the populace and the tributes of poets. Of one of these athletes the sixth-century poet Luxorius wrote in part: " . . . the walls and towers of Carthage could not bear you when you triumphed in the arena. But you will lose nothing among the shades of the dead because of your bitter death. The fame of your glory will live everlastingly after you, and Carthage will always sing your name." Another North African black had apparently attained a degree of financial success, suggested by the scenes commissioned for a mosaic found at Thaenae, dating from the third or fourth century. He and his white wife are portrayed taking part in their own funeral banquet: each in a semi-reclining position, holding a golden goblet in the right hand.

There were blacks who were at home in the culture of Greece and Rome and who were to be counted among those who had assimilated, in varying degrees, Greek and Roman culture. Children from Meroë received instruction in Greek. The Ethiopian King Ergamenes in the third century B.C., according to Diodorus, had received a Greek education. Children of well-to-do Nubians, one preserved in bronze, studied in Alexandria. Included in a list of the distinguished followers of Epicurus were two named Ptolemaeus from Alexandria, otherwise unknown, one black, the other white. Much better known are the careers of two other Africans, perhaps of Negroid descent, the dark-skinned Terence, an ex-slave from Carthage, and Juba II, king of Mauretania (one of whose portraits suggests Negroid ancestry). Juba, whose lost works, written in Greek, included a history of Rome, books on Libya and Assyria, and treatises on drama and painting, strove to introduce Greek and Roman culture into his African kingdom. A black student of Herodes Atticus, Memnon, whose head has been preserved in Pentelic marble, was one of three students whose deaths the sophist and patron of learning mourned as if they had been his sons because they were noble-minded, honorable youths, fond of learning and worthy of their upbringing in his household.

In sum, what we know of the daily lives of blacks in various parts of the Greek and Roman world points to another noteworthy aspect of the racial pattern in antiquity: blacks fared no differently than others of alien extraction and suffered no measurable consequences, no detrimental distinctions which excluded them from opportunities—occupational, economic, or cultural—available to other newcomers.

RELIGION

The structure and creeds of organized religions are often important factors in the assessment of racial attitudes. What was the experience of blacks in the religions of the Greek and Roman world? Evidence on this point comes primarily from two sources—Isiac worship and especially Christianity.

In the daily ritual and diffusion of the cult of Isis, deeply rooted in Nubia and Egypt, blacks played an important role, especially at Philae, the Jerusalem or Mecca of the cult, near the First Cataract, where they met Isiac pilgrims from many countries. But the influence of blacks in Isiac worship was not limited to Africa. A substantial Ethiopian influence on the Isiac cult in Greece and Italy is strongly suggested, if not proved, by the evidence of black priests and cultists in Athens, Herculaneum, and the area of Rome. A vivid example appears in scenes depicted on frescoes from Herculaneum showing Isiac cultists—black and white, men and women—including black priests and one black choirmaster directing a chorus of both sexes, another playing a flute, and in another fresco a black, the central figure, executing a dance, with eyes of most worshippers focused upon him. Strangers though Ethiopians may have been far from their native Africa, the reception of fellow cultists who welcomed their expert ritualistic knowledge and the authenticity of their music and dances gave them a spiritual security in new lands. A black man, far from his homeland, may have been like Apuleius' Lucius, "a stranger to the temple but at home in the faith."

The strong bond that had united blacks and whites in the common worship of Isis was reinforced by Christianity. Like the Isiac cult, Christianity swept racial distinctions aside. When the early Christians proclaimed that it was the whiteness of the spirit, not of the skin, that mattered and that it made no difference where a man was born, they were echoing the poet Menander and were adapting the familiar Scythian-Ethiopian formula, which left no doubt as to its meaning and comprehensiveness. The Ethiopian's blackness gave rise to a deeply spiritual imagery of black and white in early Christian exegesis—in which Ethiopians came to occupy a privileged position. Origen and St. Augustine made significant adaptations of an "Ethiopian" symbolism, perhaps inspired by their first-hand knowledge of blacks in Africa.

Origen's interpretation of scriptural allusions to Ethiopians was especially important because it is reflected in later Patristic treatment of "Ethiopian" themes. For Origen, the Ethiopian was a symbol of peoples out of whom the church was destined to grow. The marriage of Moses to the Ethiopian woman, in Origen's interpretation, represents the symbolic union of the spiritual law (Moses) and the church (the Ethiopian woman) gathered from among the Gentiles, and Origen recalls the suffering of Aaron and Miriam when they spoke against Moses, emphasizing that God never praised Moses, in spite of his great achievements, so highly as when he married the Ethiopian woman. Another use of the black-white imagery emphasized the applicability of "Ethiopian" to all men. Origen declared that *all* men are "Ethiopians" in their souls before they are illumined by the light of the Lord. In commenting on lines from the Song of Songs, which appear in the Septuagint as "I am black and comely," Origen reminds all that "if you repent, your soul will be 'black' because of your former sins, but because of your penitence your soul will have something of what I may call an Ethiopian beauty."

Explicating a verse from the Psalms, St. Augustine wrote: "How do I understand 'Ethiopian peoples'? How else than by them, all nations? And properly by black men (for Ethiopians are black). Those are called to the faith who were black, just they, so that it may be said to them, 'ye were sometimes darkness but now are ye light in the Lord.' They are indeed called black but let them not remain black, for out of these is made the church. . . ."

The use of the Ethiopian and his color was much more than a literary device: it was based on a cardinal tenet of equality before God that was to be translated into practice from the very beginning. The Ethiopian whom Philip the Deacon baptized came to be admired as a diligent reader of the scriptures, and his baptism foreshadowed what was to be the practice of the church in the first centuries after Christ.

From Northwest Africa came a dramatic application of Augustine's statement that the "catholic church has been foretold not to be in any particular quarter of the world, as certain schisms are, but in the whole universe, by bearing fruit and growing even unto the very Ethiopians, indeed the remotest and blackest of men,"—peoples whom Augustine knew to inhabit the southern fringes of his bishopric. An exchange of letters between a deacon of the church of Carthage in the first-half of the sixth century A.D., and Fulgentius, Bishop of Ruspe (in southern Tunisia), concerned with the spiritual welfare of a black catechumen, was vivid testimony that the vision of Augustine, "Aethiopia credet Deo," (Ethiopia shall believe in God), had become a reality in a distant region of Northwest Africa.

But blacks were not to be only humble converts. The lives of two men, one perhaps and the other certainly black, illustrate another aspect of the spirit of early Christianity. St. Menas (third-fourth century A.D.), sometimes represented as a Negro, was a national saint of Egypt but was also venerated in Rome, and elsewhere in Europe. One of the most outstanding Fathers of the Desert was a tall, black Ethiopian, Moses, whose fame spread far from the Desert of Scetis, where he acquired a reputation as a model of Christian virtue, and left some seventy disciples when he died at the age of seventy-five, at the end of the fourth or in the first years of the fifth century A.D.

The demons who troubled the visions of some early saints and martyrs were frequently black. The devil was black, according to Didymus the Blind, because he fell from the splendor and spiritual whiteness that only those who have been "whitened" by God can possess. This use of color, like earlier black-white imagery, had in origin nothing to do with skin color but was derived from a belief held by those for whom *black* evoked a negative and *white* a positive image. The emphasis of the symbolism of black demons and devils was on the color black—on the contrast between the blackness of evil and the light of God. This symbolism, like the earlier association of black with death and ill omens in the secular sphere, does not seem to have had a negative effect on the generally favorable view of blacks dating back to the Homeric poems. And with respect to fundamental Christian beliefs, exegetical interpretations, much broader in scope than the limited demonological references, set forth a coherent body of doctrine in which Ethiopians became an important symbol of Christianity's mission. No sterotyped concept of blacks as evil or as personifications of demons arose. Blacks were summoned to salvation and were welcomed in the Christian brotherhood on the same terms as other converts. Philip's baptism of the Ethiopian was a landmark in the evangelization of the world. In interpretations of the major scriptural references to Ethiopians, influential figures like Origen, Gregory of Nyssa, Jerome, and Augustine made it clear that all men, regardless of the color of their skin, were called to the faith. The early church—both credo and practice—was unequivocal: the Ethiopian imagery dramatically emphasized the ecumenical character of Christianity, and adumbrated the symbolism of the black Wise Man in later depictions of the Adoration of the Magi.

CONCLUSION

I have called attention, all too rapidly, to some important areas in which white-black relationships in antiquity differed from those in later societies. The time has come to summarize. The differences between ancient and modern black-white racial patterns are striking. In the ancient world there were prolonged black-white contacts, often beginning at an early date; first encounters with blacks frequently involved soldiers, not slaves or so-called savages; initially favorable impressions of blacks were explained and amplified, generation after generation, by poets, historians, and philosophers; the central societies developed a positive image of peripheral Nubia as an independent, viable state of considerable military, political, and cultural importance; both blacks and whites were slaves, but blacks and slaves were never synonymous; blacks were not excluded from opportunities available to others of alien extraction nor handicapped in many of the most fundamental social relations; they were physically and culturally assimilated; in science, philosophy, and religion, color was not the basis of a widely accepted theory concerning the inferiority of blacks. Reports of imaginary creatures of "primitive" tribes inhabiting the extreme south, the somatic norm image of "Mediterranean white," and standard black-white symbolism—all contained the potential for the vastly different roles that these factors have obviously played in the later development of anti-black sentiments.

But the Egyptians, Greeks, Romans, and early Christians were free of what Keith Irvine[20] has described as the "curse of acute color-consciousness, attended by all the raw passion and social problems that cluster around it."

It is difficult to say with certainty what conditions may have been the most influential elements in the formation of the attitude of the ancient world toward blacks. Scholars may disagree as to the precise stage in the history of race relations when color acquired the importance it has had in the modern world. One point, however, is certain: the onus of color-prejudice cannot be placed on the shoulders of the ancients. The Christian vision of a world in which "there is no question of Greek and Jew, circumcised and uncircumcised, barbarian, Scythian, slave, freeman . . ." owes not a little to earlier views of man in which color played no significant role.

NOTES

For a development of the points discussed in this lecture and for a detailed bibliography, especially for the ancient sources, see Frank M. Snowden Jr., *Before Color Prejudice: The Ancient View of Blacks* (Cambridge, Mass. and London, 1983).

1. J. Bryce, *The Relation of the Advanced and Backward Races of Mankind* (Oxford and London, 1902), 18.
2. E. Baring, *Ancient and Modern Imperialism* (London, 1910), 139–40.
3. E. E. Sikes, *The Anthropology of the Greeks* (London, 1914), 88.
4. A. E. Zimmern, *The Greek Commonwealth*, 5th ed. (Oxford, 1931), 323.
5. W. L. Westermann, "Slavery and the Elements of Freedom," *Quarterly Bulletin of the Polish Institute of Arts and Sciences* 1 (1943): 346.
6. T. J. Haarhoff, *The Stranger at the Gate* (Oxford, 1948): 299.
7. D. S. Wiesen, "Juvenal and the Blacks," *Classica et Mediaevalia* 31(1970):143 and 149.
8. A. Dihle, "Zur hellenistischen Ethnographie" in H. Schwabl *et al.*, Fondation Hardt: Entretiens sur l'antiquité classique VIII, *Grecs et barbares* [*Six exposés et discussions*], (Vandoeuvres-Genève, 1962):214–15.

9. G. H. Beardsley, *The Negro in Greek and Roman Civilization: A Study of the Ethiopian Type* (Baltimore, 1929), 37.

10. C. T. Seltman, "Two Heads of Negresses," *American Journal of Archaeology* 24 (1920):14.

11. A. Lane, *Greek Pottery*, 3rd. ed. (London, 1971), 55.

12. A. W. Lawrence, *Greek and Roman Sculpture* (New York, 1972), 42.

13. W. R. Connor, Review of F. M. Snowden, Jr., *Blacks in Antiquity: Ethiopians in the Greco-Roman Experience* (Cambridge, Mass. and London, 1970) in *Good Reading: Review of Books Recommended by the Princeton University Faculty* 21 (May, 1970), 4.

14. P. L. van den Berghe, *Race and Racism: A Comparative Perspective* (New York, 1967), 13.

15. "The second voyage to Guinea . . . in the yere 1554. The Captaine whereof was M. John Lok" in Richard Hakluyt, *The Principal Navigations, Voyages, Traffiques, and Discoveries of the British Nation* (London and New York, n.d. [Everyman's Library], IV, 57.

16. W. D. Jordan, *White over Black: American Attitudes toward the Negro, 1550–1812* (Baltimore, 1969), 3–34.

17. E. Shils, "Color, the Universal Intellectual Community, and the Afro-Asian Intellectual," in *Color and Race,* edited by J. H. Franklin (Boston, 1968), 2.

18. H. Hoetink, *The Two Variants in Caribbean Race Relations: A Contribution to the Sociology of Segmented Societies,* trans. E. M. Hookykass (New York, 1967), 120.

19. K. J. Gergen, "The Significance of Skin Color in Human Relations," *Color and Race,* 120.

20. K. Irvine, *The Rise of the Colored Races* (New York, 1970), 19.

Black History's
Diversified Clientele

Benjamin Quarles

Along with many other denials since he arrived on these shores, the black American has until recently been denied a past. The consequent damage to his psyche can hardly be imagined. In a poem entitled "Negro History," appearing in *From the Ashes: Voices of Watts* (Budd Schulberg, editor), young Jimmie Sherman depicts the past as his grandfather viewed it:

> A ship
> A chain
> A distant land
> A whip
> A pain
> A white man's hand
> A sack
> A field
> of cotton balls—
> The only things
> Grandpa recalls.

Such an outlook on the past has a stultifying effect, making for apathy and despair. Hence black leaders since the birth of the Republic have been advocates of Negro history, obviously envisioning a far broader coverage of it than Jimmie Sherman's grandpa had come to know. Black scholars, led by Carter G. Woodson in 1915, began to remove the layers of ignorance and distortion that had encrusted the Afro-American past. One of these scholars,

W. E. B. Du Bois, in the closing line of his autobiography, written during his last months, bespoke anew his lifelong devotion to history: "Teach us, Forever Dead, there is no Dream but Deed, there is no Deed but Memory." A quarter of a century earlier Du Bois fired back a sharp rejoinder to a magazine editor who had rejected a Du Bois essay because it had touched upon the past. "Don't you understand," Du Bois wrote, "that the past is present; that without what was, nothing is."

During the past decade the cry for black history has been stronger than ever before. Numbered among the proponents of such history are the newer black militants. We blacks, writes Imamu Amiri Baraka (LeRoi Jones), must "learn our collective past in order to design a collective destiny." Of his period of confinement at the Norfolk (Massachusetts) Prison Colony, Malcolm X wrote: "I began first telling my black brother inmates about the glorious history of the black man—things they had never dreamed." On another occasion he referred to history as "a people's memory" without which "man is demoted to the lower animals." In his assessment of the past, Malcolm X did not ignore the less glorious aspects of the black pilgrimage in America. Speaking to a ghetto audience in Detroit in 1953 he evoked a deep response with the words: "We didn't land on Plymouth Rock, my brothers and sisters—Plymouth Rock landed on *us!*"

Eldridge Cleaver who, like Malcolm X, became a serious student of history while serving time in prison, spoke history's praises. In his essay, "To All Black Women, From All Black Men," in *Soul on Ice*, he writes:

> Be convinced, Sable Sister, that the past is no forbidden vista upon which we dare not look, out of a phantom fear of being, as the wife of Lot, turned into pillars of salt. Rather the past is an omniscient mirror: we gaze and see reflected there ourselves and each other—what we used to be and what we are today, how we got this way, and what we are becoming. To decline to look into the Mirror of Then, my heart, is to refuse to view the face of Now.

One of the sable sisters who has needed no convincing about history's role is poet Sarah Webster Fabio, who writes:

Now at all costs, we must heal our history.
Or else our future rots in the disease of
our past.

Although black history is now coming into its own as never before, not all of its proponents are in pursuit of the same goal. Indeed today black history is being called upon to serve an increasing variety of publics, four of whom we may scrutinize briefly. These are the black rank and file, the black revolutionary nationalists, the black academicians, and the white world, both scholarly and lay. Not mutually exclusive, these groups often overlap. But this four-fold typography enables us to illustrate the major contemporary uses of black history. We may take these in turn, first describing their aims and then noting their general content and style.

For the black rank and file, the man in the street, the laity, black history's main objective is to create a sense of racial pride and personal worth. To the rank and file the new black history is good therapy, its end result an improved self-image. In a world that has traditionally equated blackness with inferiority, black history serves as a balm to make the wounded whole. In a world that has traditionally equated blackness with low aim, black history serves as a stimulus to success. To a black person seeking to resolve an identity crisis, black history is ego-soothing; it places one in the thick of things, thereby diminishing his sense of alienation, of rootlessness. Black history is a search for the values and the strengths imbedded in the black subculture. Black history strikes at the black American's legacy of self-rejection, the burden of shame that he had been taught was his to bear going back to the curse of Cain. "I always wanted to be somebody," runs the title of the autobiography of a black tennis champion. Black history tells the black reader that he is somebody, however vicariously.

In its content black history for the masses reflects somewhat "the great man" theory of history. White or black, the typical American, himself individualistic, conceives of his country's past as the achievements of a group of outstanding characters, pushing on against herculean odds. History is a tableau of heroes set in bold relief. To the generality of blacks their men of mark constitute their history, the bulk of their attention falling on individual achievers—an underground railroad conductor like Harriet Tubman, a dedicated bishop like Daniel A. Payne, an educator like Mary McLeod Bethune, a sports celebrity like prize fighter Peter Jackson or jockey Isaac Murphy, and a singer like Elizabeth Taylor Greenfield (the "Black Swan") or Bessie Smith. The list is endless, ranging from an early African king to a present-day ghetto leader.

Upbeat and achievement-oriented, black history for the rank and file stresses victories—the peak that was scaled, the foe that was vanquished, the deep river that was crossed. Moreover, to the masses youth makes an especial appeal, the younger Frederick Douglass arousing more interest than the Sage of Anacostia. Local black historical figures, likewise, meet with a readier response than out-of-staters, however more nationally important the latter may be. Moreover, history designed for the laity will, of necessity, devote as much attention to popular culture and the lively arts as to the more traditional staples, politics and economics, particularly since the black stamp on the former is more readily discernible.

The emphasis on the lively arts and popular culture lends itself to the mass media. Hence black history for laymen has found a natural ally in television, commercial as well as educational, but obviously of far greater proportions in the latter. Radio, too, especially in the folkways recordings, lends itself to black cultural history. Other mass media such as newspapers and magazines are increasingly carrying black history articles, biographical sketches and pictorial materials. Sensing the growing interest in black history, commercial firms have brought out coloring books, alphabet books, black history games, and black history in comic book format.

History as hero-worship is hardly the kind of history espoused by the second black group under survey—the black revolutionary nationalists. This group focuses upon exploiters and oppressors, a case study in man's inhumanity to man. This group views history as grievance collecting, a looking back in anger. Black nationalist history is essentially the story of a powerful white majority imposing its will on a defenseless black minority. Black nationalists hold that American society needs to be reconstructed and that black history is, or should be, a means of ideological indoctrination in the revolutionary cause of black liberation.

Black nationalist history is not without its traces of paranoid thinking, one of which holds that the forces of evil are banded in an eternal conspiracy to maintain their oppressive sway. Of very ancient origin, this devil theory of history is deeply rooted in the human psyche and hence should occasion no surprise when met in any of its multiple guises.

Like so much else in American life, black nationalism has, as it has always had, a variety of forms—cultural, religious, and economic, among others. Revolutionary nationalism moves a step beyond the others in its goals and does not rule out violence in achieving them. Revolutionary black nationalists, having carefully examined the almost unbelievable pervasiveness of color prejudice in our society have, in essence, given up on America. Estranged from the land of their birth, they ponder its dismantlement.

As to content, revolutionary black history is not as interested in historical spadework as in providing new interpretations of that which is already known. Black nationalist history emphasizes racial contrast, physical and cultural. It propounds a black esthetic and implies a black mystique. It bespeaks the essential kinship of black people on whatever continent they may be located or in whatever walk of life. Its central theme is oppression, slavery in one guise or another. Rebelliousness against the oppressor likewise looms large in nationalist lore.

A compound of black rage and white guilt, revolutionary black history makes much of the analogy of colonialism, holding that black Americans live in a state of vassalage to white Americans. Black America is a semi-colony of white America.

Going further, the revolutionary school of thought stresses separatism, insisting that black Americans have always constituted a nation. To those who hold these views, black history has one overriding purpose, namely, to promote nation-building.

In tone, black revolutionary history is judgmental, with over-tones of recrimination, moral condemnation, and prophetic warning. Apocalyptic and polemical in temper, it scorns objectivity, which it equates with a defense of the status quo. Revolutionary black history may, on occasion, read like social commentary, sometimes taking on a man-the-barracks urgency.

Selective in content, black revolutionary history ignores as irrelevant those aspects of the past which do not relate to its philosophy. As will be noted in just a moment, however, this tendency to pick and choose is nothing new in the historical profession.

The third group under survey are the black academicians—the intellectually sophisticated, the college and university trained, the well read. Like the revolutionary nationalists, they operate on a more studious level. They would concur with the revolutionary nationalists in holding that history is a weapon in the warfare. But to the academically oriented mind, the basic foe is ignorance, be it willful or otherwise. It hardly need be added that ignorance is a somewhat impersonal foe and hence less easily pinpointed, less starkly isolated.

To the black academician, history is a discipline, an attempt to recapture and mirror the past as accurately as possible. Admittedly this is a tall order, considering the nature of the evidence and the unreliability of so many of the witnesses. Black academicians hardly need to be reminded that history as we know it is not neutral, not value free. Who can tell the black academician anything new about the insensitivity of past generations of white scholars, of their neglect or distortion of the role of black peoples? But the black academician would question the viewpoint that prejudiced history must be met with prejudiced history; he would doubt that the best way to strike at the myth-makers of history is to imitate them. In *The Fire Next Time,* James Baldwin has observed that "an invented past can never be used; it cracks and crumbles under the pressures of life like clay in a season of drought." White Americans have made some use of an invented past, but black Americans must realize that a powerful majority may, for a time, be able to afford the luxury of fantasy. Such indulgence on the part of a minority is a species of living beyond its means, a minority having to husband carefully its limited resources.

Like the layman and the nationalist, the black academician finds in black history a deepening sense of racial worth and of peoplehood. He, too, reads black history with pride. The black academician views America as a civilization upon which his ancestors have left their stamp. Hence he does not regard America as a white civilization exclusively; to him it also has its black, red, and yellow components. The black academician holds that his forbears helped to build America and this being the case no one should sensibly expect him to pack his belongings and leave for other shores.

In addition to personal and racial gratification the black academician reads black history because he feels that it will contribute to his knowledge and understanding of mankind, of his fellow travelers in time and space.

For academicians, the content of black history would be more selective than for the laymen, in an attempt to avoid the obvious or the well known. Black history for the academician would deal less with persons and more with processes, less with general black history than with selected topics in black history. It would include comparative studies and pose methodological problems. On the grounds that academicians do not shy away from the unpleasant, black history for them would not ignore the less glorious aspects of the black past—the African tribesmen who engaged in the slave trade, the slave drivers on the Southern plantations, the black informers who divulged the slave conspiracies or those who revealed the hiding-place of a runaway slave. History has its share of those blacks who turned out to be all too human.

The academician would grant that more often than not the truth makes one sick, but he believes the New Testament adage about truth also making one free. The academician holds that truth, including the search for it, has a liberating effect. To be truly free is to be free first and foremost in the great franchise of the mind. To a group like black Americans, who have been subjected to so much falsehood by others, it would seem that the quest for truth should be held in high favor, having a relevance never failing.

Black history written for the academic fraternity will, in the main, take on a reflective, judicial tone, taking its cue from the careful winnowing and sifting that preceded it. The style will be sober, the rhetoric restrained. Passionate and deeply emotional language is highly necessary and desirable in human affairs, but such expression is more the province of the poet, the orator, and the charismatic leader than of the professional historian. An orator may give full vent to his innermost feelings, and to the innermost feelings of his audience, but a social scientist works in a discipline which has imperatives of its own, imperatives which may point to conclusions that run counter to his private wishes.

The codes of his discipline bring the black academician face to face with one of the major problems confronting every social scientist; namely, whether his citizen role should overshadow his professional role, whether he should give priority to social action or to scientific inquiry. Should an academician strive for competence in his discipline or should he seek primarily to become personally involved and relevant? To the black academician this dilemma takes on an unusual urgency inasmuch as he is fully aware of the long-standing discriminations against black people in the American social order. Addressing himself to this question of citizenship role versus professional role, sociologist Ernest Q. Campbell comes to the conclusion that "there is no intrinsic reason why the roles of scientific inquirer and staunch advocate are incompatible." ("Negroes, Education, and the Southern States," *Social Forces,* March, 1969). But to play these two roles simultaneously would seem to require unusual abilities and energies. In their absence, each black academician must come to some hard choices as to his own major commitment.

To the final audience under survey, the white community—academic and lay—black history has an important message. Black history should not be confined to blacks alone—this would be like confining the Gospel to those already converted, to use a familiar figure. Black history, like other phases of black studies, is no longer a matter of limited concern. Whites need to know black history. As Theodore Draper points out in *The Rediscovery of Black Nationalism* (New York, 1970), "In the interest of the entire society, white students need Black Studies as much or even more than black students." At a meeting of the Organization of American Historians in 1969, C. Vann Woodward voiced much the same sentiment in his presidential address, "Clio with Soul." Woodward spoke of black history as being "too important to be left entirely to Negro historians."

To begin with, whites should realize that the major reason for the long neglect of black history falls upon the historical guild itself. As Carl Becker has pointed out, "The historian selects from a number of particular facts certain facts which he considers most important to be known." Historians, continues Becker, "unconsciously read the objective facts of the past in the light of their own purposes, or the preoccupations of their own age." To point out that written history has a subjective element is certainly nothing new—Becker's observations were made in 1910. But to mention this matter at the outset makes for the openmindedness so essential to a proper perspective on the black American. Whites who read history should know by now that white historians have until recently dealt with the American past in such a way as to ignore the black presence or to minimize its importance in the making of America.

The aim of black history for white readers is two-fold; first, to eliminate the myth that our county's past was rosy and romantic, a new Eden "with liberty and justice for all," and second, to illustrate the centrality of the black American in our national experience. White historians have until recently tended to play down the somber aspects of black-white relationships in America— the deeply ingrained sense of white superiority dating back to Jamestown and Plymouth, the brutality of slavery, the mockery of post-Reconstruction, and the twentieth century offshoots of these persistent pathologies. The American past has a tragic component which cannot be brushed away. White Americans must take a second thought as they sing the familiar lines, "Thine alabaster cities gleam,/Undimmed by human tears."

Black history would enable whites to more realistically appraise some of our country's boasted achievements and some of its acclaimed public figures. For example, whites generally view the age of Andrew Jackson as one in which the right to vote was extended to the common man. But whites need to know that it was during this period in which states like North Carolina and Pennsylvania were explicitly prohibiting blacks from exercising this privilege. White readers of American history have thought highly of Woodrow Wilson for his espousal of the "New Freedom" and for his doctrine of "making the world safe for democracy," but white readers need to know that during Wilson's presidency and with his acquiescence black federal workers in the District of Columbia were systematically segregated and were given inferior working conditions and restroom facilities such as had not existed up to this time in the federal government.

Black history would be remiss if it did not call attention to these sobering aspects of the American past. But black history does not consist solely of white denial and discrimination. Hence black history for whites would indicate the myriad ways in which this country's history and culture would have been different without the presence of the black man. Many of these ways—economic, political, constitutional and military—are more quickly spotted than others. In some fields—art, literature, music, the dance, and popular culture in general—the black contribution centers in the common core, making its stamp more difficult to isolate. But whether obvious or subtle, the black man's gifts to America have been freely received if slowly acknowledged. To this extent all Americans are part black in their cultural patrimony. Blacks in general would concur in the sentiment expressed by a stanza from James Weldon Johnson ("Fifty Years, 1863–1913," in his *Fifty Years and Other Poems*, Boston, 1921):

> This land is ours by right of birth,
>   This land is ours by right of toil;
> We helped to turn its virgin earth,
>   Our sweat is in its fruitful soil.

The acceptance of black history by whites has been greatly facilitated by the current emphasis on social history. "It is a good moment to be a social historian" writes E. J. Hobsbawn (*Daedalus,* Winter, 1971), history professor at the University of London. This branch of history pays particular attention to the anonymous common man and to the manners and customs of everyday life.

And even more important for a black orientation, this branch of history emphasizes social movements and the phenomena of social protest.

For the white reader of black history the content would, at least initially, suggest the centrality of the Negro American and his identification with this country's great, professed goals. Therefore such history would comprise a general presentation of the American past with the black component interwoven throughout, appearing at its proper chronological juncture and not separately, somewhat like a disjointed sub-theme for the curious, Clio's underworld.

In style and technique black history for whites would differentiate between the white layman and the white intellectual. For the white layman the approach would be much the same as for his black counterpart, that is, an emphasis on biographical sketches, the lively arts, and popular culture, including sports. Again, as for the black layman, books would be greatly supplemented by the mass media. Indeed, of course, the mass media outlets used to reach black people will inevitably reach many whites.

For the white academician the approach to black history might be broader than the biographical and less fearful of the recipient's short attention span. Black studies for white intellectuals would back assertion with documentation, present proof, and cite authorities. A footnote is not an end unto itself. But those of an academic bent have been trained to look for the hard evidence; to them a statement must be intellectually tenable, its sources as trustworthy as possible. For the open-minded scholar—the seeker after truth—the will to believe is not an acceptable substitute for the data that corroborate.

We have dealt with black history for four different audiences. But in written history the use of different approaches and viewpoints need come as no surprise. No one category of events, no single interpretation, can furnish the cloth for that seamless garment we call history. There is no single compass by which to unravel the course of historical causation. Written history, in form and content, is many-sided, however much this may disconcert the doctrinaire types.

This short excursion into black history has taken note of varying viewpoints as to its function. Although varied, these approaches are often complementary rather than contradictory. More than anything else they demonstrate that there are alternate ways of looking at the past. The viewpoints of the revolutionary nationalist and the academic historian are not necessarily antagonistic. The academician, for example, may disavow an activist role and say that he is dealing with ideas for their own sake. But ideas are weapons and, as a rule, action is germinated by ideas.

In the formation of the new black history the academician—the traditionalist—will continue to be of major importance. But if black history is to come of age, revolutionary black nationalists will also have much to contribute. The nationalist historians will force a reexamination of the historic patterns of color prejudice in America, not only in its grosser, more obvious manifestations but in its manifold subtle forms, its protective coloration, one might say. The nationalist will bring into purview the blacks of the so-called Third World, comparing and contrasting them with their counterparts in America. The tone of moral outrage that characterizes the nationalist school has its value, too—a healthy anger often acting as a social catalyst.

And finally, the revolutionary black nationalist has made it clear that to properly assess the black past we need newer, non-traditional techniques. A multidisciplinary approach is called for, one not relying so largely on written records. Historical inquiry is already profiting from the methodology of the behavioral sciences—sociology, anthropology and psychology. Interdisciplinary history opens vistas across and beyond the traditional chronological and geographical boundaries. These widening approaches to appraising the past have led to such newer periodicals as the *Journal of Interdisciplinary History,* its first issue appearing in the autumn of 1970 and its avowed purpose to "stimulate historians to examine their own subjects in a new light, whether they be derived from psychology, physics, or paleontology."

This is the age of ideological cross-fertilization. It is to be noted, for example, that today in the study of early man on this planet no fewer than twelve different special skills are necessary—six field skills and six laboratory skills. In properly assessing the black role in American history a comparable if less numerous list of skills is needed. Without the use of these newer tools the past will remain incomplete. In fine, historians of the black past must take into consideration "the changing character of historical evidence, the development of new techniques and concepts in related disciplines, and the growing body of research by non-historians into historical problems," to borrow a phrase from David S. Landes and Charles Tilly ("History as Social Science," in *Social Science Research Council Items,* March, 1971).

The newer black history, looking afresh down the corridors of time, has a revolutionary potential of its own. For blacks it is a new way to see themselves. For whites it furnishes a new version of American history, one that especially challenges our national sense of smugness and self-righteousness and our avowal of fair play. Beyond this the new black history summons the entire historical guild—writers, teachers, and learners—to higher levels of expectation and performance. History, as all of its disciples know, is both continuity and change. Change stems from our readiness to challenge the current order, using the best tools of our trade. A new black history would revitalize education, quickening whatever it touches.

In 1925 in the foreword to his path-breaking volume, *The New Negro,* Alain Locke, one of the many illustrious Howard University scholar-humanists, said many things that have a contemporary ring: "Negro life is not only establishing new contacts and founding new centers, it is finding a new soul. There is a fresh spiritual and cultural focusing. . . . There is a renewed race-spirit that consciously and proudly sets itself apart." Locke of course was speaking primarily of creative expression in the arts, but his words aptly characterize the current black thrust in history. In its work of restoring history's lost boundaries, the black history of today is establishing new contacts and finding a new soul.

NOTE

For this and other essays by Professor Quarles, see *Black Mosaic* (Amherst, Mass., 1987). [Eds.]

Rayford W. Logan Lectures   1970–88

1970 John Hope Franklin, George Washington Williams and Africa
1971 Benjamin Quarles, Black History's Diversified Clientele
1972 John W. Blassingame, Sambos & Rebels: The Character of the
      Southern Slave
1973 C. Vann Woodward, History from Slave Sources
1974 Joseph E. Harris, The East African Slave Trade and Repatriation
1975 Mary Frances Berry, Toward Freedom for the Freedmen: Military
      Policy Origins of the Thirteenth Amendment and the Civil
      Rights Act of 1866
1976 W. Montague Cobb, The Emergence of the Afro-American in
      Medical Research
1977 Herbert G. Gutman, The Afro-American Family: Why It Survived
      Slavery
1978 Frank M. Snowden, Jr., Before Color-Prejudice: Black-White
      Relations in the Ancient Mediterranean World
1979 A. Leon Higginbotham, Jr., Racism in American Legal History
1980 F. Roy Augier, Reconstruction in the Caribbean, 1838–1965
1981 Ali A. Mazrui, On Race and the Arms Race: The Black World
      in the Nuclear Age
1982 George M. Fredrickson, The Black Image in the White Mind: A
      New Perspective
1983 David Levering Lewis, Parallels and Divergences: Assimilationist
      Strategies of Afro-American and Jewish Elites in the Twenties
      and Thirties
1984 (No lecture)
1985 Louis R. Harlan, Twenty Years with Booker T. Washington
1986 Vincent G. Harding, The Last Days of Martin Luther King, Jr.
1987 Nathan I. Huggins, Uses of the Self: Reflections on Black
      Autobiography
1988 David J. Garrow, The Evolution of Martin Luther King, Jr.

Contributors

MARY FRANCES BERRY has been professor of history and law in the Howard University Department of History since 1980. She earned a Ph.D. in history and a J.D. at the University of Michigan. A scholar-activist, Professor Berry was appointed to the United States Commission on Civil Rights in 1980. Her books include *Black Resistance/White Law* (1974); *Military Necessity and Civil Rights Policy* (1977); *Stability, Security and Continuity* (1978); *Long Memory* (1982), which was co-authored with John W. Blassingame; and *Why ERA Failed* (1986).

JOHN W. BLASSINGAME is professor of history and chairman of Afro-American Studies at Yale University. He received his Ph.D. in history from Yale. Among his numerous publications are articles published in the *Journal of Southern History* as well as the *Journal of Negro History* and such books as *New Perspectives on Black Studies* (1971), which he edited; *The Slave Community* (1972, 1979); *In Search of America* (1972) and *Long Memory* (1982), both of which are co-authored volumes; *Black New Orleans, 1860–1880 (1973); and Slave Testimony* (1977).

JOHN HOPE FRANKLIN is professor of legal history at Duke University Law School and the James B. Duke Professor Emeritus of History in the Department of History at Duke University, a position to which he was appointed after more than a decade of service as the John Matthews Manly Distinguished Professor of History at the University of Chicago. He received his Ph.D. in history from Harvard University. He is the author of scores of articles and numerous books, including *From Slavery To Freedom* (1947, 1956, 1967, 1974, 1980, 1987); *The Militant South, 1800–1860* (1956); *Reconstruction After the Civil War* (1961); *The Emancipation Proclamation* (1963); *A Southern Odyssey: Travellers in the Antebellum North* (1976); *Racial Equality In America* (1976); and *George Washington Williams: A Biography* (1985).

GEORGE M. FREDRICKSON is the William Smith Mason Professor Emeritus of History at Northwestern University. He was graduated from Harvard University with a Ph.D. in American civilization. Among his many publications are *The Inner Civil War* (1965); *The Black Image in the White Mind* (1971); *A Nation Divided* (1975); and *White Supremacy: A Comparative Study in American and South African History* (1981).

VINCENT G. HARDING is the Professor of Religion and Social Transformation at the Iliff School of Theology of the University of Denver. He received his Ph.D. in history from the University of Chicago. His publications include *Must Wall Divide?* (1965); *Beyond Chaos: Black History and the Search for the New Land* (1979); *The Other American Revolution* (1980); *There Is A River* (1981); *Black Heritage*, which he co-edited with John H. Clarke, (1969); and *Eyes On The Prize,* edited by Vincent G. Harding, et al. (1986); and *Martin Luther King, Jr., and the Company of the Faithful* (1986), which he co-authored with Rosemarie Freeney Harding.

LOUIS R. HARLAN is professor of history at the University of Maryland. He holds a Ph.D. in history from Johns Hopkins University. In addition to being the co-editor of the Booker T. Washington Papers, Professor Harlan is the author of scholarly articles and books that include *Separate and Unequal* (1958); "Booker T. Washington and the White Man's Burden," *American Historical Review* (January, 1966); *Booker T. Washington: The Making of a Black Leader* (1972); and *Booker T. Washington: The Wizard of Tuskegee* (1983).

JOSEPH E. HARRIS has been professor of history at Howard University since 1975. He earned a Ph.D. in history at Northwestern University. His many publications include articles, reports, and books such as "Protest and Resistance to the French in Fouta Djallon," *Genève-Afrique* (1969); *Afro-American History Interpretation at Selected National Parks* (1978); *The African Presence in Asia* (1971); *Africans and Their History* (1972, 1987); and *Repatriates and Refugees in a Colonial Society: The Case of Kenya* (1987). He has edited several volumes, among them *Pillars in Ethiopian History: The William Leo Hansberry African History Notebook* (1977), and *Global Dimensions of the African Diaspora* (1982).

A. LEON HIGGINBOTHAM, JR. is a judge of the United States Court of Appeals for the Third Circuit. Educated at Antioch College and Yale

University, he became a member of the Pennsylvania Bar in 1953. In addition to serving as an adjunct professor at the Wharton Graduate School of the University of Pennsylvania, he has taught at the law schools of Harvard, Yale, the University of Michigan, and the University of Pennsylvania. From 1964–77, he was a United States District Court judge for the Eastern District of Pennsylvania. He has served as a trustee of the University of Pennsylvania and a regent of the Smithsonian Institution. A contributor of articles to many professional journals, he is also the author of *In the Matter of Color: Race and the American Legal Process, The Colonial Period* (1978).

NATHAN I. HUGGINS is the Director of the W. E. B. Du Bois Institute for Afro-American Research and the Du Bois Professor of History and Afro-American Studies at Harvard University. He received his Ph.D. in history from Harvard University. His books include *Harlem Renaissance* (1971); *Black Odyssey: The Afro-American Ordeal in Slavery* (1976); *Slave and Citizen: The Life of Frederick Douglass* (1980); and *Afro-American Studies: A Review* (1983). His edited collections include *Key Issues in the Afro-American Experience* (2 vols., 1971), *Voices of the Harlem Renaissance* (1976), and *W. E. B. Du Bois: Writings* (1986).

DAVID LEVERING LEWIS is the Martin Luther King, Jr. Professor of History at Rutgers University. He received his Ph.D. in economic history from the London School of Economics. His publications include *King: A Critical Biography* (1970); *Presence of Honor: The Dreyfus Affair* (1973); *District of Columbia: A Bicentennial History* (1976); *When Harlem Was In Vogue* (1981); and *Race To Fashoda* (1987). Professor Lewis is the co-author with August Meier, of "History of the Negro Upper Class in Atlanta, Georgia, 1890–1958," *Journal of Negro Education,* 1959; and he contributed "Martin Luther King and the Policy of Non-violent Populism" to *Black Leaders of the Twentieth Century* (1983).

BENJAMIN QUARLES is professor emeritus of history at Morgan State University. He was graduated from the University of Wisconsin with a Ph.D. in history. He is the author of numerous books, including *The Negro in the Civil War* (1953); *The Negro in the American Revolution* (1961); *Lincoln and the Negro* (1962), *Black Abolitionists* (1969); *Allies for Freedom: Blacks and John Brown* (1972); and *Black Mosaic* (1987). He is also the editor of *Blacks on John Brown* (1972).

FRANK M. SNOWDEN, JR. has been a professor of classics at Howard University since 1945. He received a Ph.D. in classical philology from Harvard University. His publications include articles, essays, and books such as "The Negro in Ancient Greece," *American Anthropologist* (1948); *Some Greek and Roman Observations on the Ethiopian* (1960); *Blacks in Antiquity: Ethiopians in the Greco-Roman Experience* (1970); "Ethiopians and the Graeco-Roman World," *The African Diaspora: Interpretive Essays* (1976); and *Before Color Prejudice* (1983).

C. VANN WOODWARD is professor emeritus of history at Yale University, a position to which he was named after serving sixteen years as the Sterling Professor of History at the same university. He received his Ph.D. in history from Columbia University. Among his numerous publications are *Tom Watson* (1938); *Reunion and Reaction* (1951); *Origins of the New South* (1951); *The Strange Career of Jim Crow* (1955, 1966); *The Burden of Southern History* (1960); and *The Comparative Approach to American History* (1969), of which he was both an editor and contributor. Professor Woodward is also the editor of *Mary Chestnut's Civil War* (1981).

Editors

GENNA RAE MC NEIL is chairman and associate professor of history in the Howard University Department of History. She earned a Ph.D. in history at the University of Chicago. Professor McNeil's scholarly articles and essays include " 'To Meet the Group Needs': The Transformation of the Howard University School of Law, 1920–1935," *New Perspectives on Black Educational History* (1978), and "Community Initiative in the Desegregation of District of Columbia Schools, 1947–1954," *Howard Law Journal* (1980). She is the author of *Groundwork: Charles Hamilton Houston and the Struggle for Civil Rights* (1983).

MICHAEL R. WINSTON is vice president for academic affairs of Howard University and associate professor of history. He earned his Ph.D. in history and sociology at the University of California. He is the author of *The Howard University Department of History, 1913–1973* (1973); "Through the Back Door: Academic Racism and the Negro Scholar in Historical Perspective," *Daedalus* (1971); and "Carter G. Woodson: Prophet of a Black Tradition," *Journal of Negro History* (1976). He is co-author with Rayford W. Logan of *The Negro in the United States: Ordeal of Democracy, 1945–1970* (1971), and with G. Franklin Edwards of "The Washington of Paul Jennings: White House Slave, Freeman, and Conspirator for Freedom," *White House History* (1983); and co-editor with Rayford W. Logan of the *Dictionary of American Negro Biography* (1983).

Index